The Girls Who
Went Away

The Girls Who Went Away

The Hidden History of
Women Who Surrendered Children
for Adoption in the Decades
Before Roe v. Wade

ANN FESSLER

The Penguin Press
New York
2006

THE PENGUIN PRESS
Published by the Penguin Group
Penguin Group (USA) Inc., 375 Hudson Street, New York, New York 10014, U.S.A. ·
Penguin Group (Canada), 90 Eglinton Avenue East, Suite 700, Toronto, Ontario, Canada
M4P 2Y3 (a division of Pearson Penguin Canada Inc.) · Penguin Books Ltd, 80 Strand,
London WC2R 0RL, England · Penguin Ireland, 25 St. Stephen's Green, Dublin 2, Ireland
(a division of Penguin Books Ltd) · Penguin Books Australia Ltd., 250 Camberwell Road,
Camberwell, Victoria 3124, Australia (a division of Pearson Australia Group Pty Ltd) ·
Penguin Books India Pvt Ltd, 11 Community Centre, Panchsheel Park, New Delhi – 110 017,
India · Penguin Group (NZ), Cnr Airborne and Rosedale Roads, Albany, Auckland 1310,
New Zealand (a division of Pearson New Zealand Ltd) · Penguin Books (South
Africa) (Pty) Ltd, 24 Sturdee Avenue, Rosebank, Johannesburg 2196, South Africa

Penguin Books Ltd, Registered Offices:
80 Strand, London WC2R 0RL, England

First published in 2006 by The Penguin Press,
a member of Penguin Group (USA) Inc.

Copyright © Ann H. Fessler, 2006
All rights reserved

Grateful acknowledgment is made for permission to reprint selections from the archives of
the Florence Crittenton Collection, Social Welfare History Archives, University of
Minnesota. By permission of the National Florence Crittenton Mission.

LIBRARY OF CONGRESS CATALOGING IN PUBLICATION DATA
Fessler, Ann.
The girls who went away : the hidden history of women who surrendered children for
adoption in the decades before Roe v. Wade / Ann Fessler.
p. cm.
ISBN 1-59420-094-7
1. Birthmothers–United States.   2. Adoption–United States–Psychological aspects.
I. Title.
HV875.55.F465 2006
362.82'98–dc22   2005058179

Printed in the United States of America

1   3   5   7   9   10   8   6   4   2

DESIGNED BY AMANDA DEWEY

For my two mothers,
Hazel and Eleanor

Contents

The Girls Who
Went Away

1

My Own Story
as an Adoptee

MY MOTHER TOLD ME that on my first three birthdays she lit a special candle on my cake for the young woman who had given birth to me. She never explained why she did this for three years—no more, no less. I don't remember this private ceremony, but I do remember that there were times in my childhood when she looked at me in a particular way and I knew she was thinking about this young woman, my mother.

Three generations of women from my family have been brought together by adoption. Neither my maternal grandmother nor my mother nor I have given birth to a child. I am the first for whom this was a conscious choice.

My mother was never told that she was adopted. For my grandmother to admit this would have been a public declaration of her own inadequacy, her inability to bear children for her husband. But my mother knew. She had found her birth certificate taped to the back of a painting at her aunt's house. Her name had been Baby Helene before it was Hazel, and when she brought me home she named me Ann Helene.

My mother suffered her own private insecurity at not being able to bring a child to full term. But by the time she and my father turned to adoption there was no public stigma attaching to those who chose to adopt. In post–World War II America, families that wanted to adopt were carefully screened and represented a kind of model family–one with a mother and a father who really *wanted* to raise a child.

Although it is doubtful that families vetted through this process were actually any better or worse than other families, I was lucky enough to have parents who were loving and supportive and mindful of my development as an individual. They knew that they could guide me, but they also understood that I was not the sum of their parts. I was the product of two young people who had themselves, perhaps, been too young to fully understand the characteristics they had inherited from their own parents and passed on to me.

My adoptive mother and father were offered very little information about my biological parents. She was nineteen and from a big farm family of English and German descent. He was athletic, a college football player from a family of means. Their parents felt that this was no way to start a family.

My mother cried whenever she told me this story. She knew it could not be so simple. I did not. The story of that young couple sounded like the plot of a movie to me. I liked being part of this soulful story of ill-fated love, of having a mysterious past, of not being related to my family, of being my own person.

When I became sexually active, I imagined that if the worst happened I would do as my mother had done: go off to another town to a home for unwed mothers and return with a story about a kidney infection, or about an Aunt Betty in Sandusky who needed my care. This is what young women who got caught in this unfortunate situation did. Almost every graduating class had a girl who disappeared. Everyone knew where she had gone, and that she had most likely been told, "If you love your child you must give it up, move on with your life, and forget."

It never occurred to me that those girls may not have forgotten, that it might not have been so easy for them to just move on with their lives. But then I had never gone through pregnancy and childbirth myself. And I had never heard the story from a woman who had surrendered her child.

Then something happened that forever changed my understanding of adoption. In 1989, I was attending the opening of an exhibition at the Maryland Institute College of Art, where I had been teaching for seven years. Not long after I arrived, I noticed a woman who looked very familiar. I had a distinct and clear memory of having recently talked to her but I couldn't remember where or when. I asked several people if they knew who she was, but no one did, so I continued to look at the exhibition.

Later, this woman walked toward me from across the room and with no introduction said, "You could be my long-lost daughter. You look like the perfect combination of myself and the father of my child." I said, "You don't know what you're saying to me. I *could* be your daughter–I was adopted." There was a long silence and I saw her start to react as I had. Eventually we compared dates, but they were one year and one month apart. She kept asking, "Are you *sure* about your birth date? Sometimes records are changed." But I was sure.

We continued to talk. She asked me if I had looked for my mother and I responded that I didn't know if I wanted to invade her privacy. I said, "When you gave up a child for adoption in 1949, you didn't expect her to come knocking on your door forty years later." And she said, "You should find her. She probably worries every day about what happened to you and whether you've had a good life." I could see in her eyes that she was speaking from her own experience, and the thought that my mother might feel the same sense of loss was shocking to me. I felt guilty and empathetic and naïve all at once. Why had I never considered this possibility? How could I not know? How could everyone not know?

I continued to listen, realizing that I had never heard the story of adoption from the perspective of a mother who had surrendered her child. It seemed incredible to me that after forty years of life as an adoptee I was hearing the other side of the story for the first time. As I listened I finally understood why this woman seemed so familiar to me: the image of the two of us talking had been in my dream the night before we met. I went home and wrote down every word of our conversation. I started to wonder if my mother's worrying had caused the dream.

A year later, the woman I had met in the gallery had separated from her husband and was living down the block from me. I began to wonder if she really was my mother but had not told me because I seemed ambivalent about a reunion. Had she left her husband and home to be near me?

My parents had always been very open about any information they had surrounding my adoption. There was a file in my father's cabinet with "Ann" neatly printed in my mother's hand that contained all of my original paperwork. As a child, I periodically opened that file drawer as slowly and quietly as I could to look at the papers containing my original name, a carbon copy of a letter on tissue-thin paper from the minister of our church congratulating my parents on their recent adoption, and records of what I had been fed during the three-month waiting period before my parents could take me home. Now I returned to that file for the name of the adoption agency. I needed to know what information I was entitled to. I needed to know if *this* woman was my mother.

The man at the agency informed me that because I was born in Ohio before 1964, all I had to do was fill out a form, send it to the Department of Vital Statistics, State of Ohio, and the department would send me a copy of my original birth certificate. After all the stories I had heard about sealed records and professional searchers, it never occurred to me that I might be able to get a copy of my records with just a phone call, a notarized piece of paper, and two forms of identification.

When the envelope from the Department of Vital Statistics arrived, I was in the middle of making travel arrangements for a lecture I was to give about my artwork in an exhibition entitled "Parents." I unfolded the single sheet of paper and saw my mother's full name, her place of birth, and her permanent residence in 1949. The right side of the form, where information about my father should be noted, was blank.

I located my Ohio map. The trip I was planning would take me within an hour of the rural community where she was born. So I allowed an extra day and set off through a landscape of corn and bean fields, and an occasional white house and barn, in search of a yearbook picture. I wanted to see what she looked like. I wanted to see if I looked like my mother.

When I arrived I couldn't find the public library, so I went to the school. The halls were empty; students had left for the day, but teachers were still in their classrooms. I could hear the rustle of papers and blackboards being wiped clean. The door to the library was locked, but the teacher in the next room offered to help. He said the yearbooks in the library did not go back that far but there was a chance one could be found down in the main office.

We entered the office and he announced that I was looking for a yearbook from 1948, and the secretaries, principals, and vice principals all went to work rooting through their office bookcases. No one asked any questions. This is the rural Midwest. When they couldn't find the right yearbook they wrote down names of people who graduated that year so I could call them, maybe go to their house and look at their yearbook. I felt sick. Things had gone too far—I just wanted to look at a picture.

I tried to leave but a man came through the door and they all turned toward him and said in unison, "Do *you* have a yearbook from 1948?" The man said, "Who are you looking for?" And they all turned back toward me.

I had to say a last name. I acted as if I were asking for somebody else. I tried to sound unsure, but he knew the name and he said her whole name out loud. And then he said, "She doesn't live around here anymore, but there's a house with a business out on Route 30 with that same last name. They might know where you can find her."

I cleared out and started driving. I didn't know where I was headed other than away from that school. I hadn't wanted her name to get out. I just wanted to look at a picture. Then I realized I was on Route 30, the road with the business and the people with the same last name.

As I got closer I passed a road with the family name, the farm where I must have been before I was born. Then I saw the house and the barn and the sign for the business and I thought, I'll just go in and buy something. I don't know what. I pulled in, past buildings, past tractors, past corncribs, and reached the end of the driveway. But there was no business, just a sign out front, a number to call, and then a man came out of the barn waving. I had driven too far back into his driveway to pretend I was just turning around, so I rolled down my window and heard myself say, "I see your name up there on the barn. You wouldn't happen to know someone by the name of Eleanor, would you?" And he said, "Yeah, that's my sister."

Then he started talking. He talked for an hour. He told me about her life, her husband, two boys, and a girl. But what he didn't know was—there was *another* girl: two boys and *two* girls. He talked about growing up on the farm, the old Victorian house, and the banister they loved to slide down. Then he talked about her and how she was different from her sisters. He said, "She would much rather spend time in the barn than help in the house." And he told other stories that sounded familiar.

Finally, he asked how I knew her and I told him my mother had lived around there when she was young and had moved away. She wondered whatever happened to Eleanor. So he went into the house and brought out her address and phone number. And when I left, I drove to the town where she had lived all these years, just to drive by, to make sure she was okay. I had always worried that her family had disowned her and she had lived in miserable conditions. Maybe I thought I might catch a glimpse of her.

It occurred to me afterward that she might get suspicious when her brother told her the story of a woman who had been asking about her. Maybe she had not told her children. She might be living in fear that I would show up on her doorstep next. I couldn't decide whether I should contact her right away or wait. I waited fourteen years.

During the years that followed, I created several autobiographical installations about adoption. Whenever possible I offered space in my exhibitions for members of the community to display their stories of adoption along with mine. I was overwhelmed by what I read. The writings left behind by women in New York, California, Texas, and Maryland were the same. What the mothers had been assured when they signed the papers giving up all rights to their children turned out to be a lie: they did not move on and forget. I think my adoptive mother knew this when she lit those candles. I think three years was all that she could bear. *She* needed to move on and forget.

2

⚓

Breaking the Silence

You asked me why I agreed to be interviewed and I think it was because you were here, because you came here and it spoke to me—that's all. There's still that voice in me that says, "Who would be interested? No one cared then, why would they care now?" I was abandoned when it was right in everybody's face, so I still believe that nobody cares. My personal struggle is to get beyond thinking I'm not worth caring about. I am here. I do exist. Maybe by adding my two cents I can help other moms who feel the way I do. Maybe they will find someone who cares.

—*Suzanne*

I N JUNE OF 2002, I began tape-recording the oral histories of women who surrendered a newborn for adoption between the end of World War II, in 1945, and the 1973 passage of *Roe v. Wade*, which legalized abortion throughout the nation. These years were a time of enormous change for young women as barriers to equality and independence broke down. For the young men and women growing up in the postwar years, especially those of the baby-boom generation, this liberation from the past also applied to sexual behavior. And though premarital sex was certainly not a new phenomenon, it became increasingly common among those who had no plans to marry. For women born after 1949, the odds were that they would have sex before they reached age twenty.[1]

Despite the increase in the number of young people having sex in the 1950s and 1960s, access to birth control and sex education lagged far behind.

Fearing that sex education would promote or encourage sexual relations, parents and schools thought it best to leave young people uninformed. During this time, effective birth control was difficult to obtain. In fact, in some states it was illegal to sell contraceptives to those who were unmarried. The efforts to restrict information and access to birth control did not prevent teens from having sex, however. The result was an explosion in premarital pregnancy and in the numbers of babies surrendered for adoption.

Though sexual norms were changing among the young, the shame associated with single pregnancy remained. The social stigma of being an "unwed mother" was so great that many families—especially middle-class families—felt it was simply unthinkable to have a daughter keep an "illegitimate" child. These women either married quickly or were sent away before their pregnancy could be detected by others in the community. Between 1945 and 1973, one and a half million babies were relinquished for nonfamily or unrelated adoptions.[2]

> I've tried to explain to my kids that it wasn't like it is today. Nobody knew that much about birth control. What used to bother me a lot was I knew lots of girls who were having sex; they just weren't caught. If you were caught, somehow you were different, and you needed to be horrified and shamed. I was thinking, "But everybody's doing it. Why am I a bad person now?"
>
> It was just totally, totally different. You didn't keep your child. You didn't. I knew one girl who got married and immediately divorced afterward. At least that would keep the people who talk at bay.
>
> —*Laurinda*

Just about everyone who lived through this era has a memory of a girl from their high school, college, or neighborhood who disappeared. If she returned, she most likely did not come back with her baby but with a story of a sick aunt or an illness that had kept her out of school. If her peers doubted her story, they probably did not challenge her directly. They simply distanced themselves. According to the prevailing double standard, the young man who was equally responsible for the pregnancy was not condemned for his actions. It was her fault, not their fault, that she got pregnant.

> This was in that period of time when there wasn't much worse that a girl could do. They almost treated you like you had committed murder or something.
>
> *—Toni*

The girls who went away were told by family members, social-service agencies, and clergy that relinquishing their child for adoption was the only acceptable option. It would preserve their reputation and save both mother and child from a lifetime of shame. Often it was clear to everyone, except the expectant mother, that adoption was the answer. Many of these girls, even those in their twenties, had no other option than to go along with their families or risk being permanently ostracized. For them there was generally little or no discussion before their parents sent them away. Those who went to maternity homes to wait out their pregnancies often received little counseling and were totally unprepared for either childbirth or relinquishment. They were simply told they *must* surrender their child, keep their secret, move on, and forget. Though moving on and forgetting proved impossible, many women were shamed into keeping their secret.

> As soon as the time was near and we were going to do this interview, all these physical things started happening. My jaw doesn't want to open and my lungs are all tight. I thought, "I wonder why I can't open my mouth." Then I realized, I'm supposed to be silent. I'm not supposed to tell this story. The secrecy has dominated everything. It's so powerful and pervasive and the longer you keep a secret, the more power it takes on.
>
> *—Diane IV*

I've never really felt like I could talk to anybody about it. You know, society has this picture—you hear about people giving their babies away. That whole terminology is just so misleading. I didn't give him away. I think one of the reasons I don't talk to some people about it is because they are so judgmental. Quite frankly, it's not that society can't understand, it's that they won't understand. People choose to not understand.

—Carole II

Afterward I never told, unless it was somebody I was very, very close to. I never opened up to anyone unless I felt that they would accept me. I felt like I lived a lie because people didn't really know me. I was afraid that people would not accept me if they knew the truth. It was something that I carried with me for thirty-five, thirty-six years.

—Carol I

The secrecy has, in part, allowed some of the old myths about women who surrendered babies to survive. One assumption was that they were women who were having a lot of sex with a lot of different young men. In fact, a majority of the women I interviewed became pregnant with their first sexual partner, some from their first sexual experience.

I'm being very honest with you by saying I was a very late bloomer. When I got pregnant, it was the very first time I had ever had sex. Very first time. I'm sure I probably didn't even like it. I went all through high school and never had sex.

My parents' generation, that greatest generation, thought it didn't happen to nice girls. You just have to know that's what society and parents felt: nice girls didn't get pregnant. But nice girls do get pregnant, and nice girls get pregnant now. People saw us as loose women. Well, I wasn't a loose woman! It wasn't that way for me. I didn't sleep around. But that's the label. That is absolutely the label. Oh, well. I could be called worse things. I could be called a liar. I could be called a cheat.

—Cathy II

Another prevailing myth is that these women were all eager to surrender their child and be free of their problem. The assumption that these babies were unwanted by their mothers is ubiquitous. The act of relinquishment seemed to confirm this, since it is commonly believed to be a personal decision made by the mother based on her lack of interest or desire to parent— a decision that is independent of social, family, and economic pressures. This misguided and simplistic notion has been hurtful not only to the mothers but also to many adoptees who believe that they were thrown away. Over the years, I have had many conversations with adult adoptees who say, "She didn't want me. Why should I want to know her?" They clearly have no idea how infinitely more complicated their mother's circumstances were and a short conversation could not possibly explain it. This book is partly a response to their comments. It is a story best told by the mothers themselves, and best understood within the context of the time period.

> Chances are the baby wasn't unwanted. It was a baby unwanted by society, not by mom. You couldn't be an unwed mother. Motherhood was synonymous with marriage. If you weren't married, your child was a bastard and those terms were used. I think I'm like many other women who thought, "It may kill me to do this, but my baby is going to have what everybody keeps saying is best for him." It's not because the child wasn't wanted. There would have been nothing more wonderful than to come home with my baby.
>
> *—Glory*

Nobody ever asked me if I wanted to keep the baby, or explained the options. I went to the maternity home, I was going to have the baby, they were going to take it, and I was going to go home. I was not *allowed* to keep the baby. I would have been disowned. I don't even know if they had programs to help women and children back then. I don't know what was available. I was made to feel very ashamed of the situation that "I had created for myself" and for my mother and for my family and friends, so I felt all those avenues were closed. I guess maybe I had to convince myself that I didn't give him *away*; I gave him a way to have two parents, a way to have a home. Maybe that's a cop-out on my part. I don't know, but that's the only way I can live with it.

—Joyce I

I never felt like I gave my baby away. I always felt like my daughter was taken from me.

—Pollie

Yet another myth in common currency is that these women did move on and forget. In truth, none of the mothers I interviewed was able to forget. Rather, they describe the surrender of their child as the most significant and defining event of their lives. Given the enormous number of women involved and the impact the surrender had on their lives, not to mention the lives of their parents, their subsequent partners and children, the fathers of their babies, and the surrendered children, it is remarkable that so little is known about these mothers' experiences even now, decades later. This silence has also kept many of these women from learning about one another and understanding that their feelings of loss were normal and consistent with thousands of other mothers who had surrendered children.

I am shocked at how much it has impacted my life. I really tried to move on and forget, I tried to do what they said, but it didn't work. I was convinced that there was something wrong with me. There *must* be something wrong with me. It was supposed to work; everybody said so. But it didn't. No matter how many degrees I got, how many credits I had, how many years I worked, I was empty.

—Glory

The surrender was the beginning of a long cycle that colored my entire life. Your identity is formed in your teen years and if you take on this identity of a worthless, horrible, guilty person, then that's going to affect you your whole life. Guilt was always such a pervasive part for me. Not that I was sexual, or not that I was pregnant, but that I let somebody take my child. That's the guilt.

People talk about the worst thing that could happen to you is to lose a child. And no one talks about that in terms of a birth mother. What do they think that is for her? Why would it be any different? It's in your cells, and in your guts, and in your consciousness, and in your heart.

—Diane IV

As I listened to story after story, what impressed me so powerfully was the commonalities in the women's experiences. How the surrender was not only a deeply personal experience that affected the life of each woman but also a profound collective experience. Taken together, these experiences offer evidence of the lack of individual choice and the pervasiveness of surrender as a social phenomenon. For most of the women I interviewed, it was not a question of choice but of doing what society demanded—a demand that society has never fully acknowledged.

You know, it was such a long time ago and I started thinking, "Just let it go. Just let it go and move on," yet I couldn't, and I can't. It's a big issue to those who lived it. There are women out there who lost their firstborn child and never got to grieve. I can't even put it into words. It's a weird thing, this whole adoption thing where people think that someone could just hand their child over and it will be okay. Obviously it's not. We're still alive. We're still here. We haven't died. Our issues are every day. We live this every day. Every day.

—Suzanne

DOROTHY II

I was fifteen that summer. And I was in love with the Rolling Stones. My girlfriend Patty and I spent a lot of time listening to their music. One day my brother came home with his best friend. He introduced me to this guy and I remember being singularly unimpressed. But I noticed he stared at me in a way that no other guy before had. And it frightened and fascinated me all at once.

Meanwhile, I went on with my life as a Rolling Stones fan. And he started calling the house. He would call and ask for my brother. And we began to play this voice game where I would sound more and more seductive and he would sound more and more interested. And so that's how we began. Then one day when he called, he actually asked me out. It was my first real date. I felt safe because he was my brother's friend. I don't even remember what we did that first time—probably drove around in his car. He had a baby-blue '57 Chevy that was his pride and joy. He spent a lot of time talking about the car and all these little gadgets he had attached. And I kind of liked riding in that car. I felt really important. I'm fifteen years old and I'm thinking, "Wow, this is what dating is like."

Then one night he decided we should go parking. I thought it was just gonna be a make-out session. But the very first time, he was already pushing me back in the seat and I remember thinking, "Boys are a handful," then thinking, "Well, he's nineteen, maybe that has something to do with it." And I think the very first time we went parking I began to be afraid. That this was going in a direction I was either not ready for or in some way I felt threatened by. And yet something else took over—a kind of fatalistic inability to say no. And I am not sure to this day why this happened. I've wrestled a lot with that.

I began to be very secretive with my family, and not tell them I was meeting him. I can't remember the first time we actually went all the way. I don't remember how many dates, in other words, it took. But I do remember feeling betrayed, because he refused to wear a condom. I remember saying, "I don't wanna do this, because I don't want to get pregnant." And he said, "Well, I promise you, you won't get pregnant." And I said, "How are you gonna manage this?" He said, "Well, I'm going to pull out," and he explained what that meant. So he stopped trying to convince me and just took over and sort of pushed me back, and again I felt unable to act. I was stunned, dazed. I could not say no.

It was very quick. I was not even sure that it had happened. It didn't hurt terribly—it just felt a little uncomfortable. There was this wet feeling between my legs and I said, "Was that it?" He was unable to speak for a few minutes and then he said yes. Then he said, "You're mine now." And I think in my whole life that is one of the moments when I was the most afraid. In my whole life. Even now, to this day. That feeling of being *owned* was horrifying. And that's when I began to think, "I don't want to see this person ever again."

I began to make excuses not to see him. He was very possessive. I think we carried on for another month or so, and then I skipped a period. I was terrified. And I was just, I remember feeling like I was falling down this hole. I was just falling and falling and everything was spinning. And I thought, "No, not me. Why me?" My first love, and it wasn't even a love. Why me?

I didn't know what to do. I was very ashamed. This was not something that good girls did. Because I came from a very kind of poor family, I was more acutely aware than most people, maybe, about reputations and how easily they are lost. I knew from the experience of living in that small town that girls who got pregnant really lost their ability to have any kind of decent life. It was over for you. Your best hope in those days was to marry the boy and have done with it, and in the years to come hope that people would just forget it. The thing was, I was fifteen. I didn't love this boy. This was 1966— abortion wasn't an option. I mean, we didn't even think about it.

He said, "I've told my mother" and his mother wanted to talk to me. Her answer was "You're gonna get married." She said, "We'll help you get through this, *but* you have to marry him." And I said, "I'm not really ready for marriage." It's one thing to deal with being pregnant, and quite another to deal with being someone's wife. They said I was selfish. They called me some terrible things.

I finally realized I had to tell my own mother because I knew she was my only ally. So he and I took my mother out to Carvel's, which is this little ice-cream place in town. And I remember being really afraid of how she would react. I was the one child of her four who just might make it through school, might make it out of our little town.

It turned out that I couldn't tell her. We were sitting in Carvel's in the parking lot, and he had gone in and bought us all banana splits. As soon as I saw mine, a wave of nausea just swept over me. I had to escape from the Chevy. I ran to the back of the parking lot, and I threw up. My mother was sitting in the back of this car watching me getting sick. And I saw the two of them talking from my vantage point and I realized he was telling her.

She got out of the back of the car and walked toward me. I felt so afraid and I started crying. I remember thinking, "Please, Mom, you're all I have. Just stick by me." And I waited, and I watched her walk to me. And she just put her arms around me and said, "It's okay, babe. Because no matter what, we'll get through this together." We cried in each other's arms for about ten minutes, I guess. And finally she waved him away. She waved him away. She said, "Just *go*."

And she and I walked home from Carvel's. We took this road, this detour that was one of our favorite walking spots. It was along the Housatonic River and it was a road that was lined with these wonderful weeping willow trees. It was the most beautiful place I think in our town at that time, at least for me. We walked with our arms around each other's waist. The willow trees were blowing in the wind and we hardly talked at all. By the time we got home, I knew that she was gonna watch out for me, and that she was gonna make sure that everything was okay.

I had to start school. I was going to school and throwing up in the bathroom. I was absent chronically during that month of September. By then I was about six or eight weeks pregnant, I guess. It became difficult to go to school at all. I decided to go see my priest and tell him about it. He was the only male authority figure that I trusted.

I talked to my priest and he said, "You know, there *is* a way, Dorothy." And I said, "Well, I can't imagine what that is because I don't want to marry him." And he said, "Well, I wouldn't advise you to marry him anyway, because he isn't a Catholic."

I didn't understand a lot of things about the Catholic religion. I was a convert and had only been officially a Catholic for maybe three years by the time I got pregnant. I didn't understand a lot of the details—things like you can't marry a non-Catholic. I said, "So you're saying marriage isn't even an option for me? Is that what you're saying?" He said, "Unless you can find a good Catholic man who would be willing to adopt the child, no, we can't accept your marriage." On the one hand, I was glad, because this gave me ammunition to tell his mother, "I'm sorry, it's against my religion," of all things.

But the worst part was yet to come. He said, "You know what purgatory is? We've talked about that." And I said, "Yeah, I know what purgatory is." And he said, "We can't baptize your baby if you have her out of wedlock. So if you don't marry a Catholic man there's only one other option, or your baby's going to stay in purgatory when she dies. She can never be baptized into the Church."

I was devastated. Here I am, fifteen years old, having to deal with the metaphysical complications of what happens to a soul when it passes from this earth if I don't do the exact right thing at this moment. I said to him, "Well, what would *you* do?" Like I was six years old. I said, "What would you do?" He said, "I would give the baby to a family who could take care of those things. A Catholic family—a good Catholic family." I said, "You mean adoption?" And he said, "Yes. I think that's your only out in this situation. You don't want to ruin your reputation. We can find a place for you to spend the last few months of your pregnancy. There's no reason for you to feel embarrassed or go through the pressure that you're currently facing with your boyfriend's mother."

I was sort of enamored of the idea of running away, sure. He made it sound like this place he was going to send me to was a country club. He said, "There will be other girls like you. You'll be able to talk and have fun for the last few months of your pregnancy, no one will bother you, and you will be able to make an informed choice." He said, "Nothing is final till it's final, but I think you'll do the right thing." And that was just the first time I heard "do the right thing" in that whole nine-month period.

So I went home after that long meeting and tried to explain to my non-religious mother what purgatory was, and how my child would end up there if I didn't give her away. She finally just gave up on trying to understand,

and said she respected this priest. She said, "If the priest says you should go away to this place, then I think you should go. 'Cause I don't have an answer for you, babe. I'll help you if you want to stay here, but I don't have an answer for you."

So for me the easiest thing to do was to go away. It was a running away; it was a place where I really thought I could go and think. But before I could go there a social worker had to get involved. And it was explained to me that the state of Connecticut would be paying my tuition at this home for unwed mothers called St. Agnes. I was told it was located in West Hartford, and that they would take care of bringing me there. I could stay until my baby was born and then come home. They would take care of the adoption and I wouldn't have to worry about anything. Sounded wonderful, but it was very hard for me to say good-bye to my mother. I had never been away from home except for an overnight visit to a friend's house. I was devastated to be away from her.

She had said, "Write me letters. You won't feel as lonely." So I did. And that started my little pattern. Every night before I went to bed, I would write my mother a love letter. I think she kept them for most of her life. And it kept me in touch with the one person who really loved me.

And I just, to this day, cannot get over that feeling of loneliness and abandonment and being in that place with so many young people. Everybody I saw was just a kid. I noticed one thing very quickly at St. Agnes, and that was that nobody wanted to talk about what was going to happen to them at the end of their pregnancy. They really wanted to live in the moment. They didn't want to talk about "going over"—that became a metaphor for the birth. We would come to breakfast in the morning and we would look around to see who wasn't there. "Oh, she went over last night. She went over." That meant she had gone to St. Francis Hospital and had her baby. We would envy that person because she was out of jail, so to speak. But we were a little afraid, because we didn't know what this was all about.

I remember that one of my best friends at St. Agnes was a girl named Brenda, who was like a movie star. She just was very glamorous and had long blond hair. She was one of those people who didn't really look pregnant. She just had a little belly and she looked *great*. We were all so envious of her. When she went over, we were all very interested to know what she had. After Brenda's four days, she came back to say good-bye to all of us. Being so popular, she almost had to. She held court in one of the rooms on the second floor, and we were all allowed to go in. We asked her all kinds of questions. "What was it like? What was it like?"

She had changed. In just those four days. She was very mature in a way that frightened me. She was not the same person. She looked fabulous, but she looked about four years older. She didn't want to talk about the details and we thought that was kind of curious. If Brenda didn't want to talk about it, it must not be good. She said she had a little boy, and she had said good-bye to him, and she hoped he had a better life. But that's all she would say. She said good-bye to us all, and we were a bit chastened after that. We all went upstairs. And that night I remember not many of us had dinner. We were just very, very worried. There were a group of us that were all due around the same time, and we kind of bonded. One by one, we went over.

By the time I was in my third false labor, they decided to induce me. I had no one there to hold my hand. I had no one. I didn't even know who was going to deliver me. It was the loneliest thing I've ever gone through in my whole life. The loneliest.

The baby was born at seven o'clock. I had only been in labor maybe seven hours, I guess. And most of it I don't remember. I woke up at about seven-thirty, maybe seven-forty-five, and I was in the recovery room. There was this nurse changing my sanitary napkin. I looked down and my stomach had caved in. I no longer had a child in there. I looked at the nurse and I said, "What happened?" She said, "You've had your baby," in a very kind of businesslike, matter-of-fact way. She wouldn't look at me. And I tried to get her to meet my eyes, because I wanted to ask her all these questions. It was a very important moment for me. "I had the baby?" And she was just very— she was doing her job, and I said, "Well, what was it?" And she said, flatly, "It was a girl." I said, "Oh, it was a girl."

I remember thinking I wished it was a boy, because boys can't have children. I thought, "I gave birth to a little girl who's going to have to go through this, that poor little thing." I had always thought boys had it better than women. All my life, you know? And that whole experience made me feel even more so—that it's the girls who get punished, the girls who suffer through all of this stuff, and the girls who can't talk about it.

But, of course, once I got used to the idea that it was a girl—which took me all of twenty seconds—I wanted to see her immediately. And they said, "You can't. We have to take you back to your room, and in the morning when they bring the children around for feeding time, you can see her." I said, "What's feeding time?" Because it sounded like the zoo. And she said, "Well, the hospital is on a feeding schedule, and they bring the children at ten and two," and something else—I forget. I thought, "Oh my gosh, I have to wait until ten in the morning to see my child?" And they said, "Well, that's the way we do things here." I said, "Well, where is she now?" "Well, she's in the nursery. They're taking good care of her."

They took me upstairs to this room. It was a room with four beds. Two of the beds were empty and one had one of my friends in it. She had delivered three days earlier. The next day would have been her last day. When I came in, she was awake. By then it was maybe eight-thirty, nine o'clock, 'cause it was dark outside. She said to me, "Dottie, is it you?" I said, "Yeah! How are you?" I was all happy. I was in the euphoria that—right after birth you have this euphoria, "I'm done, I'm done!" She was in the throes of postpartum depression already. I could sense that this was a serious *down* that she was on. She said she had had a boy, and she said, "Tomorrow's my last day of seeing him, and then I gotta go home."

I couldn't even relate to that sadness at that moment. I felt bad, but at the same time I couldn't relate. I said, "Oh, I can't wait till the morning, because I'm going to see my daughter. I had a little girl!" We were at opposite ends of this spectrum of grief. I hadn't seen it yet, she had already and it was very hard. She said to me, "Dottie, I have one bit of advice for you before they bring her: don't get attached." I said, "Oh, I won't. I just wanna see her and count her toes and make sure she's okay." I was always a kind of brave kid, and thought, "I can do this."

Well, when they brought her I wasn't prepared. All that pain and all those months of waiting were nothing compared to what I felt when they put her in my arms. When I saw her for the first time, I knew what real love really was. And I've never been the same since that moment. I remember her cuddling up against my neck, and I held her as close as I could, and the feeling of her little face just nuzzling my neck, and I thought, "Oh my God, it's a real, live person." And I loved her so much. I thought I loved my mother,

I thought I loved my friends, I thought I loved Mick Jagger, but this was something else. This was like looking at another version of myself. I never thought you could feel like that in the whole world. And then I wondered, "What am I supposed to do now?"

I held her, and the first thing I did was unwrap her. I wanted to see her entire body. She was very tiny. She had the most beautiful, perfect little toes. I remember counting them, and I thought, "Well, this is what everybody said I would do." I did exactly what everybody said. I looked at her little fingers, and I remember caressing every single inch of the fingers and toes, and saying, "This is really her. This is really Tracy." And I started to talk to her, and to say, "I love you. You're just so beautiful." I started talking baby talk. And I remember her turning her face into my neck and nuzzling. I just knew it was her way of recognizing me. I thought, "She knows me!" And I called across to my friend, who was seeing her son for the last time—at the same time that I was seeing my daughter for the first. She was in grief and in tears. I said, "She knows me! She knows me!" And she couldn't speak. She couldn't even be glad for me. And I just looked back at my child, and I thought, "In three days, I'm gonna be her."

Finally, on the third day, I had to say good-bye. I remember being very out of it, and not being able to come up with the right words. I felt somehow that whatever I said to her was really significant—that if I didn't say the exact words that it would somehow curse her. And I have no reason for this except for, possibly, it was the influence of the medication. But I told her to be a good girl. That I would never forget her. And to understand that I just did what I thought was best. And to forgive me.

When it was over, the last thing I remember was that little pink blanket. That little shred of pink blanket that I could see over the nurse's white shoulder, going out the door. And that's the last time I saw my daughter.

The next couple of weeks were horrifying. I got sick. They didn't know what was wrong. They wanted to do an emergency exploratory laparoscopy. I guess at one point I was in critical condition. So during that couple of weeks of recovering from the surgery, that's when the real loss of my daughter hit me. I was able to think at that point. It was then that I felt seriously depressed.

The person who drove me home from the hospital happened to be the social worker. Again, me trying to think the best of people, I thought she was just being kind. Then I remembered she wanted me to sign that piece of paper. And, sure enough, halfway home, she pulls over by this little lake. She had taken the scenic route. I guess she thought that would make it easier. She pulls over and brings out her little briefcase. My mother was in the backseat. I think she had picked up my mother before she had come to get me. And again I thought this was so kind of her, but it turns out she needed my mother's signature. That's why. It wasn't anything altruistic at all.

So I'm in the front seat with the social worker. My mother's in the backseat. And out come the papers. She said, "We need you to sign these so we can place your baby." I said, "You know, I really don't think that I can sign these papers. I really don't think I can do this. I really don't want to do it now—I'm just coming out of this surgery." And she said, "Well, look. The baby's been in foster care this whole time. You haven't bonded with her at all." She said, "As far as we're concerned, she's only known the foster mother at this point. The adoptive family is waiting for her. And why would you want to just do this to *them*? They've been waiting all this time while you were sick to get this done." On the one hand, I was outraged that I should care that they were waiting, and on the other hand, that was the deal I had made. As young as I was, I understood what making a deal with the devil means: you just can't win.

So my mind is racing, trying to think up ways to get out of this. And I said, "Well, I really need to see her one last time because then I'll know for sure." And, of course, I was planning on making a break for it. She refused to tell me where the baby was. She said, "I'm not at liberty to disclose that." And I said, "Well, have you seen her? How do you even know she's all right?" She said, "Oh, she giggles and coos and she's happy as heck." She didn't say "heck." She said, "She's very happy. She's a happy baby, and she's ready to go with her new family."

I said to myself, "Well, she's got it all sewn up good and proper, doesn't she?" Everything I could think of, she had an answer for. And as things got a little tense, and I was about to say, "No. I'm not gonna sign these," she said, "You know, the state paid for you to go to St. Agnes. That's quite a bit of money that we put out in good faith. Do you have the money to pay for that?" I said, "No." I looked at my mother, and I said, "Mommy, what am I going to do?" And she said, "Babe, I don't know. We don't have any money." I wanted to know from an attorney—I wanted to know from some-body what my rights were. But for every question I asked this woman I got the answer that I didn't want to hear: that I had no rights. That I had already given her away. That it was the best thing. And that it was all my fault. Somehow, it was all my fault that things weren't going well. And that I needed to just go home and I would forget about it and I would be fine.

We sat there for a long time, wrangling back and forth, and she wore me down. I was still sick, I still had not recovered. I was very weak and needed to lie down. She wasn't moving that car until I signed those papers. I re-member almost grabbing them from her at one point and saying, "All right, I'll sign them." I remember just scrawling my name and handing them back to my mother and my mother signed. The social worker took the papers, put them in her briefcase and we drove to my house without saying one more word. And life for me was never the same.

That fall I went back to school. I was a junior in high school but all I cared about was escaping. I couldn't concentrate—it was very difficult. I re-alized that I could find escape in drugs and, later, in alcohol. And that be-gan a lifelong problem, with trying to realize you can't bury your emotions. You just have to talk about them. So for about fifteen years, I smoked pot really heavily. I drank. I couldn't hold a job. I didn't know what I wanted. I remember just being really wild and not caring about anything. I was court-ing death, certainly. This went on for years.

I never had another relationship with a boy. I would never let anyone close enough to me. I no longer associated pleasure with sex. I associated death and pain and loss with sex. At some point I cleaned up enough to get a job, and I met my ex-husband in the late eighties. By then I was, like, thirty-six or something. And he taught me to enjoy sex, which I'm really grateful for. Before the age of thirty-six, I did not know how to enjoy sex.

I also noticed another phenomenon: I couldn't talk about what had happened to me, about my daughter and giving her up, because every single person I told the story to judged me. Not one single person said, "I know how you feel. If I were in your spot I would have had a hard time." Every single person judged me.

ANNIE

I was a junior in high school and an above-average student. I finished in the top 10 percent of my class, but I had no aspirations for continuing my education. I simply wanted to work for a year as a secretary and then get married and have babies. I had my husband picked out. He and I had been going steady since I was fourteen and he was fifteen. I was madly in love with him and he with me. That was the thing then. Around age fourteen and a half, we started having sex. Unfortunately, that was not that unusual for young people at that age, though no one admitted it then. When I returned to school in September of my junior year, that would have been 1957, there were about a half dozen girls who didn't come back because they had gotten married over the summer. So in this area of Milwaukee, and our socioeconomic class, it wasn't all that unusual.

We were so serious at fifteen and sixteen. We talked about getting married. We talked about the children we would have. We never thought about any birth control. Neither one of us really knew much about it. It just was not talked about then. Young men certainly couldn't get condoms, and there was no such thing as the birth-control pill. I doubt if I'd ever heard of a diaphragm. Maybe they didn't even exist. We just didn't really face the issue. The feelings that we had for each other were so strong, it never occurred to either one of us that we wouldn't be allowed to get married, because that's what happened if you got pregnant. I didn't know anything about girls being sent away. I never knew anyone who was sent away.

I missed a period and I worried and I worried. I missed another one and we decided that we had to tell our parents because we would both require their written permission to get married since we were underage. We dreamed up some excuse to take my mother somewhere in the car. We got a few blocks from home and he parked the car around the corner. She said, "Why are we stopping here?" I said, "Mother, we didn't go to the circus last night.

We went to a doctor." And she said, "Oh my God, don't tell me you're pregnant. Let me out of this car. Let me out of here right now." She was just crying and angry and we kept saying that we wanted to get married and she said something like "We'll see about that." She wanted to know if his parents knew and he said, yes, he had told them and they were willing to sign for us to get married and that his boss had offered us a room in their home rent free until we could be more established. She said, "I don't know those people."

Within a few days, she took me to her doctor, who was not very nice. He said, "Well, you know, there's a place where they send girls like her down in Kansas City," and he handed her a brochure. He said, "It's pretty expensive. If you have any money put aside for her, use it for this. She doesn't deserve to have it anyway." That was when the shame began. Before that, I had not really felt ashamed.

My mother and aunt went to his family's home and did not like what they saw. She said, "They have linoleum on the living-room floor. They're not good enough for you. Do you want your life to be like that twenty years from now?" When it became obvious that we were not going to be allowed to be married, he decided to enlist in the Marine Corps.

Then one day my mother said, "We are leaving for the Willows Friday night." That was the maternity home in Kansas City that her doctor had told her about. She said, "You're going there and you're going to stay there until you have the baby. Then you're going to give your baby up for adoption and you're going to come home and forget that this ever happened. Someday you'll thank me." I was very compliant. I respected authority and I did what I was told. At sixteen, back then, you couldn't get a job other than working at the local custard stand or as a car hop and earning two dollars in tips. I don't even know if welfare existed. I had no exposure to anything like that. I just had to do everything that my mother said. That was it. There were no options. The only option was to get married and she wouldn't allow it. So that was it. It was all decided for me.

We left for the Willows after dark so that nobody would see us. We rode the train all night long, in coach. I still remember those horrible seats. They were like the old streetcar seats. We took a taxicab to the maternity home and the owner came to greet us. My first thought was, "She seems pretty nice. This might not be so bad." My mother waited in Mrs. H's office while she took me on a tour. There were two vacancies, and they were both semi-private rooms. One of them had a washbasin and the other didn't. As soon as I found out that the room with the washbasin cost five dollars more a week, that was the one I wanted. It was one of the few things I could do to get back at my mother.

We spent the day in downtown Kansas City. We went out for supper and it was quite a treat because we didn't normally dine in restaurants. We stayed at a hotel and on Sunday morning my mother took me back to the Willows in a taxicab. They had a front entrance with thirty, forty, fifty steps, but nobody used it except the adoptive parents when they came to get the babies. Everyone else used the rear entrance. The taxi driver knew exactly where to go. I imagine he had delivered quite a few young women. My mother briefly got out of the cab and hugged and kissed me, and I remember that she was sobbing when she left. I remember that her shoulders were shaking and I think now of how difficult, how heartbreaking, that must have been for her. I was so nasty to her—oh, I was nasty to her. I made her pay five dollars a week more. She had on a red-and-white sleeveless blouse and a rust-colored skirt. Horrible color combination but, you know, this was 1958. But I'll always carry that picture in my mind of her with her shoulders shaking as she got into the taxicab.

I NEVER TOLD my husband about my first child. People used to say, "Never tell a man, because he'll think that you're used merchandise." They thought men should have all this experience and women should be virgins. You were supposed to fake it. Well, that's what I did. My obstetrician knew, and he said I made a very good decision. I believed what I was told, and I went along with it. The person that I am today looks back on that young girl and thinks, "Didn't she have her own mind?" But it was a totally different time. There's just no way that it can be compared to today.

When our second child was about seven, things started to fall apart between my husband and me. It seemed like we disagreed for the sake of disagreeing on just about everything. At that time in Wisconsin, the grounds for divorce were horrible things: physical abuse, mental cruelty, abandonment *or* voluntary separation of one year or more. So we separated. I had quit a really good job about two and a half years before because I was doing better at work than my husband and, you know, in 1972 that was an issue. I had been earning more money, and I hadn't told him about the last couple of raises I had gotten, and when he found out it was a big problem. So I quit the job because I thought the job was not as important as the marriage. The man was supposed to be the provider. It was getting to the point where it was okay for the woman to work, but only to supplement the family income. This was in our circle, anyway.

Everybody was very surprised to see that we were separating; we had put on a really good show. When I went around and told my family members, the first thing my mother said was "I hope you never told him about that baby you had in Kansas City, because if you did he can have you declared an unfit mother and take the girls away from you."

So my husband and I had separated and I don't remember why, but one Saturday when he came over I told him about the daughter I placed for adoption. And I saw something in him that, after living with him for fifteen years, I'd never seen before. I saw a caring, a depth, a compassion, and that was really . . . that was big. He had always been kind of surface and cavalier about everything, and I was the one who spoke about feelings. That was a big, big issue between us. I told him very matter-of-factly. I didn't elaborate a great deal. I did not cry. I just said that I'd never told him because I had been advised not to, but I did not like having this between us. I'd never felt honest about it and I just felt that I wanted him to know. He was so caring. He said, "It must have been so horrible for you to carry that all those years." This was one of the finer moments of our marriage, it really, truly was, but by then it was just too late. There was so much else that had happened. It was just too late.

3

-⫚-

Good Girls
v. Bad Girls

It was 1959 and I was living in a dormitory at the University of Toledo and working two or three part-time jobs to work my way through school. I was dating this guy who was a couple of years older who was an engineering student and I cared about him very much. I don't think in those days we knew about birth control. I didn't know anything. It was something good girls didn't talk about. I never talked about sex with anyone, including my family. I didn't know about ovulation or anything. Good girls didn't talk about those things.

—*Carole I*

I F YOU ARE A WOMAN over fifty who had sex before marriage, you are one of the so-called bad girls. I would put myself squarely in that category. The only difference between me and the women whose stories appear here is that I didn't get caught. These women and I were certainly not alone in our badness. As early as the 1950s, about 39 percent of unmarried girls had gone "all the way" before they were twenty years old, and by 1973 the percentage had risen to 68 percent.[1] Because of the difficulty of getting contraceptives, the frequency of premarital pregnancies rose right along with that number. In the mid-1950s, about 40 percent of first births to girls age fifteen to nineteen were conceived out of wedlock.[2] Thereafter, the numbers rose sharply. By 1971–1974, the number of first births conceived outside of marriage to teenage girls had reached 60 percent.[3]

In the post–World War II years, young people's attitudes toward premarital sex, as well as their actual sexual behavior, began to change. A revolution in dating behavior had actually begun back in the 1920s as teens, rather than their parents, started regulating dating behavior. Unlike their Victorian predecessors who courted on the front porch where their behavior could be closely monitored, the young people in the 1920s enjoyed a degree of privacy and mobility. As dating moved off the porch and into the community, parents were no longer present to set limits. Teens themselves began to determine what was appropriate sexual behavior and to enforce their own standards through peer pressure.[4] At the same time, they were being influenced by notions of love and romance disseminated through movies, magazines, and popular music rather than by local customs.

In 1924, for example, when the sociologists Robert and Helen Lynd conducted extensive interviews with the residents of Muncie, Indiana, the young people there were already having petting parties, going to the movies on their own, and parking.[5] As more and more families owned cars, they afforded young people increasing independence and provided the privacy that allowed them to engage in sexual activity. Henry Ford, it seems, may have been at least partly to blame for the sexual revolution.

Over the decades cars have, of course, continued to play a significant role in dating life, and that was certainly true in the postwar years. Not only were they safe havens, they also served—as they continue to—as a measure of a young man's status.

> We were middle-class folks; I had a pretty normal childhood. I was in my senior year of high school, still kind of quiet and shy, not one of the popular cheerleader girls, but I had my own little clique of friends. And there was a guy who had moved to town that all the girls just thought was so cute, and so cool, and we talked and whispered, "Weren't his blue eyes so pretty," and all this kind of stuff.
>
> He drove a really hot car, which was real important at the time. I think it was a pumped-up Super Sport Chevelle—big tires, big engine, souped up, beautiful, fast, noisy because noisy was impor-

tant, with a stick shift, which was also very important. And for some reason he decided to ask me out. It wasn't my first date or anything, it wasn't even my first sexual experience, but he was very cool and I was cool because I was going out with him.

—Barbara

The economic boom that followed World War II increased young people's independence from their parents and escalated the revolution in sexual behavior. An increasing number of nonmarried coeds left home to attend college and joined the nearly six million returning veterans whose education was funded by the GI Bill.[6] This younger generation became a cultural force to be reckoned with and much of the new energy seemed to be sexual. As early as 1952, panty raids were being conducted on campuses all across the country. Gangs of nice college boys were breaking windows and entering women's dorms just to get hold of girls' underpants.[7]

More overt expressions of sexuality not only became common among single people in their twenties but trickled down into high-school age youth culture as well. Young people took their cues from older teens and mass media, decidedly not from their parents. For girls, magazines like *Seventeen* were looked to as the fonts of wisdom about what was popular and sexy. Increasing one's sex appeal, of course, required a whole host of products that mothers thought their girls were too young to buy or wear. I remember the many battles over skirt length, lipstick, and blusher—which my mother insisted on calling rouge—that raged routinely in my house and I'm sure in households across America. The first-floor girls' restroom in my high school was packed every morning with young women rolling the waistbands of their skirts so as to raise their hemline to the maximum distance above the knee permitted by school law. A considerable amount of elbowing was required to make it up to the mirror and apply makeup, which was promptly removed after seventh period.

Interestingly, as young people expanded the boundaries of permissible sexual activity a movement toward forming steady relationships took hold. Sociologists in the early fifties noted a significant new trend among young people to get into serious relationships rather than date around,[8] which had been more popular in previous decades. This new emphasis on commitment might well have been due to the fact that it provided something of a safety net for pre-serving a girl's reputation, as more and more young people engaged in sexual intercourse. During the postwar decades, the question that the youth grap-pled with became not so much *if* as *when* premarital sex was considered per-missible. Permissible by their peers, that is, because sexual activity was still not discussed, or even acknowledged, by most parents.

And though the rules about who could have sex without risking reputa-tional suicide surely varied from group to group, town to town, and region to region, they followed a general progression over the years. At first, sex was permissible only for couples who were engaged; later for those who were pinned or going steady; then for those in love; and finally widening all the way to include those who were simply attracted to one other.

> If you got pregnant outside of marriage you were a whore, a slut, whatever. You had no morals, therefore you deserved this. But if you didn't get caught you were smart. When you got a fraternity pin on your boob, that meant you were allowed to have sex. That meant you were engaged to be engaged or whatever. I never un-derstood all that, but that's the way it was.
>
> *—Nancy III*

In the early fifties, many women engaged in heavy petting but refrained from sexual intercourse until a promise of marriage was forthcoming, and the majority waited until their wedding night. But as the years progressed not only did more young couples begin having sex before marriage, but they had it at younger and younger ages. Comparing white, unmarried women who turned eighteen between 1956 and 1958 with those who did so between 1971 and 1973, the percentage who had their first premarital sexual intercourse at age fifteen quadrupled, from 1.3 percent to 5.6 percent. Those in the same cohort who had premarital sex before age twenty jumped from 33.3 percent to 65.5 percent.[9] And though eventually a commitment was no longer re-quired, what sexual intercourse signified in a relationship often varied quite a bit among partners. Plenty of young women, and some young men, pre-sumed sex would solidify a commitment where one was never intended.

In some cases, young women who did not feel ready to have sex did so anyway because of continual pressure from a boyfriend and the lack of assertiveness required to put a stop to the steady progression of sexual advances. More recent studies have shown that sexual coercion from partners still plays a powerful role in the timing of a young woman's sexual debut. In a survey from the 1990s, 25 percent of women indicated that they did not want to have sex the first time they did so.[10] Sometimes sexual aggressiveness went beyond coercion and women were date-raped, though neither the concept nor the terminology was well understood or defined at the time. About 7 percent of the women I interviewed became pregnant as a result of rape—not by the violent sex criminals who have become the staple of television dramas but by *nice* young men.

> I think it was in about February, and a friend's brother was home on break from his school and called me up and said, "All my friends are having this party at the summer house that we're opening up. I don't have anybody to go with. Would you go with me?" I said, "Sure, I'll go." And we went off to the party, and I really remember very little about that night.
>
> I remembered standing in a kitchen, talking to this fellow about calculus and all these Latin things, and somebody handed me a drink, and the next thing I know everything was spinning. I felt desperately sick and I said, "I'm going to get sick. I've got to go lie down." I remember walking and trying to find someplace to lie down. That's the last of my memory.
>
> The next morning I thought, "Oh my God, what has gone on?" I was still feeling so out of it that I wasn't really quite sure, but I started to suspect what may have happened. Back then date rape was not a term, but apparently that's what it was. So I don't know the birth father at all. I have no visual memory of him. My reaction was "I don't ever want to think about this again. Whatever happened, happened. I don't want any part of this."
>
> When I went home for Easter break, I started feeling really sick and I thought, "Oh gosh, I have the flu." Well, when it didn't go

away I thought, "Could I have become pregnant?" Two months later, I thought, "This is not right." I went to the library, and I started reading all these books about pregnancy to try and figure it out. I had no idea what the symptoms were. I don't know when I really figured it out, but I knew I absolutely could not tell anybody because I would be expelled from college. It was just automatic expulsion, no questions asked, and I was halfway through my senior year. I knew I had to hide it in order to get out of school.

I was so devastated that this happened to me, because it was the antithesis of everything I was and how I was brought up. It really just shattered every sense of self I had, and I went into denial. By denying it, I could be who I really was, and not what I had become, or at least what I thought I had become.

—Carol II

One might expect that with premarital intercourse becoming more frequent among the youth, a loosening of the stigma associated with engaging in sex would have followed. But one of the great ironies of this time period was that the social policing of youth by their peers was intense, and could be psychologically brutal. The girls bore the brunt of this social condemnation as the sexual revolution evolved. For young men, being known as sexually active was a badge of honor among their peers, whereas for young women sexual activity had to be kept secret, and if word got out, their reputations could be devastated. Throughout the fifties and sixties, women had to be highly discreet about their sexual behavior; a reputation lost was almost impossible to regain. An unattached girl thought to be "putting out" was a threat to the social order of the peer community. More specifically, she was a threat to other young women who were following the rules and feared losing their boyfriends to someone more sexually adventuresome.

There was this business then that girls are only two types, you were either a Madonna or a whore, and not the singer Madonna, the virgin Madonna. You were good or bad. Between the culture of the family and the culture of the religion, you were very bad if you had sex. So you couldn't really *plan* to have sex; it had to just *happen*.

We had been petting and you get all the, "Oh, we have to go
further, we have to go further." I said, "I don't want to get pregnant, don't get me pregnant." He said, "Oh, don't worry, I won't."

                                                              —Diane IV

In my Midwest high school even in the late 1960s, women did not admit
having sexual intercourse even to their closest friends. There was very little
talk about sex apart from boys' locker-room talk, which often stretched the
truth but could make or break a girl's reputation. Being well liked and popular among one's female and male friends, and being sexually active behind
closed doors, required a set of advanced social skills. There were very defi-
nite and complicated rules about what was and was not permissible, and under what conditions. Careful calculations had to be made about the number
of dates and the number of bases that a boy was allowed to reach. The sum
of these calculations then had to be weighed against the seriousness of the
commitment and how others perceived the relationship. Going steady was
the pinnacle of commitment in my school and held a kind of false promise
of a future together. It was, for all intents and purposes, a practice engagement. Often young people practiced quite a bit and had one "steady" after
another, ostensibly in search of the ideal mate.

Once a young woman was going steady, she removed herself from the
competitive dating scene and her sexual behavior fell off her classmates'
radar screen. Having sex with a steady did not presume a promise of eternal
bliss, but at least if a young woman had sex with her steady she would not
be labeled promiscuous. Everyone silently agreed on a "Don't ask, don't
tell" policy when it came to the activities of committed couples.

If a young woman had not gotten to the going-steady stage before having sex, her reputation was more vulnerable. There were always a few young
women who were either unfamiliar with the rules, unfairly targeted, or more
sexually adventurous, all of whom were labeled "sluts." Those of us who escaped being the target of rumors did not, to our shame, befriend these girls
because we feared guilt by association. After all, our status was tenuous and
could be preserved only by keeping our distance and maintaining our hyp-
ocritical stance through steadfast denial.

The deep and damaging irony of the "bad girl" myth is that those who became pregnant were assumed to be less moral—to be transgressors—by others who were engaging in the very same behavior. A young woman's pregnancy was thought to result from her "badness." The scorn and blame heaped on these women seem to have been partly a mechanism of denial: by focusing attention on women whose sexual behavior was evident, others could continue to deny their own.

You were shunned if you were pregnant. That's the way they reacted to girls who were pregnant in high school. The girls who didn't get pregnant were all virgins. We swore up and down we were virgins. If you fooled around, nobody else knew about it. It was never a thing where you could say to a friend of yours that you went to bed with somebody—that was just taboo.

You were all supposed to be virgins and the ones that got pregnant it was like . . . oh, she was no good, she was promiscuous. Guys were supposed to be that way. They have their oats to sow. So that's the way it was. Girls weren't supposed to do it, and guys were always trying to do it with them.

—Carol I

There were good girls and there were bad girls and I played a good girl, but I was really a bad girl. A lot of people didn't know that I was sexually active. There was such shame associated with being pregnant and unmarried at that time. When I was in high school, there was a girl who became pregnant. She had PE with us and then she was gone. I remember being in the locker room and the girls were snickering and making jokes. She was such a nice person and a good athlete, and they turned their back on her. They could at least have said, "It's okay, we still like you."

—Joyce I

I was a sorority girl and I was going into my junior year at the University of Minnesota. I conceived on September 20, 1968, in the Gopher Motel. I was from a small town, so I didn't tell anybody because in 1968 you were considered trash if you were pregnant.

The symbol of being a good, white, middle class family was a lily-white daughter.

—Sue

The other fateful irony about the explosion in premarital sex in the postwar years was that society at large failed to acknowledge the magnitude of change under way, and failed to act responsibly to educate the youth about pregnancy and prevention. Young people were clearly secretive about their behavior, but by the 1960s so many pregnancies were occurring that the warning signs should have been clear and troubling enough to sound an alarm. Instead, adult society effectively turned a blind eye to the situation, and in the main simply continued to profess that young people should hold out until marriage.

Women were expected to wait and learn about sex from their husbands, who would bring their sexual experience to the marriage. I've never quite figured out how that was supposed to be mathematically possible, but presumably the theory was that the future husbands gained their experience with a few bad girls who were not marriage material and who were having sex with the majority of the male population.

Most parents simply did not want to acknowledge that their sons and daughters were having sex. Not my son. Not my daughter. But with millions of young people having sex with no planning and no protection, there was a high likelihood that parents' denial would be short-lived. School systems had not yet begun offering substantial sex education and, incredibly, in the late 1960s were still referring to sexual intercourse as "the marriage act." Sex education generally consisted of watching a scratchy movie that showed egg and sperm meeting. Wherever this mysterious meeting place was, it seemed to have nothing to do with being in the backseat of a car with your boyfriend. Many of the women I interviewed were utterly uninformed about sex and pregnancy and learned what little they knew from their boyfriends.

I can remember in sixth grade we had a film. You know, the sperm and the egg and that whole thing. There was no sex education. My mom sent away for the Kotex kit in the mail and it came and there were all the different sizes and shapes of pads. Of course, this was before tampons. She didn't really talk to me but she sort of supplied the information. That was probably the best she could do. I remember there was controversy about should we have sex education in high school at the time, but I don't think we ever had any. And condoms weren't as available to kids as they are now. We were oblivious. I mean, certainly I knew that if you had sex you could get pregnant. I wasn't that naïve. But abstinence wasn't thought of. You were just horny teenagers and that was that.

—Becky

If there was any talk of sex in the home, it was usually the sex talk the girls had with their mother around their first period and mainly concerned itself with the wearing of Kotex pads and the stretchy belts that kept them in place.

I think I was in the fifth or sixth grade and I went to the bathroom and I'm pulling my panties down and they had blood on them and I started screaming because I didn't know what was going on. They called my mother and she came and picked me up from school. We stopped by a drugstore, she left me in the car and went in and then handed me a bag and told me go in the bathroom and put it on. I sat in that bathroom probably an hour trying to figure out how all this mess worked. There was a stretchy thing with clamps on it, and then these pads. Scared me to death.

—Joyce I

When parents did talk to their daughters about sex, they often began the sentence with the word *don't,* as in "Don't ever let a boy touch you." Or, if pregnancy was even acknowledged as something that could *occur* before marriage, "Don't ever come home pregnant." This directive rarely included an explanation of how one might actually get or not get pregnant. Since most adolescents are eager to grow up as quickly as possible, the silence and mystery surrounding sex surely only made it all the more intriguing.

My mother talk about sex? Oh, God. Please. "You can't be kissing boys. You can't be letting anybody touch you. Sex is dirty. Sex is bad." It was always bad things. Always taboo. It was never healthy, never, never a healthy talk. My mother was twenty-four with four kids. Probably that's why sex was bad.

We did not have sex education in school. I mean, I graduated high school in '64, and sex was not discussed. You were not supposed to have sex until you were married and that was it. My goodness. You just didn't talk about sex. It was all negative, it only got you in trouble. She was right about that, though, when you think about it. She was right. I should have listened to her.

—Carolyn I

I was throwing up and one of my friends said, "You're probably pregnant." And I said, "Oh no, no, no, you can't be pregnant unless you're married." That's what my parents told me: "You have to be married to have a baby." So I couldn't be pregnant because I wasn't married. Sex education was in sixth grade all the Campfire Girls went and saw this film. I didn't understand it. I mean, it was just the man has the sperm and the woman has the egg, and somehow or other they make a baby. They didn't talk about body parts, ever. Oh gosh, no. Men and women, back in that day, slept in separate beds on television. I'm adopted and my parents were older. They were scared to death to talk about sex, scared to death to talk about anything.

—Nancy II

Sex was just not discussed in those days. You found out from your friends. The girls would talk at pajama parties or if they got together at somebody's house after school, but sex talked about in school? Oh, my God, no! I remember when *Peyton Place* was published. It was banned, so we all had a copy of *Peyton Place*. We would stick it inside a book in study hall and read it. If you ever got caught reading that book—I mean, you can't even imagine the detentions and the phone calls home. Life would not be worth living.

And you did not discuss sex at home. I can see my mother sitting there knitting. My mother was a great knitter. She was like

Madame Defarge in *A Tale of Two Cities*. She would knit, knit, knit to avoid conversation. I remember her knitting away and all of a sudden I said to her, "What is sexual intercourse?" She looked me right in the eye and said, "Don't bother me, I'm counting."

—Maureen II

The mothers' denial of the reality that their daughters might need some facts about sex and pregnancy is especially illogical given that, statistically, almost half of the mothers themselves had had sex before marriage, and some had walked down the aisle pregnant. But then again, logic usually has little to do with sex, and parents usually don't think *their* child is having sex. That has likely not changed over time.

Even for those who were somewhat aware of how to prevent pregnancy, effective contraceptives were hard to come by. The legacy of blame and shame that so many of the women who became pregnant have had to live with has been perpetuated in part by a current lack of awareness about just how difficult contraceptives were to get hold of in those postwar decades. This was particularly true of contraceptives for single women.

Many of the laws in effect in the 1950s and 1960s had been in place since the Victorian era. In 1873 for the first time in U.S. history, birth control was prohibited by law with the passage of the Comstock Law, which criminalized sending "obscene" matter through the mail.[11] In the mid-1800s, women could send away for informational pamphlets, and ads for douches to prevent pregnancy were common in women's magazines and newspapers, though they were often veiled in nonspecific language having to do with cleansing or health.[12] In fact, information about birth-control methods had been passed down through generations of women, long before devices were regulated through the medical establishment. Women were using vaginal sponges several thousand years before Christ.[13] Whether through herbal potions, vaginal suppositories, diaphragms, the rhythm method, or douching, women have tried to prevent unwanted pregnancy.

But in 1872, Anthony Comstock, a religious reformer and the founder of the New York Society for the Suppression of Vice, drafted an anti-obscenity bill, which included a ban on contraceptives. He argued that contraceptive devices were obscene and sinful because they *prevented* conception. Comstock successfully campaigned for the enactment of the bill as a federal law, and he was also instrumental in twenty-four states adopting their own versions of the Comstock Law, restricting the sale of contraceptives at the state level. Despite the diligence of birth-control advocates like Margaret Sanger in the early 1900s, as late as the 1960s some states still criminalized merely dispensing information about birth control or making contraceptive devices available to women.[14] Even as laws changed state by state, the moralistic attitudes endured and few unmarried women were willing to attempt an appointment with a doctor to obtain contraceptives.

> I mean, the lack of information in 1966 was astounding. If you wanted to get birth-control pills, you had to be flashing a diamond solitaire. Doctors really didn't give them to you. Why would you need those? You shouldn't be having sex anyway.
>
> *—Nancy III*

During the late 1950s and through most of the 1960s, the most effective means of birth control—the pill and the intrauterine device—were either unavailable or inaccessible to single women. The pill was available for the regulation of menstrual periods beginning in 1957 and was approved for contraceptive use by the FDA in 1960. The IUD also became available in the 1960s. But both the pill and the IUD posed safety concerns when they were initially released and it was not until the early 1970s that both were generally considered to be safe. It was not the safety of contraceptives, however, that prevented doctors in the 1960s from prescribing the pill or the IUD to unmarried women but state laws or personal moral values.[15] The diaphragm was the device most widely used by married women in the 1950s, but it was also largely unavailable to single women because a doctor's visit was required.[16]

> I had finished nursing school and I was working as a nurse. And, you know, one thing led to another and we had sex. That's what happens. Birth control just wasn't available. I mean, condoms were available but hardly ever used. The birth-control pill was on the market, but in those days you really had to be married to go to a doctor and ask. There weren't walk-in clinics. There wasn't any of

that stuff. Birth control just was not a subject that was talked about. If you knew somebody who was not married and was taking oral contraceptives, they were taking them to regulate their period. I couldn't even tell you how many people had *that* story.

—Maureen II

I knew I should be doing something to prevent pregnancy but I would never have gone to a doctor. You had to pretend you were married to get birth-control pills. I could never have done that. I'm not an actress. There was a girl in our dormitory who sold them—I don't know how she got them. I started taking them, but I felt terribly guilty because it went against what I had been taught. So I sort of took them and then I didn't take them, and then I took them and I didn't take them, and I got pregnant. I mean, I just didn't really understand that you had to continuously take them.

—Maggie

The most readily available contraceptive for nonmarried couples was condoms but they were often kept behind the counter at the pharmacy, and in some towns just asking to purchase one might result in a phone call from the pharmacist to the boy's parents. Sometimes prophylactics were found in gas-station vending machines, but for a number of reasons—including difficulty getting them or young men feeling confident that they knew how to prevent pregnancy without a condom—they were not often used by young people.

I got pregnant at the end of July 1969. I remember, I went to the drive-in movie to see *Easy Rider* because the birth father loved motorcycles. He was just home from Vietnam and the first thing he did was buy a motorcycle. So we had to go see that movie.

I mean, this was before the days of birth control. You had to be eighteen to buy a rubber. They didn't have them in Stop & Shop, like they have today. They were down at the corner drugstore. The boys would maybe buy them, sneak them, or something. But as a female? To go and buy rubbers? Oh, my God, that did not happen. (I probably should have said "prophylactics" but you'll white that out.) There's no way. They wouldn't have given them to you. And you think, "Aw, it's not gonna happen to me. I'll never get pregnant."

We had dated for about two and a half months before I got pregnant. But that was the first time I ever had sex. In the backseat of that car, watching *Easy Rider.*

—Cathy II

The state of Connecticut, home state of Anthony Comstock, still had a law in 1961 that prohibited counseling and medical treatment to *married* persons for the purposes of preventing conception. The constitutionality of that prohibition was struck down in 1965, when the Supreme Court decided the case of *Griswold v. Connecticut.*[17] Estelle T. Griswold, the executive director of Planned Parenthood League in Connecticut, and Dr. C. Lee Buxton, a Yale professor and physician who served as medical director of the league, were arrested in 1961 for giving information and instruction to a married woman to help her prevent contraception. The Supreme Court's decision in *Griswold v. Connecticut* guaranteed all married couples in the country the right to receive information and services to prevent pregnancy based on the right of privacy in marital relations.

By 1970 most women, whether married or single, were able to get prescriptions for the pill or other contraceptive devices and control their own pregnancy prevention. But in the state of Massachusetts a law still prohibited the dispensation of any kind of birth control to an unmarried man or woman. In 1967 William Baird, longtime reproductive-rights crusader, challenged the state's anticontraceptives law—which also stipulated that only doctors or pharmacists could provide contraceptives—by giving vaginal foam to a woman after a 1967 lecture on birth control at Boston University. Baird was not an authorized distributor of contraceptives and he was promptly arrested, convicted of a felony, and spent thirty-six days in jail for "crimes against chastity." Only when his case, *Eisenstadt v. Baird,* reached the Supreme Court and was decided in his favor in 1972 was access to birth control guaranteed to all single men and women in the United States.[18]

With little information or access to effective birth control, until the early 1970s most young people either took their chances or took ineffective precautions such as the rhythm method and withdrawal—more commonly called "pulling-out"—which required no access or planning. Boys were convinced that withdrawal was a surefire method and most girls took their word for it. Interestingly, a survey conducted by the Kinsey Institute in 1989 indicated that one quarter of those surveyed still believed that withdrawal was an effective method of contraception.[19] In fact, withdrawal, the rhythm method, and vaginal foam are the least effective methods.[20]

He knew all about the rhythm method, so he asked me when I had my last period. That's why it was okay to have sex without any condom. What else was there in 1963? There wasn't anything. I guess there was a diaphragm, but who knew?

I became paralyzed by the fact that I was pregnant—I was so unprepared for it. When I was in high school, I remember there were a couple of girls who got pregnant and there was just all that negative gossip. That was not me. I wasn't part of all that.

—*Judith III*

My mom hadn't been real big on telling me about sex. I think, like most girls my age, we kind of tried to figure it out on our own. I knew having sex could get me pregnant but I didn't think I *would* get pregnant. I don't know why, but that's what I thought.

—*Barbara*

I had no idea what I was going to do. I mean, abortions were not legal. The world wasn't going to accept a white, Anglo–Saxon, Protestant single mother in 1966. I knew I wasn't going to tell the father. There was another girl who was pinned to a guy in the same fraternity and when she got pregnant he trotted out three or four of his fraternity brothers to say they'd all had sex with her.

—*Nancy III*

I was twenty-three years old at the time. I was not educated at all about sex. In Catholic school they just constantly, constantly, put in your mind that you never had sex before marriage—you didn't need to know anything about it. The only time I heard anything about the reproductive system was when I was a senior in high school and one of the nuns got up and tried to tell us about two frogs having sex. When I stop and think back, I never even knew that parents slept in the same bed until I went to a girlfriend's house and her mother and father did. I thought that was a mortal sin.

—Bette

Most of the women I interviewed had been wholly uninformed about sex and pregnancy prevention. Few reported that they or their partner had used protection. Many did not think they could become pregnant after only a few sexual encounters. Some had boyfriends who used condoms on occasion, and others tried the rhythm method with only a vague notion of the days during which conception was likely to occur. They had been left to figure it out for themselves and they were ultimately unsuccessful. Given sexual activity and inadequate precautions, there was a high likelihood that pregnancy would occur. A sexually active teenager who does not use contraceptives has a 90 percent chance of becoming pregnant within a year.[21]

Hearing these women tell their stories today, one can't help but acknowledge the unfairness of calling them "bad girls" and of the social scorn that was inflicted almost exclusively on them, and not on the young men with whom they had conceived.

I was a senior in college and I was getting ready to begin my student teaching, which was very exciting. I had been dating somebody for a few years and he was the person I was going to marry. We had gone through the traditional steps of that time. First it was the friendship ring—everybody got that pearl ring—and then the Christmas right before I was given a hope chest. It was a beautiful hope chest and everybody was giving me gifts and planning for this marriage.

Once I finished school, the next step would be the engagement. Of course, I was thinking maybe that summer after graduation. He was a couple of years older than I and he was teaching at the time. So, you know, we had a relationship and we had plans for the future. But the plan didn't include my becoming pregnant at that point in time. But it was still going to be okay. We went out and we ordered wedding rings and we were having them engraved. I don't believe those rings were ever picked up.

I knew that my parents would be upset but I didn't know how bad it would be. My mother was screaming and yelling and my father threw him out of the house and then hit me so hard that I went across the kitchen. It was horrible. I just never expected that. Then we went to tell his family and they were horrible, too. He left me sitting there in his house with his mother screaming at me and the last thing I remember her saying to me was "What have you done to my son? What about my son's life?"

My parents said that if I agreed never to see him again and do exactly as they told me to do, everything would be taken care of. I remember calling him and telling him that, and he said that might be the best thing because we had too much going against us.

—Kathi

NANCY I

Things began to get fairly physical between us. I had never entertained the idea of sex before, because it just wasn't done in our family. In those days, there was just a certain decorum in puritanical families. We were never even allowed to say the word *pregnant;* we had to say *expecting.* Everything I learned about sex was off the walls in the A-wing bathroom. We would talk about it at lunchtime: "Can you believe this is what they do?" "No. You're kidding." I mean, we were seniors in high school—how pathetic is that?

I could tell that he knew a little bit more than I did and, as ridiculous as it sounds, I was learning from him. He had come out to visit me one evening and we went for a walk, and he decided that that was going to be the evening he would "have his way with me," and he did. I was scared. I just didn't know . . . I mean, the whole biology of it. He kept saying, "It's okay. It's okay. It's really hard to get pregnant. Don't worry." What did I know? I didn't see a lot of pregnant people, so I figured, I guess it *is* really hard. Maybe you have to do this a lot to get pregnant.

Later, I began to notice that there was something awry. I started getting sick in the morning. I knew something wasn't right. I got clothing for Christmas and I knew that however badly those clothes fit me then, it was only going to get worse. I remember taking a particular green-and-white dress that my father had bought me up to my room. I looked at myself in the mirror and thought, "This is a joke. This is going right back to the store." I took it back and later my father said, "I'm not gonna buy you kids' clothing anymore. Soon as I do, you hightail it right back to the store and take it back."

I had stayed after school for a student-council meeting and I was sitting on top of a desk in a classroom, participating in this meeting, and I saw my mother's face through the door. She was a teacher at the elementary school in town, but I don't think she had ever set foot in the high school. I knew when I saw her face that she knew. She motioned for me and I got my books. We walked down the hall and she said, "I need you to come with me." In the car she turned to me and said, "Are you really four months pregnant?" I was, like, "Me? Pregnant? Of course not. What are you talking about?" My sister had heard a rumor and told her. She reached over and sort of pulled my shirt up ever so slightly and touched my stomach and said, "Are you?" I said, "I have no idea what you're talking about."

She starts driving and we wind up in the parking lot of our church. My father's car is parked there at three-thirty in the afternoon, next to the minister's car. This is a party I don't want to be going to. The Reverend and my father were sitting in his living room. I had never been in the Reverend's home before. My mother sat down and my father said, "Okay, what's going on?" I said, "Beats me. I have no idea what you people are up to." He dismissed that. He talked right over that and said, "We've got a problem here. We're going to get this taken care of. We have to figure out what to do with the baby." That was the first time I had ever heard that phrase, "the baby," and it was almost like a safety net for me. It wasn't *my* baby, it was *the* baby. I could separate myself from this problem and I knew I wasn't going to have to make any decisions about it, because it wasn't *mine*.

I continued to deny it up and down: "I don't know what you're talking about. There's no baby." My mother finally said, "Okay, if it's not true, would you at least do us a favor and go to the doctor's tonight, just to get it confirmed?" I said, "Sure, there's nothing to confirm." My father, my mother, and I drive to the doctor's. He meets us there at eight at night. It's this big, huge Victorian home that I'm terrified to be in. I had never met this guy in my life, never had any kind of exam at all, except for a dentist appointment.

He takes me to the examining room, has me take off all of my clothes and put on a johnny. He does an internal exam and then he says, "Okay, you can put your clothes on." I considered leaving through the back door, in the middle of the winter, to go to another planet. All I knew is I did not want to go back out into that room where my parents are waiting. We went home and there were some tears and I remember my mother saying those classic words "Why?" and "How could you?" until finally, out of emotional exhaustion, we all went to bed.

Arrangements were made for me to be sent to this home. It was presented as an option at the time: "It would be more comfortable for you. If you'd like to do that, we'll help you." The night before I was scheduled to leave, my mother was starting to feel the effects of the impending separation and I had the very first, possibly the only, honest conversation I'd ever had with her. I felt safe enough, as we do when we're feeling close, to ask her this question: "How do they get rid of the mark when they take the baby out?" I'd seen people in bathing suits and I could never tell if they'd had children. She stood there, three feet from me, with a look of horror on her face and said, "My God, Nancy, that baby comes out the same way it went in." I said, "You have got to be kidding me." She said, "No."

I mean, it's borderline child abuse not to share this kind of information. How can anyone think that we will just absorb it naturally, or that it's our responsibility as children to figure it out? It just mystifies me. I had no idea. I mean, we had never had pets. I didn't live on a farm. We had a very puritanical, Beaver Cleaver lifestyle, and it just wasn't anything that was ever discussed. I mean, as amazing as it sounds, I was sixteen and pregnant and I did not know how babies were born. It's pathetic, but it's true.

At the maternity home there was a roster on a bulletin board, near the stairway, that indicated people's chores. The chores rotated. They were minor, like cleaning the bathrooms, running a vacuum cleaner, helping out in the kitchen, setting the table, that kind of stuff. As new girls came in, their names went to the bottom. So, over the time you were there, you would watch your name continue to move up that list—that was one indicator of how close you were. When a girl left we would never see her again. A few girls, revolutionary girls, talked about keeping their babies but we knew they were crazy. We knew: no one was allowed to keep their baby.

When I went into labor, someone from the home drove me to the hospital. She left the car running, went into the emergency room, and said, "I've got a girl from the home here" and she turned around and left. They put me in a room and I lay on a bed holding on to the bars above my head, enduring contractions in silence. I was afraid to make any noise. I lay there almost all night. It got worse and worse and I held on for dear life. Finally, someone came by and said, "What are you doing in here?"

They took me into the delivery room. It was a huge room with a lot of people milling around. Here I am, up in stirrups, and all these young doctors are kind of walking by chitchatting, like they're at a baseball game. I remember being so humiliated. Finally, a doctor comes in. He starts saying, "Push," and I'm thinking, "Push what?" I didn't know what he was talking about. I didn't know how to help. I couldn't help; I had no control over my body at that point. He started yelling, "Who gave this girl so many drugs?" Then two other people started pushing on my stomach, and I could see, in that round light above my head, the reflection of what was happening. My child was being born. And this guy saw that I could see and moved the light. He tipped it away once he realized I could actually see this event that was mine. He took that away from me.

Every day I asked if I could see my baby, and every day they said, "Yes, we'll come and get you and take you to the nursery." But they never did. Then the day I was being released, someone took me upstairs and wheeled me in front of the nursery window. She pointed to the one that was mine and said, "That's him." I asked if I could hold him, and she said no. I just looked through a piece of Plexiglas and she stepped back from the wheelchair and said, "Are you done?"

Afterward, I sort of fell into my old ways and started seeing my friends again, but I wasn't the same anymore. I mean, you just can't be the same after the experience of becoming a mother. I knew that my son was gonna be part of my life again one day. I never let go of that from the very beginning. I remember writing to the agency because I had some things I was making for him that I wanted to send. I got a note back saying, "Don't send anything else." I remember thinking, "Over my dead body are they gonna tell me this is done." When he was about two, I met my husband. I remember it was one of the first things I told him: "I have a two-year-old son that's gonna be a part of my life someday." I figured, you know, I'm a package deal now and there was no way to undo that.

In the late eighties, I was reading the paper one day and there was a little block ad, which I still have, that said, "Adoption Issues group meeting at the Library." I closed the paper and then I opened it again, and I thought, "Adoption issues? I think I have an adoption issue." So I cut it out and put it on the bulletin board in the kitchen. I found myself ruminating over it constantly. I remember sitting at the table one night and my husband was looking at me and he said, "What are you thinking about?" And I said, "Nothing." He said, "You're going to that meeting, aren't you?" And I said, "Yeah, I'm going to that meeting."

I had to say it many times over the next few weeks in order to actually get my strength up to go. When I walked in someone approached me and said, "Hi, I'm Barbara. I'm a birth mother." I thought, "She just said that in front of everybody in this room with a smile on her face." And as those meetings progressed, over October and November and December, all the tears that had never come finally came. I decided that if I could go to the meetings for a year without crying, then I would be ready to pursue an active search.

In January 1989, which was the year he turned twenty-one, I was ready to search. I finally got the nerve to call the agency and the director said, "I really can't tell you anything over the phone. If you have any questions, they have to be in writing." I'm thinking, "Oh, that's just great. I could barely say the words, now you're asking me to write them?" I couldn't. Then one summer evening my husband said, "Why don't we just sit outside, you tell me what you want to say, and I'll write the letter." It seemed much easier that way. On Monday morning, I walked up the granite steps to the old post office and put that letter down on the counter, shaking.

On Wednesday, my husband called me at work crying. I've only heard him cry once, when his father died. He had done something he'd never done before, and has never done since: he opened mail that had my name on it. The letter said, "Dear Nancy, I got your letter and I've read it, and nowhere in it did you say you'd like to meet your son. If that's something you're interested in, I'd like you to call me because I opened your file and there's a letter from your son in there."

He read this letter to me and the only word I can use to describe it was, I was *paralyzed*, absolutely paralyzed at the thought that he had tried to make contact and no one told me. His letter had said, "If you're interested in talking to me, give me a call." The thought that my son might even *entertain* the idea that I hadn't held him close to my heart for twenty years . . .

I hung up from the call with my husband, picked up the phone, and called the guy at the agency. I said, "I just got your letter." He said, "I'm not sure if you know what you want to do . . . you might need some time to think about it." I said, "I don't need one more fuckin' minute, okay?" He said, "Don't get mad at me. I wasn't even here then. I've only been here thirteen years."

The phone rang at work and someone said, "It's for you. It's a young man." I took it in the back room. He said, "Hi, the man at the agency gave me your phone number." And I asked him the question I'd asked every single night, 365 days a year, for 21 years: "Where are you?" I'd look up at the stars at night and think, "We're under the same sky," and it was the one thing that made me feel close to him. I knew that he was looking at the same stars. I didn't know where he was. He could have been in Germany, if he was in the service. I was prepared for him to be anywhere in the world. When I said, "Where are you?," he says, "I'm in my bedroom." I said, "Okay, where's your bedroom?" As it turns out, he was right across the river from me. We know a lot of the same people; our paths had crossed many times. We ate at the same restaurants. I had worked in the theater department of a college where he was taking classes.

I wound up seeing a psychiatrist for about a year to deal with the grief, which I hadn't fully dealt with. It's never a good idea to delay that process. It was a difficult year for me, juggling family, a job, our relationship, and dealing with my past at the same time. My son lived near me for about eight years and then he moved to New York City. We started a small business together so we could work together and we became very close during that time.

Losing him had such a profound influence on me. You know, my siblings all had fancy degrees and very focused careers, and they drew from that in order to define who they were. This is what I had; this is what influenced most of my life decisions, the development of my family, where I lived—I would never have moved out of this state because this is the last place I saw him. It affected the choice of my husband to someone who was accepting immediately and almost passive about it. It's affected my drive in terms of politics and I think, most of all, my sense of feminism.

People say to me, "Oh well, it's not that way anymore." I say, "It's still that way for a lot of us. A lot of my sisters are still suffering in silence." And the more I read about the physiological effect that stress has on your life—you know, I'm not at all convinced that there isn't a small connection between illness and this trauma. I've known some birth mothers who died when they were fifty years old from cancers of one kind or another. I mean, trauma is not a mystery. It really attaches itself to you in a way that's very hard to undo.

It's hard to convince others about the depth of it. You know, a few years after I was married I became pregnant and had an abortion. It was not a wonderful experience, but every time I hear stories or articles or essays about the recurring trauma of abortion, I want to say, "You don't have a clue." I've experienced both and I'd have an abortion any day of the week before I would ever have another adoption—or lose a kid in the woods, which is basically what it is. You know your child is out there somewhere, you just don't know where. It's bad enough as a mother to know he might need you, but to complicate that they make a law that says even if he *does* need you we're not going to tell him where you are.

It overshadows my life. People can't believe it has had such influence. Or they don't believe that it is relevant anymore because I know my son now. But that little wet ink across a piece of paper made me *not* a mother in the eyes of society. That's all it took was the stroke of a pen. They felt they could erase it, but we just aren't made that way. It's unnatural to be separated from your child that way. And if it happens when you're fourteen, fifteen, sixteen years old, and it's your first experience of motherhood, it makes you a little crazy. Sometimes I wonder how any of us survived it and are as successful as we are in our interpersonal relationships. Not that I consider myself to be completely successful. I've sequestered myself out here in the woods for most of my life to be away from people.

It's changed my personality. I feel like I was in a car accident. You know how sometimes when people have a head trauma their personality changes? Well, it changed my personality. I don't really care if I have the popular view. I suffered this alone for twenty-one years so everyone around me would be comfortable: "Don't talk about it, because it makes *us* uncomfortable." And I didn't.

I think if anything good came from my pain it has been to encourage other women in my situation to understand that they have as much right to put their opinion out there as I do. I tell them their story is as important as the next person's story. They all have to be heard. For twenty-one years I wasn't allowed to speak about it, but I have my own voice now.

CLAUDIA

I got pregnant on my seventeenth birthday, so 1967. I was living at home. I was a junior at . . . well, nowadays it would be called an alternative high school, but it was a private prep school. I hated public school. I did okay, I just hated the social aspect of it. I went to a high school in a new suburban area where if you weren't a cheerleader you weren't anything, and I was an artist weirdo.

During that time, the most important thing in my life was my art. I was always drawing, always, always. My life mostly revolved around a few friends, music, and drawing. I went to life drawing classes all the time and there was a man in that drawing class that I thought was the most handsome man I had ever seen in my whole entire life. He was also an amazing artist. He was Cape Verdean Portuguese and he was quite a bit older than me: he was thirty-one to my seventeen. His paintings were beautiful. Those were the kind of men I would be attracted to, the hippie or artist type.

I didn't abuse any substances—I don't consider smoking a little pot abusing substances. I wasn't a big drinker, and I was not promiscuous. At that point, I had only had sex with my first boyfriend and I only had sex with him once, then he moved on to somebody with bigger breasts. That's the truth. So, anyway, it's the night of my seventeenth birthday, I was with my friend, and we're excited. We're going to hang out and maybe meet some cute university guys. I had on a polyester stretch iridescent paisley psychedelic minidress and those Indian sandals that everybody wore where your toe goes through the one thing. My friend had on a white peasant blouse with a little string and the puckering, cutoffs, and the Indian sandals.

So we're off for the evening to celebrate my birthday. We had taken the bus downtown from the suburb where we both lived and we're walking up the street and there, sitting on the front stoop of a house, was that gorgeous man from the art class. He sees us and says, "What are you girls doing?" And my girlfriend says, "It's Claudia's birthday so we're out for the night, we're going to celebrate." He says, "If you girls want to come back here at nine-thirty tonight, I'm having a party and it can be a birthday party for you, too." Well, my heart dropped down into my lower abdomen. I could not believe he was talking to us, never mind inviting us to a party. My heart was pounding. I'm dying, I just couldn't believe this, because he was so handsome and he was this wonderful artist.

So, we go up the street but, of course, nothing is gonna compare with what we've got to look forward to. We walked back down later and, sure enough, he was having a big party. The people at the party were older, probably in their late twenties or early thirties—an interesting, artsy, eccentric crowd. My girlfriend hooked up pretty damn fast. She was adventurous and already sexually active and liberated, and I really wasn't. I was pretty naïve in that whole realm. I mean, my mother told me about periods and that was it, you know. I never got anything except what I learned from friends, so I really was very naïve. I remember the older women kind of eyeballing us but I was so honored and overwhelmed just being there, and having fun. He totally focused on me, gave me tons of attention, and clearly led me to believe that he was interested in me, so I couldn't think of anything else. I was in one of those states where you're really just so joyful that you can't believe it. That was on a Friday night and before I left he asked me, very gently and respectfully, if he could have my phone number and would I like to get together sometime? I was dying, I gave him my phone number and said, "Absolutely." Now, I didn't know it, but at the time he did have a girlfriend. She wasn't at that party.

Only a couple of days passed and he called me and said he wanted to see me. And this is what we did a lot of the time: I would cut school and go to his apartment, he would get out of work, and we basically just had sex. I don't remember the sex being particularly . . . it wasn't like I liked sex or didn't like sex; I just wanted to be with him. He never said anything about birth control and I don't know what I was thinking. I got pregnant probably the first or second time I ever had sex with him. I got pregnant almost immediately.

So here I am, at this private school, wearing this uniform—the gray flannel skirt, white shirt, and cranberry blazer—and I'm taking Humphreys 11 [a homeopathic preparation for irregular or delayed periods] by the bottleful. There was this legend that Humphreys 11 would make you have your period. Nothing was happening. I wasn't getting a period. So I go to Planned Parenthood and get a pregnancy test and it's positive. But my denial was pretty huge. I don't know what I thought was going to happen. I kind of created this fantasy in my head that something would happen that would fix this.

I didn't even think of abortion. Abortion wasn't legal. I had known friends who had had private abortions. If you had money, you could always get an abortion. Their mothers' gynecologists did D and Cs, but I was terrified of telling my mother. So, little by little, my waistline is expanding and I'm trying to hold my skirt together with pins. I started off with safety pins, then bigger and bigger, and then diaper pins. The biggest pin I got to was . . . at that time kilts were very popular, remember those plaid, pleated kilts that had the giant pin? That was the last frontier, the kilt pin.

I knew I had to tell him but in the meantime it had become real apparent that I had become the other woman. I'm sneaking around behind someone else's back. I kinda know her and I feel guilty, but I'm addicted to being with this man because he kind of embodies everything that I think is spectacular about men. So that's what the relationship had evolved into. He was having an open relationship with her and I was sneaking around. I didn't feel good about it, but I continued to do it.

Anyway, I'm getting very big and I feel I have to tell him. So one night I'm babysitting. My parents are out and I go into my mother's room, shut the door, pick up the phone, and I call him. I say, "I have to talk to you. I'm pregnant." He says, "Get outta here. What are you talking about?" I said, "It's true, I am. I didn't say anything to you before, but now I'm sure. I've done the test, and I'm really starting to show. I'm almost four months pregnant." He says, "You're crazy, you can't be. There's no way." He keeps saying what I'm telling him isn't true and I'm trying to be discreet and quiet on the phone and finally I scream, "You have to believe me. I am pregnant. You are the only guy I'm having sex with. I'm pregnant!" My sister has been sitting outside the bedroom door and I hear her run down the hallway. I walk out and she looks at me and says, "I'm telling Mommy." I immediately call my other girlfriend who has a car. I pack a bag and I run away. I run away to a hippie flophouse apartment where I knew some people—you know, with the bare mattresses and Jimi Hendrix and Jim Morrison posters on the walls?

My girlfriend who was at the party with me knew where I was, but you could have put cigarettes out in her arms and she would never have told my mother; she never did. My mother went to her house and threatened her mother, she was hysterical, of course. I would have done the same if it was my daughter. My girlfriend reported to me daily. She was the most loyal friend, and she still is now. But I had another friend who lived with her fiancé, who knew where I was. She didn't have the same amount of backbone. My mom got to her and broke her down. I'm not judging because I understand now, as a mom, the terror of not knowing where your kid is.

So maybe something short of a week had gone by and my mother is absolutely hysterical. She's on Valium and diet pills, going absolutely mental. She's telling my friends I just need to come home. She eventually breaks my weaker girlfriend down. One morning there's a knock on the door. I open the door and there's my girlfriend with my mother standing behind her peering into this room with the bare mattresses. My mother is crying and freaking out and my friend is saying, "I didn't want to tell her, don't be mad. She made me tell her."

My mother grabs me and hugs me and says, "I don't care what's going on in your life. I know you're pregnant. You need to come home. We're gonna take care of this. We're going to do whatever we need to do." She sounded like a mother. So I pack my things and I go home. Within a day or so, I'm getting shipped off to Dorchester, Massachusetts, to St. Mary's home for unwed mothers. In 1968, Dorchester and Roxbury, Massachusetts, were literally burning from race riots. It was like being sent to a war zone.

At the time I went to the maternity home, my dad was commuting to Boston for work. My dad was kind of shut down, but I liked him. I felt a connection with him. He was really smart. He used to help me with my homework and we talked about politics, and he supported me going to art school. My mom didn't really respect me being an artist, but my dad respected it. He would give me art books—the really big coffee-table kind—on Picasso and on surrealism and Dalí. He didn't really like or know anything about art, but he supported and respected my interests. So those tiny little things my dad had done for me cemented our relationship, and I identified with him. My mom used to always say, "Oh, it's all fine and dandy that you're an artist, but you're never going to be able to do anything with it. You need to learn something to fall back on. You need a job with the city." That was my mother's mantra: "Get a job with the city."

The maternity home had really dark woodwork everywhere, dark woodwork railings, and lots and lots of marble stairs. It was attached to the hospital, but it looked more like a house than a hospital. It looked like an old lady's house in England or something. It had that weird, disapproving grandmother feel to it. They had big dorm rooms where four girls slept in a room. You had a little twin bed with a dresser. Then there was a lunchroom, and they always had stewed tomatoes. They gave us water pills every day so we wouldn't retain fluids, yet they were feeding us all this high-sodium hospital food.

So, anyway, this is where I am. I'm seventeen, I'm at least five months pregnant, and I'm in this really weird place run by nuns. Their disapproval was palpable. They gave me the name Marsha; everybody was given a fake name. I bonded with my three roommates and, of course, we knew each other's real names. There were probably about twenty-five girls in the home at that time. The youngest was fourteen and she was one of my roommates. The oldest was in her middle thirties. She was mildly retarded and had been raped. She had been raped and left on the side of the road.

The intake nun was this really hard-looking woman. They all had mustaches. The nuns where I grew up were from this order from Sicily that had lots of facial hair, too. Nuns do not get rid of facial hair. I felt like I was plopped in an environment and given no choices whatsoever. You know, I've done the ultimate shameful thing and this is the only answer to my problem, or the problem I've caused in my family. There was really never any counseling or therapy, but there was a dialogue and this is what it was: "You've done a really bad thing. You have really sinned. You've committed the ultimate mortal sin." There's a big difference between mortal sins and venial sins. Mortal sins are the really bad sins that you've got to really, really make amends for.

I don't remember any dialogue around having choices. You were here, you were gonna be fed, and you're going to get your schooling. You were going to be taken care of, but you were gonna have that baby and you are gonna do the only thing that is right. You're gonna give that baby to good people, decent people, people who can take care of it because you are so bad and so flawed for just having this happen, that there's no way you could possibly provide what a child would need. And if you were ever gonna redeem yourself in God's eyes, you were gonna give this baby to a good Catholic family. I never believed that only a Catholic family was good, but I definitely believed I was flawed. I already believed that from the time I was about five. So it didn't take a lot to really drill that home.

The father of my child never came to see me. There was no communication with him at all. He knew that I was going away and he knew the phone number. I wrote to him and I think I called him once or twice when I first got there. He never responded, so I just let it alone. That's what I do, I get invisible. I just got invisible from his life.

So I'm at this home and I make friends. There's the fourteen-year-old girl—she's a white girl and a wicked tomboy. She was really fun. Then there was a black girl from Massachusetts who was about my age and who was very pretty—really nice hair with a bouffant like the Supremes. We became very fast and good friends. Then there was this girl from upstate New York. She was brilliant. She reminded me of my best friend from home. She had long, straight strawberry-blond hair, and those Ben Franklin glasses. I always thought that girls my age who wore those kind of glasses were Mensa potential. The four of us really connected. I was also friendly with some of the other people and with the retarded lady who would go from room to room and talk to everybody.

The home had three levels of marble stairs, so there was a lot of exercise involved in going from the classroom to your room, or to the lunchroom. The retarded woman threw herself down those stairs to try to kill her baby. She was only mildly retarded, but that was a time when if you had a freakin' learning disability you were labeled retarded. I think that was the case with her. She really could have been anything. It was also that time period of a lot of meanness—if you looked different, if you had curly hair like I did, if you were anything but a stupid blond, no offense, blue-eyed, tall, slim cheerleader. The beach-girl thing was happening then. If you looked different, you were ostracized. If you were retarded on top of that, you were really ostracized. So she wasn't getting much warmth or compassion from the other girls. She was treated badly and she threw herself down the stairs to try to kill the baby because she was so bad. Because *she* was so bad.

During this time my dad would come to visit me alone, without my mother. It was the only time in my life I was ever with my dad alone. He came to visit me a lot. We weren't supposed to have any sweets at all. It was off-limits, against the rules. He'd bring dozens and dozens of Dunkin' Donuts for us. He'd sneak them in, in a big brown paper bag with a handle and he would take me and my three pregnant roommates out. He would sign the four of us out.

So he is going out in the community with a fourteen-year-old pregnant girl, the black girl, the eccentric intellectual, and me his daughter, and we're all hugely pregnant. He took us to movies. We'd go to Chinatown for dinner. He took us to museums. He wasn't ashamed. The only glimmer of any happiness that we had was when we knew he was coming. And when he would leave he'd give me a really big hug—the really tight kind where you don't have to say anything. My mom would always give me that nervous hug. She'd be crying and it was a weird kind of hug, you know? But he was actually there for me.

The day I went into labor my water broke and I thought I had wet my pants. They took me down to the hospital. I was alone there and nobody was friendly. Nobody was nice. Nobody said, "Don't worry, you're going be okay." It wasn't overt meanness but it was total clinical indifference: "Turn over. Roll over. We're going to shave you. You're going to get an enema." I just felt like I was being led by this invisible rope. Then they gave me a spinal and within minutes I'm numb from the waist down. They tell you that you cannot move. I remember them saying that if I moved there was a chance that I'd have some kind of permanent damage. So I also have this fear that I might be paralyzed for my whole life. You go through this whole process without anybody who is supposed to care about you being there.

I didn't know it, because I can't feel anything from the waist down, but I had shit the bed. And that's just humiliating. I mean, there's another big shame ball right there—no pun intended. Then my arms were strapped down to the side of the table like in *The Cuckoo's Nest* and they wheel me into another room and put my feet in the stirrups, and all of a sudden I'm giving birth to a baby. I remember, vaguely, a suctiony kind of emptying out, and a baby is born and I see this unbelievable mass of black hair on this incredibly beautiful reddish-brown baby. The first thing I saw was this really long, sticking-out, crazy, wild black hair like that boxing promoter guy, Don King. That was my baby. Then after I give birth I'm really, really sore because, you know, they gave me an episiotomy. I'm surprised they don't sew it completely up on teenage Catholic girls, you know? Just sew the whole damn thing up.

So I'm in my room and my roommates from the home came to see me. It was very weird because it's not something you should be celebrating, but it was like the end of this whole crazy time. The girls gave me flowers and I remember the retarded girl had her baby and she came in the room and talked to me and she brought me a gift. The girls were really very compassionate. I named my baby Raina Elizabeth—Elizabeth after my girlfriend. I did get to hold her for three days. She was beautiful. She had a little tiny heart-shaped mouth, big dark eyes, beautiful reddish-brown skin, and tons and tons of black hair. I held and fed Raina as much as I could. And then on the third day my parents came. I had everything packed. I knew it was the day that I was leaving the hospital and I was leaving the baby in the nursery.

We walked out of the hospital. My dad got in the driver's seat and my mom got in on the passenger side. I got in the backseat. We always had Chryslers because they were safe cars—they were like boats, you know, huge. So my dad's way up there driving, totally white-knuckled, and I'm looking out that back window at the hospital. And seeing the view of the hospital getting smaller and smaller and smaller, I flipped out—it was total, 100 percent, ripped terror, wailing, screaming, crying—and nobody said a word. My mother didn't even turn around. I could tell she was crying because I could see her shoulders going up and down. My dad was white. He was like a statue driving the car. I just had that kind of cry that was a giant, wailing, screaming, weeping, until you just are totally crumpled in and your whole body is crying.

It was the beginning of it being invisible. It was never, ever, brought up again. It was never talked about—not once, not ever. I was never asked, "How are you? How are you feeling?" I don't even remember the ride home. I must have gone unconscious inside.

I went back and graduated from school. Then a friend of mine had a 1950 Pontiac Chief, one of those fat cars that had the Indian chief on the hood, and he was going to Aspen, Colorado. He was taking five friends and there was room for one more person in the car. This was the summer of '69 and there was this rumor that the Beatles were gonna be in Aspen, so I said, "Definitely, sign me up." I stayed away thirty years.

When I was forty years old, I initiated a search and when I was forty-six I met Raina. When I initiated the search, my daughter from a subsequent marriage was part of the whole thing. I told her the story when she was about thirteen or fourteen in the sex talk. I said, "There's another reason I want you to be really well informed, because this is my story. . . ." I shared the whole thing with her. So I got the nonidentifying information about Raina and did the registry thing. I called my mother and I said, "Look, I have to talk to you about something that we've never talked about. It's important to me. I have decided I am going to initiate a search for my daughter." She doesn't say anything. I say, "Do you have any documents, anything?" Nobody's ever mentioned this in all these years. My mom says, "I don't think I do." She was very open to it. As a matter of fact, I think it was healing for her, because it gave her a chance to be part of something, and to say that she was really sorry.

Raina was adopted by a family sort of like my family. They're conservative Catholic, Italian. Raina was light-skinned, and she could pass for Italian. Her parents were told the truth, but they were encouraged to lie. They were dark-skinned Italian like my dad, who's Sicilian. I grew up with Italians who were darker than my black friend from the home. Catholic Charities told the couple who adopted Raina Elizabeth that there's no need to tell her that her father was black. I didn't know they were gonna tell them this. I was just told, "We have a young couple that want her. They know she's biracial, and they want her." They never said to me, "We have a biracial couple," because . . . who knew biracial couples in 1968? Actually, I did, but my parents certainly didn't, and Catholic Charities probably wouldn't let them in the freakin' door. So maybe it was a naïve assumption, but I assumed that they had somehow found a biracial couple. I remember feeling relieved because they said over and over, "Who's gonna want this biracial baby? They're hard to place."

I've met her now, so I know the story. She always knew she was different. She always knew that her skin was darker and her hair was kinkier. She knew she was adopted but she was led to believe that she was Italian. She was adopted by a family who lived maybe a mile down the street from where I had lived and where my mother still lives now. What happened was, when Raina was about nineteen, she had a boyfriend who was Cape Verdean Portuguese and her parents were absolutely ballistic. They said, "Can't you go out with boys that are your kind, Italian boys?" They were giving her a really hard time, but she's got this rebel spirit in her—I know where that comes from—and she's gonna be who she's gonna be. So they're having this huge fight because Raina is totally in love with this boy. He's smart, he's nice— there's nothing wrong with him. She can't understand why her mother doesn't want her to go out with him. They get into the fight of fights and Raina screams, "What do you have against Portuguese people?" And her mom says, "I don't have anything against them. You're Portuguese and I adopted you, didn't I?" Silence. Raina said, "What?" She got into her car and went to Catholic Charities and said, "I want to know my history. I want to know who I am," and it was all in her file.

She went back three times. The second time she got the letter that I wrote. The social worker called and said, "I'm calling to let you know that your daughter came in again and we gave her your letter." She said, "She isn't ready to meet you and, to be quite honest, she doesn't know if she ever would be." I could barely breathe. I could barely freakin' breathe. I felt re- jected, but I thought, "Okay, she's only twenty-seven or twenty-eight years old." The social worker said something that led me to believe it might be a loyalty conflict with her mother, and I understood that. I thought, "Okay, I've gotta just let her, hopefully, grow beyond this." The social worker said, "What you can do is write another letter." The first letter I wrote was basi- cally "I want to meet you." It was probably just a couple of pages. But when the social worker said to me, "If I were you, I'd write another letter, and I'll put it in the file," I sat down and I wrote a novel. And, sure enough, within six months Raina went back and wanted more information and she got that second letter. When she read it, she said to the social worker, "I'm not sure, but I think I might want to go through with this."

What she was supposed to do was write a letter and take it to the agency and then they would send it to me. But she's smart. She had all of the first names of my family members from my nonidentifying letter and she went to the public library, got on microfiche, and goes through all the death notices for July of 1978 until she found my father's first name, address, and the names of the survivors. She gets into her car and goes right to my mother's house.

I'm in Colorado working at this boutique when she knocks on my mother's door. My mother's making macaroni—what's new? She comes to the door in her apron and my daughter says, "Are you Claudia's mother?" She says yes. And she says, "I'm Raina. I'm Claudia's daughter." My mother just grabbed her and smothered her with a big hug. Then she immediately calls my sister and says, "You gotta get over here right away. Claudia's daughter is here. Drop whatever you're doing. I need you here."

So I'm closing up the register at work and the phone rings. I pick it up and I hear this voice, "Hello, is this Claudia?" "Yeah." "This is Raina." I said, "Oh my God, it's you, it's you!" She said, "I'm at your mother's house." I said, "You're what?" She said, "I'm at your mother's house." And I say, "Are you okay?" And she starts laughing. In the background, I hear my mother screaming, "Oh my God. She looks just like you did at that age." And there's crying and screaming and laughing, and Raina laughs and says, "I'm fine. I grew up just like this."

We talked for two hours, right then. I couldn't even think straight; I was mental. I hung up that phone. I closed up that store. I went home and told my daughter what happened. We were both mental. Then I called my friend the travel agent. I said, "I don't know where I'm gonna get the money, but my daughter and I are flying home within the next two days."

She met me at the airport. All of a sudden, here comes this beautiful woman. She's got on Levi's and a pair of black Doc Martens and a little black leather jacket, and she has hair like mine, really long curly hair down to her waist. She's got these really big eyebrows and this beautiful smile, which I saw her father in right away, and she's carrying one rose. We went up to a restaurant and ordered all this food but we didn't eat anything. We were looking at each other's fingers. I was looking at her ears. She's looking at my eyebrows. We're looking and we're talking and it was just amazing. It was so amazing. She said, "You know, if we're gonna have a relationship I want you to know who I am. I'm gay." I said, "I don't care." And I really don't care because, oh God, if you can find love you're lucky.

Raina says to me, "Tell me about my father." So I tell her. I tell her how magnificently beautiful he was and how I was so in love with him and what an amazing artist he is and she says to me, "I really, really want to meet him but I don't want to interrupt his life. Even if I could just see him, I don't want anything from him." Well, I hadn't seen him since I was nineteen years old. I contacted a friend of mine who knows him and he says, "I don't have his phone number, but I know where he works. I'll take you there, and then you're on your own." So my friend picks me up and I'm shaking like a leaf. I'm more nervous about this than I was about meeting my daughter.

It's about eleven in the morning. I go to the main door and it's locked. I go to a side door, locked. I go to the back door, locked. So I'm standing in the yard and I see a man with a baseball cap on. I'm way up on the steps and he's down in the yard. He sees me and he points to a door under the stairs. He says, "That door is open if you want to get in." I'm thinking, "Maybe he knows him." So I walk toward him and I go, "Excuse me, sir," and he looks up from what he's doing and takes a couple of steps forward and I say, "Maybe you can help me? I'm looking for . . ." He takes his baseball cap off and he says, "Claudia?" And it's him. He's sixty years old. When I knew him he was this gorgeous thirty-one-year-old man. He's still handsome. He's still a beautiful man.

He says, "What are you doing here?" I said, "Do you have a minute? We need to talk." And he says, "You know, I always knew that I would see you again someday." He says, "I've thought about you over the years and I always thought, "One day I'm gonna see Claudia walking down the street." I said, "Remember when I had the baby in 1968?" And he nods his head, "Yeah," and his eyes are getting kind of big. I said, "Well, I met her." He doesn't say anything. He kind of just leans forward. I said, "She's an amazing girl. She's a beautiful, smart, articulate, amazing girl, and she doesn't want anything from you, but she would love to meet you. Is there any chance that you would be willing to meet her, just meet her?" His eyes fill up with tears and he says, "She's my family, of course I'm gonna meet her." Then the very next thing he says is "I have to tell my wife." He had never told her.

He went home and he told his wife. She called me. Oh yeah, she called me, she's an amazing woman. They're amazing people. She was definitely taken aback. She told me that every April she used to think of me and would always say a prayer for me. She told me that she used to even say to him, "Remember Claudia? Remember your friend Claudia, who went to that home for unwed mothers? That was so sad." He had twenty-nine years to tell her, and he had opportunities, but he never did. Maybe he thought she would leave him. She told me it took a couple of days of praying and being alone and sitting with her rage, and then she said, "Okay, I have another daughter." And that's when she called me. When she called me and said, "Claudia?" I just got hysterical. I just started crying. I couldn't believe the courage. She said, "Look, let me just say right up front, I'm very glad that you came forward. We have a daughter now. We are family. I don't want you to feel bad about this, because we share a daughter now."

I'm in the process of some big-time healing now. I moved back here five years ago to help my mom. She's eighty now. You know, in Italian families there's usually one who stays home. Now I'm that person. She needs me. She had complete knee replacement five years ago but she's up and running now. We're taking Italian lessons together and we're gonna go back to Italy because she wants to go one more time before she dies.

4

Discovery and Shame

I called my folks from college in Madison to tell them I was pregnant and my dad said, "Don't come home." And my mom would not buck my dad. At the time, my dad was a sheriff. He would be up for reelection and he did not want a daughter like me around. It was fine while I was class valedictorian and the shining star, but not while I was pregnant, no.

—Glory

FOR SINGLE GIRLS who became pregnant during these decades, the most common solution was a hasty trip to the altar and the claim that the baby's birth was premature. One reason that the high number of pregnancies wasn't socially acknowledged was that so many premarital conceptions were effectively covered up through marriage. On average, 50 percent of these young women were married before the baby was born, leaving only half to be recorded as illegitimate births.[1] Since the average age of marriage had dropped after the war, it was not at all unusual for young people to get married in their late teens or very early twenties. Throughout the war years and until about 1972, the median age at first marriage for women remained below twenty-one.[2] Those who did not plan to attend college often got married shortly after graduating from high school.

You could always get married to give the baby a name and then get divorced afterward. That's what was done. That's what many, many, many girls did.

—Maureen II

For many girls, however, marriage wasn't an option and the reasons varied. In some cases the young men walked, or ran, away from their pregnant partners. Many simply said they weren't ready for marriage. In other cases, the young couple wanted to get married but parents or clergy discouraged or prevented their plans from moving forward. Those who were not yet of legal age—which could range from fourteen to twenty-one, depending on their state of residence—needed their parents' permission to marry.

When I told him I was pregnant, he asked me what the heck I thought he should do. And the next thing I knew he was gone. I was devastated when he just hit the road. I felt so violated, so stupid, so used. I never told anybody. I couldn't even get it out of my mouth because to *say* I was pregnant might have made it real. I don't know whether I thought an angel would appear and tell me what to do or, better yet, maybe a truck would run over me. I just thanked God that 1967 was the era of big tent dresses. I never heard from him again except for when I had the baby. I wrote him a note and he called me and said, "You sound so bitter, Lynne. You were never bitter."

—Lynne

I had been dating the father of the baby for probably a year and a half or two years. He was in Vietnam and he came home to Minnesota on leave and that's when we started up a more serious relationship. I got pregnant when he came home for good. In the beginning, I sort of fantasized that we would get married. I remember looking through the Sears catalogs at curtains and kitchen tables and things like that. Then it became clear that he didn't want to get married, so that was that.

—Susan I

I was seventeen when I found out I was pregnant and I was actually not too worried because I had gone out with my boyfriend for four years and we had talked about getting married. I was graduating from high school in a few months and I had gotten a job. My boyfriend had gone into the National Guard because his draft number was something like three. I called him and told him that I was pregnant, and he didn't say anything. I was just so sure that everything was going to be fine. A week later he came home, but he was still evading it. Then he said, "I'm not ready for this. I'm not ready for this."

I thought, "Well, he just needs time." In the meantime, he moved into his own apartment with a couple of his buddies and he still wasn't talking about what we were going to do. I was just hoping that he was going to call and say that he cared about me and about our baby. But at that point I didn't really care if he loved me. I just wanted some way to be able to keep this baby.

—Cathy I

I grew up in St. Mark's parish and later we moved to St. Ann's. Everything is parishes in Dorchester if you're familiar with Boston at all. They don't ask where you're from in Boston; it's from what parish. My boyfriend came from a similar background and we met in the fall of 1967 at UMass in Boston. He was my first real boyfriend. We were inseparable. We had been together all summer and didn't have sexual relations that whole year until December. I suspected immediately because I had never been late in my life. When I told him, he cried. He said, "It's not happening, it's got to be something else." But he said he would stand by me and we would get married.

You have to go through this Pre-Cana stuff with the Catholic Church and they have to talk to you for weeks on end. So we made our first appointment with the priest. I remember him being very suspicious. The next time we went back together, the priest wanted to see my boyfriend by himself. He talked to him for about half an hour and the next day the priest called my father and said, "There is not going to be a wedding. This boy isn't ready for marriage."

Then my boyfriend told me about this church for people who are outcast Catholics, or if you're divorced or some kind of sinner you can go there. There was a long corridor with little counseling rooms and my boyfriend went in and talked to the priest and then he came out and said, "He wants to see you now." He wasn't like my parish priest, who wore a black robe and a white collar. He was a Franciscan. He had a brown robe, and sandals, a real rope belt and I think he had a big crucifix and beads hanging around his waist, too. I was a little bit fascinated just by the look of him.

He immediately pointed out to the corridor and said that he was worried about my boyfriend. He started talking about my boyfriend's mother and about him being her only son, and making me feel that this was all about him. He said he was sure that my boyfriend was a good boy and had strong feelings for me, but I was doing the wrong thing by trying to arrange a marriage. He said, "You must know from your twelve years of Catholic education that you need to take responsibility for yourself."

—Diane I

It was not always parents or boyfriends who were against marriage as a solution to the dilemma. Some young women were determined not to marry, despite pressure to do so.

Mothers can tell that something's wrong by the look on your face. Mine said, "What's wrong?" "Nothing." She called me into the bedroom, "What's wrong?" I said, "I'm pregnant." She said, "You're the only one in the family that has ever gotten pregnant out of wedlock," which was a lie. My mother made me feel like a bag of shame. She wanted me to marry him. She said, "Marry him, marry him. Get us out of this mess." But I didn't want to marry him.

My father said, "Get out of the house—I want you out of the house." So my mother bought a Greyhound bus ticket so I could go to my grandparents in Brooklyn. They're from the old Yiddish world, from Poland. I was their first grandchild and my grandmother loved me very much, but she could not look at me.

My boyfriend sent me a ticket to come back. He picked me up and had arranged for a justice of the peace to marry us. I was in high school and I'm thinking, "This is not the way I pictured my life." I mean, I was supposed to go off to college and do better than this. I think he was working in a snack shop. I remember thinking, "This is supposed to be the happiest day of my life and I feel trapped."

Then there was a knock at my boyfriend's door and it was my father and mother. My father said, "Sheryl, I don't want you to rush into this. If you still want to marry him in a year, yes, but don't do it now." I thought, "Daddy, just get me out of here." I don't remember exactly what happened in the next few days or weeks but my mother kept saying, "Are you sure you don't want to marry him? That's what women do."

—Sheryl

I had this idea that I couldn't tell anyone. I thought I would be arrested, or they would contact my boyfriend's family and I would be forced to marry him and I didn't want to marry him. I didn't know if I ever wanted to marry anyone. I had not seen that marriage had done much for my mother.

—Toni

I had graduated and I was going with this guy. My mother and father knew his whole family and everybody thought he was Mr. Wonderful. He's the one who got me pregnant. But he had slapped me and I didn't want to be with him if he could be that mean. I told him the baby wasn't his. I knew that my mother would make me marry him and his family would make him marry me and I didn't want that kind of a marriage.

—Bonnie

Although the discovery of a daughter's pregnancy was a shock for every family, for the women who were not going to get married the ordeal was all the more traumatic. Those young women were made to suffer a latter-day version of social shunning. Once private sexual behavior was made visible and public by pregnancy, it could not be denied. Given the social stigma of unwed pregnancy at the time, members of the community who wanted to be perceived as maintaining a higher moral standard had to refrain from associating with a pregnant girl. Accepting her condition or helping her keep her child might be perceived as condoning her actions. Most members of society felt they must distance themselves in order to make their position clear. In one of the strictest forms of banishment, high schools and most colleges required a pregnant girl to withdraw immediately. It was not until Title IX of the Education Amendments Act of 1972 that federally funded high schools and colleges, by law, could not expel a pregnant girl or a teenage mother.[3]

> I got called down to the office at school and the principal said, "There's a lot of gossip about you being pregnant. We figure that you're about three to four months and you may not return to school until you have a doctor's note saying that you're not pregnant." The gym teacher helped me clean out my locker and drove me home, and the school called my mother and told her at work.
>
> I had been this girl who didn't smoke, didn't drink, didn't do anything wrong. I took care of my kid brothers and sisters, and everybody's parents wanted their daughters to be with me. Now, when I walked down the street, all the parents made their daughters cross the street. They couldn't walk on the same side of the street as me. A sense of shame and humiliation permeated the entire family.
>
> —*Margaret*

For every woman I interviewed—even those whose parents showed them a great deal of compassion—the news of their daughter's pregnancy was a wrenching shock. Many girls' parents were overtly disgusted or infuriated with them. But perhaps even more disturbing, many would not even discuss the situation with their daughters. Some families made their daughters hide in the house so their pregnancy wouldn't be seen, drawing the drapes and making them duck down when they were in the car. The girls were made to feel that they had shamed, if not ruined, their entire family.

I called my dad and said, "I'm pregnant." And he said, "Oh, no." We lived about an hour and ten minutes from my college, and he came to get me. I remember vividly that we did not say one word to each other the entire trip. Not one single word. A block from home he said, "We still love you." And the minute he opened his mouth I started bawling.

I went in the house and my mother was nowhere to be found. I just sort of wandered around and put my stuff away and I remember going upstairs and walking in her bedroom and she was ironing with her back to me. The TV was on, so I sat on the bed and chitchatted a little bit, but she wouldn't turn around. She just ironed away. Finally she turned to look at me and her lip and her chin were kind of quivering and she said, "I don't know how this happened. We took you to church." I just looked at her and said, "I wasn't thinking about church."

−Linda III

My mom took me to her ob-gyn. After the exam the doctor said, "Do you want to tell your mother or do you want me to?" About thirty minutes later, my mother came out. She was teary-eyed and said, "We'll get through this. We'll talk to your daddy." I was crying and hysterical, thinking, "Oh, my God. What am I going to do? I've just ruined my whole family." My dad came home at five-thirty, and I guess my mother told him. He came in and he had tears in his eyes and . . . this is very hard for me to talk about because it still hurts. He said, "We're going to take care of this. You don't to have to worry about a thing." My dad had been commuting back and forth from Fort Worth to Dallas and he made the decision that this would be a good time for us to move to Dallas so that nobody would know.

During the time I was at the maternity home, my mother would come and take me to Dallas to see the new house they had moved to while I was gone. When we got to the neighborhood, I would have to get down on the car seat and hide. Mother would come down the alley, open the garage door, pull the car into the garage, close the door, and then I could get up. All the curtains would be closed in the house so nobody could see me. My sister and brother were told that I was staying in Fort Worth to finish my schooling and everybody in Fort Worth thought I was in Dallas.

—Nancy II

The couple times I did go with my parents somewhere, I had to lie down in the backseat. We had a three-car garage and my father would take the car from where it was parked on the left-hand side, he would back it up to the porch, and I would go right down the stairs and get in the backseat of the car. I had to lie down until we got out of my neighborhood because my parents didn't want anyone to know I was home. I couldn't answer the door. I couldn't answer the phone. It was all "What are the neighbors going to think?"

—Cathy II

We lived in a typical Michigan two-story home with a basement. I got to be downstairs on the main level with my mom during the day and eat dinner with my father and mother, but if a neighbor came, or any company, I had to go upstairs and stay out of sight. We lived in an old house with wood floors and they creaked, so I couldn't move. I had to go upstairs and be still. I spent most of my pregnancy upstairs. One day the little neighbor lady next door came over unexpectedly and I was downstairs and I couldn't get upstairs soon enough. So I was hiding in the downstairs bathroom for two hours waiting for her to leave while she visited with my mother.

—Barbara

Meanwhile, the young men who had fathered these children largely escaped social condemnation. They were not expelled from school, and they were generally not treated with scorn, not stigmatized, and not considered a disgrace to their families. Most parents supported the double standard by holding their daughters, but not their sons, accountable, and school administrators reinforced the notion by allowing the young men to proceed as if they were not involved. Their role in the pregnancy wasn't publicly visible, thus they were not publicly condemned. Tens of thousands of girls were asked to drop out of sight, while their sexual partners, who had been so eager to couple, escaped recrimination. Some of the young men did, however, suffer emotional consequences. Several of the women I interviewed relayed stories about how their boyfriends' lives had been adversely affected by the pregnancy and breakup.

Last summer I heard from my son's father and he had a terrible life, spiraling downward from this experience. He ended up cutting himself off from his entire family. He felt like he was a screwup and couldn't do anything right. He ended up in Vietnam and he's one of those people who were adversely affected by it. That set the tone for his whole life.

—Laurinda

I lived in a small town in North Dakota. I was just about to turn seventeen and my boyfriend was nineteen and a freshman in college. We had been dating for about a year and talking about getting married after we both finished school. Then we realized that I was pregnant and we decided we'd just get married right then. He went out and bought an engagement ring and a wedding ring for me. But our parents wouldn't sign the necessary papers to allow us to marry.

He said he went through two years of pure hell. He started drinking very heavily and did things during those two years that he won't even talk about. He went through a period of extreme rage. He would not accept money from his parents or go visit them because he was so angry. He said at that time I was his whole life and that had been taken from him and he didn't know how he was going to go on.

—Connie III

The insidious nature of the double standard, which continues today, has even been apparent in the studies that try to determine why teens become pregnant. Many studies over the years have tried to identify the predictors of teen pregnancy and most have looked for answers in the young woman's psyche or personal circumstances, rather than looking equally at both parties responsible for conception. Studies have examined factors such as the young woman's psychology, her economic conditions, her age at first menses, her relationship to her parents, her religion or lack thereof, her educational aspirations, her history of sexual abuse, her love for her partner, and her use or nonuse of birth control. And though these indicators offer insight, they are only half of the picture. Little attention has been directed toward the young men who are equally responsible. Few have speculated that a young man impregnating a girl is a sign of his neurosis, his low self-esteem, his need for affection or attention, or a sign of his need to prove his virility. In fact, several of the young men implicated in these stories impregnated more than one girl who was subsequently sent away.

> When I had been divorced from my second husband for a couple of years, I contacted my daughter's birth father. I was feeling strong: "I am woman, hear me roar." I was out in the working world again, I was making money, I was supporting my family, I was taking care of business and, damn it, I was going to take care of that, too.
>
> I looked him up and I called his house. I pretended I was JC Penney's and I needed to speak with him. I got him on the phone and I said, "This is Barb and I've got some questions to ask you. I want to talk to you—when can you meet with me?" This is embarrassing now.
>
> It was the first time I'd seen him in all those years. I said, "You know, we have a daughter together somewhere out there and you never acknowledged it. You walked away, you never talked to me again, you left me. Why?" Well, turns out he had two other women pregnant at the same time. One was a girl I used to go to Brownies with when I was a little girl; the other one was married to somebody else. The girl I had been in Brownies with was further along than I

was, so he married her. The babies were about three months apart. He was a nineteen-year-old boy with three pregnant girlfriends.

—Barbara

The standards of the day dictated that a young woman was responsible for stopping the advances of a young man. Thus she was ultimately responsible both for his behavior and for her pregnancy if it occurred. It was "her own fault" if she got pregnant. Occasionally, the young man's family took the blame a step further, suggesting that the girl was trying to trap their son. Perhaps their son wasn't even the responsible party.

In fact, before the 1970s the most reliable blood tests available could not absolutely prove paternity. The best they could do was eliminate 40 percent of the male population from being the father based on blood type. Tests developed in the 1970s could exclude about 80 percent of men. It was not until the 1980s that DNA testing could determine a 99.9 percent likelihood of paternity. Since there was no way to prove fatherhood with absolute certainty in the 1950s and 1960s, if a man denied fatherhood his proclamation often went unchallenged. But very few boyfriends of the women I interviewed denied their role in the pregnancy. Since most of the young women's families wanted to keep their daughter's pregnancy a secret, and did not want her to keep her child, proof of fatherhood was not a primary concern. They tried to settle the matter with as little fuss as possible. If the young man's family was involved at all, they often offered to pay some of the maternity-home expense and considered that the end of their involvement, and of their son's responsibility.

My boyfriend talked to his parents and then he came over to our house. They wanted me to see their doctor because they thought maybe I wasn't really pregnant; maybe I was just trying to get him to marry me. He went home and his parents took him back to the University of Florida that night. He called me sobbing, saying, "My parents won't let me get married." His mother called my mother and said, "I just wanted you to know if there's anything that we can do to help you, or if you need any money, we will be glad to give it to you."

—Leslie

Whether the young women's parents were compassionate or enraged, nearly all the women I interviewed reported feeling ashamed—not so much for being sexual but for bringing shame upon their families. Many felt that they would do anything their parents wished in order to get back into their good graces.

> I think my biggest fear was to be ostracized from everything that I had known up to that day, and from my family. I was a sixteen-year-old high-school student. I had never had to think about anything beyond that. So what I was facing was the look on their faces and just that fall from grace, in my neighborhood, and in my community, and with my family. Not with my friends—I had several other friends who were also pregnant. I mean, it was a thing that was happening. We accepted that it was going to be in the hands of our parents. It was not something that we were going to be able to say, "Here's what we want to do."
>
> —*Lydia*

The treatment young women received from family, friends, professionals, and members of their community deepened their sense of abandonment and often contributed to lifelong struggles with low self-esteem. Those who were still dependent on their parents were cast out of their communities or sequestered in their parents' home. Many dreaded reentry into their schools and towns, because they were unsure about who knew the truth of their experiences. They were asked by families and professionals to lie to everyone about where they had been and to keep up this charade indefinitely. Most of the women I interviewed have carried with them for the rest of their lives the emotional pain of being ostracized and then having to live a lie, pretending to be someone they were not. Yet they were soon to learn that the shame they felt as a result of their banishment would prove to be only the tip of the iceberg. They had yet to learn about the emotional impact of relinquishing their child, a child who was not yet real to them.

MARGE

I lived in a small town in southwestern Kansas. By small, I mean a town that has twelve hundred people in it—so really small. Of course, everybody knows everybody. This new guy came to town to live with his uncle and there were stories about him but he had a brand-new Camaro and he must have been nineteen and he was, like, wow, really, really exciting.

His uncle owned a filling station, so he started working there and I started hanging out at the station because I had it in my mind that I was going to be the girl who got him. He was really cute, so I set out to see if I could get him to pay attention to me. He asked me out and then immediately my dad said, "No, this guy's too old for you. What are you doing? He's been out in life, you haven't." I said, "Well, I like him." And I have a really rebellious spirit anyway, so that's all my dad needed to say to set all this in motion.

I was bound and determined to go out with him. I don't even remember when it was, but he decided that we should have sex, so I went to his apartment and we got undressed and got into bed and then I thought, "Oh, my gosh, I can't do this." I said, "No, I can't do this." But by then it was too late and he had sex with me. I don't say that *we* had sex because I was really just frozen.

I had a lot of hickeys on my neck and my dad and mom grounded me and told me I couldn't see him. I couldn't see anybody. I couldn't go anywhere without one of my sisters or brother with me. I had to have rides to school and rides home from school. I couldn't go anywhere.

But being the person that I am, I figured out a way around that because I babysat a lot. After the kids would go to bed and after they would get to sleep I'd just have him come over to wherever I was babysitting. I continued this relationship with him. At this point it wasn't about him, and it wasn't about love or anything; it was about showing my mom and dad that I was in control. I was going to be able to determine who I spent my time with and how I spent my time.

Along the way, I got pregnant. I was sixteen, and I knew that if my parents found out there would be big trouble, so I just ignored it—except that I was throwing up with morning sickness. We had to go outside every morning on the way to band and I'd throw up on the playground. I was, like, "Oh my God, what am I going to do? I'm pregnant." I didn't feel there was anybody I could tell, or anyone to talk to, but this guy.

So I told him and he started talking about it around town. And I mean this was a small town and news travels really fast. It wasn't long before the school counselor called my parents in and said, "There's a rumor going around that Margie is pregnant and I don't know if it's true or not but I think you should know." That same day a couple of girls cornered me and said, "We hear you're pregnant." And I said, "How did you hear that?" "Well, your boyfriend is telling everybody, he's telling the whole town." I said, "He doesn't know what he's talking about." Then my mom came into my room after school and she said, "The counselor called us in and said he'd heard a rumor that you're pregnant. Is it true? Have you had a period?" And I just broke down and started crying and said, "Yeah, I think I am."

My mother understood. My mother had known my dad six weeks and had gotten pregnant and they got married. She said, "I need to talk to Dad about it and we'll decide what to do." Obviously, I could not have a voice in the decision. I couldn't make good decisions in their eyes, right? They decided that as soon as I started showing I would need to go to this home for unwed mothers in a city that was 250 miles away.

It was weird because the purpose of sending me there was to hide it, but everybody in town already knew. You can't keep a secret like that in a town of twelve hundred, so I didn't get why I had to go away. The only sense I could make of it was that I had done something so awful and so wrong that I needed to be sent away.

When I was about four months pregnant, they loaded me up in the car and drove me on the longest drive of my whole life to this home for unwed mothers. I remember crying all the way, looking out the window and just crying, and still not understanding why I had to go away—I just didn't. They drove me out to this place. It was this old brick building that was three stories high—just what you envision as the stereotypical home for unwed mothers.

We went in there and all the social workers were so nice and oh, this poor little girl got pregnant; we'll take care of her. There were a lot of eighteen-, nineteen-, and twenty-year-old women. There were some sort-of-tough women and then some of us really naïve girls who had no idea what was happening. There were very few young girls, but there was one other girl who came the same week that I did. She and I bonded. We were pretty much in the same boat and we were about the same age, so we had a lot of talks and got really close.

I stayed in that place for months. My parents would come once a week, religiously. Every Sunday they would take me out. We'd go to the park and take a walk and go buy a soda or something to eat, and then they'd drop me back. Those visits were so painful. I mean, everybody just had to act like everything was okay and it was going to be over one of these days. My mother wrote me letters every single day that I was there. I'd get some mail every day when they did mail call.

I've just blocked a lot of it out. I mean, it was okay if you have to live somewhere, but it was kind of like being in prison. We couldn't really go out on the grounds; you couldn't go out of the place unless you had your parents with you. The older women could, but the younger ones couldn't. All these months confined to this place. This other girl and I started walking the stairs—all the way up and all the way down. We thought if we exercised the babies would come faster, and at least this gave us something to do. We were bored. I mean, we all had to do the jobs. You'd have to be on the kitchen crew and cook the meals, you'd rotate jobs. Then we'd have groups on birth control and we're like, you know, it's a little late for that.

I just hoped that my baby would come before school started so I could go back to school in September for my senior year and act like nothing had happened, just like my parents wanted me to. Just go on with life and have it all be over. I mean, my parents had decided that I would give the baby up for adoption and there was never a door for talking about anything else. There was never any other option.

I couldn't go back to school in September, I was still there. So that was really difficult, knowing that I was going to have to go back to school after it had already started. How was I going to deal with all the questions that I'd get? What would I say about where I'd been?

I delivered at the end of October and the very next morning a social worker shows up. It must have been the same day, because I delivered early in the morning, like 2:00 AM or something. The social worker comes and says, "Here, sign this paper." She said, "You can have the choice—do you want to see your baby before you sign the paper or not?" I said no. I chose not to because it was going to be too painful. I asked her what the paper was and she said, "This signs him over to adoptive parents. It says you'll never try to find him and you'll give him his privacy." So I signed it. I didn't feel like I had any choice. She said, "Okay, it's all done. Your parents will be here in a couple of days."

I've dealt with that my entire life, trying to find my sense of power and voice. Because this whole experience was just totally taken away in so many ways. I don't know what happened to my baby. I've always had to assume that he's okay. I got the message from the social worker that this was all done. It's all over and there's nothing else to say about it.

It was just a couple of days later my parents came and picked me up and we went out to eat. I was trying to eat and I fainted, because it was way too early to be out doing anything. Then I went home and I had to go to school. My parents were, like, this has ended, there's nothing else to say about it, nobody in town has to know. I mean, everybody knew but it was never, ever, ever talked about.

I just had this huge sense of shame and I went back to school and acted like nothing was wrong, nothing had happened. The spirit of the town was nobody ever said, "Where have you been? Why are you coming to school two months late?" But everybody knew. Friends that I had weren't my friends anymore. Then all the boys wanted to go out with me because, "Oh yeah, she's had sex—she's loose, she's a tramp, she's a whore." I ended up in some weird situations. I mean, one guy had a gun and tried to make me have sex with him. I guess I had shown that I would have sex, so boys decided they could take advantage of me. I guess they thought I didn't have any sense.

I just was wanting to get my senior year over. I did a lot of crying but it was all private. I never talked about it with anybody. It was never mentioned in my family and I just went on like nothing happened. But deep down I was feeling all this shame and all this pain and loss and sadness. Really, really sad but ignoring it all, and just numbing. That's when I really learned to dissociate from my feelings and just go about life and not feel.

I went away to college and started drinking. I found out that worked pretty good to numb the pain. I drank a lot in the first few years of college. I drank a lot and I had a lot of sex, trying to do something with all these feelings. None of it really worked but I kept with that game plan. And all the time I was wondering what happened to this baby. You know, just feeling this big, big sense of loss, and crying a lot. I would get drunk and cry, get drunk and cry. In the dorm, people would say, "Why are you so sad all the time?"

I was finishing up my degree and then I met the guy who's now my husband. Our early years were not good. He was messed up, too. It took me a lot of years. I lived with that pain and loss and it was never really expressed. A few years ago, I went to therapy and this was what came out: giving up that baby. Along the way I kept thinking, "I'm really, really sad. I need to go to therapy," I mean, I didn't realize that's what it all was about, that deep sense of pain. But when I sat down with the therapist and started talking, this was where I was stuck. I had just lived in that grief for thirty-some years.

It's still not talked about in my family, still not mentioned. If I bring it up, people will say, "Oh, that was so long ago, why are you thinking about it now?" I mean there have been a lot of times over the years when I've thought I need to find him, make sure that he's okay. Every fall, every October, I get really, really sad.

I just felt wrong most of my life. I mean, I got a doctorate degree to try to make myself better, to try to prove to myself that I'm okay, and I still didn't feel okay. It's affected my self-confidence, my ability to be intimate with people and let myself be close to other people. I just couldn't have long-term friends or friends who were close because I was afraid that they'd be taken away, or that they'd leave and I'd feel all that pain again. I've lived most of my adult life disassociated from my feelings, just numb, in order to exist.

It's had a profound impact on my relationships with other people, bigtime trust issues. I mean, that's one reason I couldn't get to therapy–I didn't think I could trust the therapist. Then, living with the secret. That's another thing that kept me away from intimacy. I've had a secret. It's been a secret my entire life and there have been very few people I've talked to about it. Having a child out of wedlock at that time was just not an okay thing to do. You were not an okay person if you did that. And that's fueled my feelings of low self-esteem, low self-confidence.

If I could have stayed home and had the baby and it had all been out in the open, or just had a choice of whether or not I wanted to surrender this baby. . . . I don't know what choice I would have made. I was living in my parents' house, I didn't have a job, so it would have taken some cooperation on their part. But, you know, I've seen students of mine who've done that and they've done okay. Things have worked out.

YVONNE

I was eighteen years old. I was working and trying to make enough money to go to college. None of my family members had gone, just a couple of aunts who had gone to nursing school. My dad is the child of German immigrants and he had to drop out of school in sixth grade when his father died to work and support his mother and younger brother. So his idea of accomplishment was getting all his kids through high school. When I said I wanted to go to college, he said, "I'm not spending money on that." I wanted to study art, which he also thought was perfectly useless.

I think I was a normal eighteen-year-old. I mean, I liked to goof off and have fun. When I met my son's father he said it was love at first sight, but he was a hopeless romantic. I was still a virgin. What I thought was making out turned into sex and that was my first experience. I was shocked and horrified and was sobbing my brains out. So we had sex, and then we didn't have sex again until about two weeks later. Because of my good Catholic background, I was feeling like we had to be married before we did that again. He moved into my apartment with me. I would go to work every day and he would be there with supper when I came home. We did do it again and the next day at work I just knew I was pregnant and I knew I was having a son. I just had this premonition.

I panicked. When I told him, he got all excited: "Oh, I'm going to be a dad." He could teach his little boy how to play the guitar and take him horseback riding and fishing. So, yes, we were going to get married. He came up with this plan. His grandparents had a resort in northern Wisconsin, so we were going to move up there and live. I was going to get a job. He was in a band with some rather strange people, and he was going to get, whatever they call them, gigs.

So I did my part. I moved back to a small town in Wisconsin where my parents lived to work and save money. I worked the night shift in a battery factory. And he moved up there with his band and a herd of other guys. Some of them I thought were really old guys, they were, you know, twenty-four. His friends convinced him to tell me to sleep with other guys so he could say that I didn't know who the father was. So here's somebody who had professed he loved me, and he tells me this. He didn't have to tell me twice. It was, like, "If you don't want me, I don't want you."

I had to resort to telling my parents. My dad freaked out and he loaded my brother in the car with me in the backseat. "We're going to go find that miserable son of a bitch and I'm gonna castrate him." Which, gee, I didn't really want my dad to do anything but help me raise the baby—somehow just make sure I could do this. Well, we found him and my dad took one look at this long-haired guitar player, which was his worst nightmare, and told him what he thought, which was "If you don't get a real job and a haircut you're never going to see my daughter again." Then he picked him up by the collar, threw him across the room into the refrigerator, and dented it with his head. We got back in the car and left and I didn't see my boyfriend again.

My parents took me to Catholic Social Services, where I met with a social worker who—I don't know, when I was eighteen I had a hard time judging other people's ages—I thought was really ancient, so I would say she was probably in her fifties. She was the first person I heard the word *adoption* from. It never, ever crossed my mind. I thought, "Well, I'm having a baby and I'm going to raise him."

I kept working and I had to go see her once a week. I worked the evening shift, so I'd get home from work at maybe one in the morning and then I had appointments with her in the early morning, so most of the time I wasn't on time. That convinced her even more that I was a horrible, irresponsible person because I was always late. I would go there to have her tell me what a lowlife I was. "How do you think you could ever raise a child? Look at you. What do you have to offer a baby?"

I had really long bangs at the time, and I'm sure that's because I was trying to hide. I had terrible posture. I was just trying to be invisible. She'd always say, "Brush those bangs out of your face." But she used to marvel at my eyebrows. I think it was the only feature about me that she thought was passable. When I got a copy of my records after my son found me, there was a physical description in there that said I had sallow skin, dark circles under my eyes, thick lips, a snub nose, and I lumbered when I walked. The only nice thing she had to say about me was that I had wonderful, naturally arching eyebrows.

So it was always, "What are you going to do? How are you going to support this kid? What makes you think that you could possibly be fit to raise a baby?" And this was week after week after week. "What are you going to do with your life?" I think I was working for less than a dollar and a half an hour at the battery factory. We made big battery packs with about twenty-one cells in them. We soldered the little wires together and they were used for radios for soldiers in Vietnam, which always made me very sad. You know, is somebody going to die if this isn't right? So it was dirty, dirty, dirty work. It was filthy, but I religiously went off to work every night, even though my friends were out socializing.

My dad said, "I'm not going to spend one damn cent on that little bastard." He dragged me off to the welfare office to apply for welfare. The plan was that I would go to a maternity home. I went along with it because obviously my wages were not going to pay for anything. He also took me to the district attorney's office to file paternity charges, which were sent off to my boyfriend's family. Of course, they totally denied it: "Not our son." So the welfare was approved to pay for a maternity home and medical care.

I had some time off from work, so I tried to track down my ex-boyfriend. I went to his parents' house and I remember his mother came out on the front steps holding his youngest brother, and there were I'd say probably six other siblings with her. I'm standing down on the sidewalk below her. It was a bright sunny day and there was a beautiful blue sky and a couple of his siblings had the most incredible blue eyes that matched the sky. I remember that. I told her who I was and she proceeded to scream at the top of her lungs, telling me I was nothing but a whore and a slut who had led her son astray and given him clap or something like that. I said, "What's that?" Then I just turned around and left.

I went back home and kept on working at my job. There was a dance hall that had live music where my friends and I spent the weekends dancing and I met, wow, the most incredibly gorgeous guy I had ever seen. He actually gave me a ride home. We stopped and walked around a golf course until four in the morning and talked. He walked me to my door and said good night and I went inside and I thought, "Hmm, if I'm ever going to marry anyone, this is the person I'm going to marry." But of course I wasn't going to breathe a word about this to him. We saw each other from July until I went to the maternity home in October.

I think it was after Thanksgiving, and the social worker at the maternity home rounded up the girls and gave us a presentation about the wonders of adoption: how all these infertile people are just feeling so heartbroken and what a wonderful thing it is for us to give our babies to them. I couldn't handle it. I left the room just sobbing my brains out, "You just can't do this to us, you just can't do it." I locked myself in my room and refused to come out for the rest of the day.

My baby was due on December 26. All the other girls wanted to be with their parents on Christmas, so they decided that I should be with my parents and induced labor on December 14. The grown-ups told me to do it, so I did it. You know, all my life I really, really tried to be doing the right thing. I just didn't always get it right.

On the morning of December 14, I took the tunnel over to the hospital, which was right across from the maternity home. They put me in a room and shaved me, which I was shocked by, then they did the internal, broke my water, hooked me up to an IV, and left the room. There might have been some kind of little light on, but it was just a really cold winter day and the light was just as cold. It was kind of a gray light and I just lay in that bed for hours and hours. I always had horrible, horrible cramps when I was a teenager when I got my period. Well, this was like, ugh, the worst thing I could have imagined. So finally at about one in the afternoon a nurse peeks her head in and I said, "Isn't there something you can give me because these cramps hurt so bad I can't stand it." She said, "You should have thought about that nine months ago!"

I didn't do any screaming, I cried. Finally, it was just so bad that I rang for the nurse and somebody decided to see what was going on. They panic: "Oh my God, the baby's gonna be born." They wheeled me out of there into the blaring bright lights of the delivery room. I remember them transferring me to the table, tying my arms and my legs—you know, spread-eagle. She's putting the mask over my face and the last thing I remember was wanting my own mother, which was probably the only time in my life I ever did. I had never in my life felt as alone as I did right before my baby was born.

And then I don't know how long it was, but this nurse-anesthetist brought me out of it enough to show me my baby, so it must have been right after he was born because he was still all covered with newborn baby stuff. And, of course, I couldn't touch him because my hands were tied down. Then I was out again.

The next thing I remembered I was in recovery and I started throwing up, and I kept throwing up. Finally, I think they got sick of me throwing up in there and they put me in a room all by myself, down at the end of the hall with the door closed. Which was fine because I didn't want people looking at me. I kept on throwing up, but I managed to get myself out of bed. Every step I took I felt like the guy had sewed my heel to my butt. Honest to God. I think it was around eight-thirty at night that I called home and my dad answered and I said, "Guess what? You're a grandpa. You have a grandson." And his reply was "When are you coming home?" I said, "I don't know." That was it.

I was in the hospital probably five days and my son was in the baby nursery. At first he was in one of the front rows and I could see him. He looked just like my aunt Katie, who is my favorite aunt on my dad's side. I thought, "Wow, that's a narrow little group of genes there." I guess we all think this, but he was really a beautiful baby. When they realized that I was there looking at him, he was suddenly moved waaaaaaay to the back. I started begging any nurse who came in to please let me see my baby and they all said, "Absolutely not."

The nun came over to the hospital and I spent a whole lot of time just sobbing my heart out to her, just crying and crying, and she finally said, "You know what? You're gonna forget all about this, you're gonna go home and you're gonna meet a nice young man, and you're gonna get married, and you're gonna have other babies, and you're never even gonna remember you had this one."

They moved me back over to the maternity home, where I refused to come out of my room. I didn't have a roommate because they didn't want people being around me. I wasn't making it look too good. Finally, I pulled my act together. I was supposed to go home and I said, "No. I refuse to

leave. I don't care where you make me go, but I'm not going back to them."
So I stayed there for Christmas and every day I would go to the newborn
nursery. After supper we folded diapers and then I would at least get to peek
in and see him. Then, just like that, one day he was gone.

On Christmas my dad called. It was the only time while I was there that
he called. "How come you're not home, god damnit. Get the hell home." I
said, "I don't care if I never see you again. I don't want to be around you."
He said, "That's bullshit, you're getting home." So the day after Christmas a
social worker picked me up and she actually gave me some Christmas pres-
ents. She gave me some really fancy stationery and some perfume and I
thought that was kind of odd. By the time we got home it was already dark
and she helped me unload my one little suitcase.

I wasn't welcomed. Within hours my mother is screaming at the top of
her lungs about how I've ruined her happy little family. She didn't want me
sharing a room with my sister. She had this room where she sewed and
ironed and where the kitty litter was, so they set my bed up in there with the
kitty litter. It was just kind of a walk-through room; there were no doors. If
it wasn't the dead of winter in Wisconsin, I'm sure she would have been glad
to send me off to the barn to sleep. That's how happy she was. When I was
at the maternity home my sister, who was fourteen at the time, wrote me one
letter and told me how I had ruined the family name because I was a whore,
and on and on. I mean, it hurt, but it didn't surprise me. I knew she didn't
come up with this stuff on her own. This is what she heard at home.

I went out with the guy I had met in July on New Year's Eve and I had
nothing to say. I just couldn't even talk. The only thing I was thinking about
was the baby. So we didn't have very much fun and then we didn't see each
other.

After New Year's my dad marched me into town, where there was a
cheese-packaging factory, and got me a job working there. I think my son
was probably two and a half weeks old when I started working there. The job
involved standing in one spot on the cement, doing the same thing all day.
I felt like absolute death when I got home. I still got up and went to work
and just kept on. It was maybe the second week at work, this guy who
worked there and was two years behind me in school, said, "Hey, I heard
you had a baby." I stood right there and I said, "Ha! Where'd you hear

that?" And he said, "Oh, I just heard it." And I said, "Well, you're wrong." I actually denied my own child. He said, "Yeah, well that's not what I heard." I just felt like . . . what a horrible, horrible mother. I mean, it was bad enough I didn't know where he was, but to deny his existence. . . .

The social worker would call at least once a week. "Well, did you make up your mind yet?" "Well, I'm trying to figure this out." By that time I was trying to weigh the options. I kept a diary: "What's worse—for a child to grow up being adopted or being labeled illegitimate? What's going to be harder for him to live with?" I thought, bottom line, if I put this off long enough she'll just say, "This kid's too old. You'll have to take him home."

I think it was early in February when I did talk to my mother about keeping him. Even after a horrible childhood with her, she was my last hope. She said she would babysit while I worked, but that scared me because of the way she treated me. I mean, she stopped beating on me when I was fourteen because I grew five inches and suddenly I was taller than she was. I was very concerned about leaving my baby with someone who was capable of doing that, but I was desperate. Of course, I'd have to pay her for babysitting, besides the room and board that I was paying.

I called the social worker. This was just the happiest day. I was calling to find out when we could pick him up. She sounded really mean, "I'll call you back tomorrow and let you know." So my mother was actually getting excited about it and was saying, "We can get the crib down from the attic," and all this kind of stuff. Then, the next day I go to work and I get laid off. When the social worker called back, she said, "You can pick your baby up, but before you do, you have to pay me for your hospital, his hospital, your doctor, his doctor, my counseling, the maternity home, and the foster home." She was going to keep the meter running at the foster home until that was paid in full. I couldn't have him until then.

I still can't remember the exact amount she told me but it was thousands. I'm thinking that even if I got called back to work at $1.57 an hour I just could not imagine how I would ever be able to get that much money. So I said, "Fine, I'll sign your f'ing paper because I'll never have that kind of money." She called me to tell me when I would be signing the papers and she wanted to know if I wanted to see him before and, of course, I did. I had one more glimmer of hope. I asked my mom to go with me to see him because I thought, "She can't let this happen if she sees him." But she said no. I found out after he found me that that was exactly why she said no.

On February 14 my dad drove me so I could sign. He parked six blocks away because he didn't want anyone to think that he had anything to do with this. I went into the social worker's office and she led me to some cold little institutional room. There was no light on, but there was light shining through Venetian blinds and it was kind of a hazy winter day. I sat in a chair and she brought my baby in. He was all bundled up. He was sleeping and she handed him to me and left. I just sat and held him and cried. I was dropping big tears on him and trying so hard to memorize his little face. He was just so, so cute, except he had some scratches and kind of a rash. I'm thinking, "Professional people are taking care of him and this is how he looks? How did I ever think I could do it?" Half an hour later she came back and said, "Okay, your time's up." He didn't see me because he slept through the whole thing.

I gave him back. It didn't even cross my mind not to give him back. I was just at rock bottom, totally hopeless. Instead of me making her break my goddamn arms to get him, like I should have, I just did it. I left and walked the six blocks to my dad's car. He drove me to the lawyer's office. I went in and the lawyer asked me, "Are you doing this because you want to?" And I just mumbled, "Yes." And he said, "Okay, I'll see you in court tomorrow."

I walked back to my dad's car and we went home and said nothing. The next day we drove to the courthouse and I think it was a judge's chambers. It was this big wood-paneled courthouse room. This time it was kind of warm, yellow sunlight. It always seemed like nobody had bright lights on. I had to go in there and the judge asked me if I was doing this because I wanted to, if anybody was forcing me to, and I answered, "Yes, because I want to. Nobody is forcing me to." I signed my name to I have no idea what and I turned around and left. I didn't shed a tear. I showed nothing. I went to my dad's car, and from there he took me to a job interview at some savings and loan. I did pretty bad. This time my dad parked right out front. Then I got back in the car and went home and we never once mentioned it again. You'd think we just dumped clothes off at the Salvation Army. The next day I went out with my friends and I drank until I puked.

I was unemployed for about six weeks, then I got a job at another factory.

This one was a piston-ring factory. I didn't know what piston rings were. I had to ride to work with these creepy guys from my hometown because they drove past our house. I had an iron bar and the piston rings were in stacks of one hundred and I had to stick the bar in the rings, tilt it, dip it in this tank of solvent, pick it up, drain it off, and then put the rings on these metal trees with arms that looked like Christmas trees. I did that for eight hours a day. Occasionally, I would be sent to this little room and have to dip stuff in tar. I still have scars on my arm where the tar splashed. I did this for six weeks. It was mind numbing but I'm trying to be a good girl.

The supervisor who taught me how to do all this stuff was a balding, not very nice woman. She walked up to me one day and said, "What are you doing?" "I'm doing exactly what you told me to, ma'am." She said, "That's not how I told you to do it! Gimme that thing!" She does some kind of backhanded little maneuver and then she said, "Now do it the way I told you." I tried to do it that way and a hundred piston rings fell all over the floor. She says, "Now pick them up." And I took the iron bar and I said, "F— you!" and I threw it at her. Thank God I missed. It bounced off the wall behind her. I just started screaming at the top of my lungs and ran to the bathroom and just sat in there screaming and screaming. Not even sobbing, just screaming. They got the personnel manager—and he's a man—to come in the ladies' bathroom and try to talk me down. I can't even explain it, you know—it was like I had tried and tried and tried to do what all these f'ing adults want me to do and it still wasn't right.

He finally convinced me to stop screaming and led me out to his car and took me back to my family. When my dad and brother found out why I was home before I was supposed to be, wow, all hell broke loose: "You useless piece of no-good shit, can't even hold a goddamn job," and on and on and on. "If you don't get back to that goddamn job . . ." So the next morning the guys from my hometown picked me up and I went back to work. I no longer had to dip rings in solvent; I got to sort them. God knows how many bad piston rings got sold. There was a little old lady there that I talked to and she'd been doing that for twenty-five years. I said, "So how do you know the good from the bad?" I had no idea what I was doing and I don't know that she did, either. The personnel guy called me into his office and told me that he didn't think I was factory material and they were going to have to permanently lay me off at the end of two weeks. He said that I really should think about going to college.

I didn't tell my family I got fired. I had the guys who took me to work take me to the employment office every day. I would sit in the Catholic church in the morning and draw pictures and write morbid poetry and then go to the employment office. I called the social worker to find out how my baby was doing. He wasn't adopted yet. She said, "He's probably too old. We don't know if anybody's going to want him." She said, "Do you have any deafness in your family, do you have ear problems?" I said, "My sister had a bad left ear and infections when she was little and had to be hospitalized. Why?" "Well, we think he's deaf. We don't think he's adoptable." I said, "I want him back." And she said, "No. I don't care if he grows up as a ward of the state, you will never get him back."

I got another job washing dishes in the kitchen at the TB sanatorium. I had to wear a little mask so I wouldn't get TB. God forbid I should die, with a life like that. Somewhere along the line it dawned on me, this thing about "If you have other kids, you're gonna forget this." I'm thinking, "I'm going to have to have another baby," but I knew that I would never be pregnant again and unmarried. I would find a way to kill myself first. There is absolutely no way in hell I would ever go through that again.

I hadn't seen the guy who I thought, "Hmm, if I'm gonna get married someday it will be to him," since January. In April I wrote him a little letter telling him I had something to tell him. He wrote back and said he'd be home from college that weekend. He showed up and I had nothing to tell him. I just wanted to see him again. We go out and by then I'm able to talk, unlike when I saw him right after my son was born. When the evening ended he said, "What was it you wanted to tell me?" And I said, "Nothing, I just wanted to see you." We've been together ever since. We've been married thirty-five years.

On my son's twenty-first birthday I dug papers out from the back of my underwear drawer where I kept them. I filled out some paperwork and sent it to the state of Wisconsin but I never really let myself hope. I didn't let myself get my hopes up that he would find me.

One day I'm at my studio and I get a phone call from Catholic Social Services asking me if I still want to know my son. I said, "Of course." "Well, do you want him to write you a letter or would you like him to call you?" I said, "Listen, I didn't wait twenty-three years to wait even longer for a letter. He can call me." I hung up the phone, burst into tears, ran across the hall to tell one of my very best friends, whom I'd never told about my son. I called my husband and said, "Guess what? The chickens have come home to roost"—our farm background here. "This will never be a secret again, from here on out."

I packed up my stuff, went home, picked up my fifteen-year-old, and said, "I have something to tell you: you have a brother." This is my A+ student. She said, "No way, dude! Cool, Mom!" That was it. No questions. We had supper and I hadn't told the two other girls. They were watching something on TV and the phone rang and it was my son. I cannot describe . . . hearing your child's voice for the first time when he's twenty-three is just, just indescribable. He sounded so much like my brother and my favorite first cousin. We exchanged statistics and covered all that basic stuff and then it was, "Well, now what do we do?" I had never read anything about adoption in all those years, so I said, "Well, I don't know what we should do next, but I'll tell you one thing: I want to know absolutely everything I missed if you're willing to tell me. I want to hear everything."

He took me at my word and we talked for four hours. I got off the phone and everybody says, "Mom, who were you talking to?" I said, "Well, it's a really long story. I'll tell you as soon as that show is over." And when it was, I told them, "When I was nineteen I had a baby. He is your brother and that was him on the phone. He wants to know us." One daughter says, "That's cool!" And the other says, "Yeah, that's great!" And they all went to bed. I didn't sleep. I got up and started writing and I have continued to write, all in longhand with old ink pens.

I had never stopped to think. I had been just running through life. I had gone from my childhood, which was a matter of just survival, to a major trauma. When the lid came off, when I reunited with him, I really think I was clinically nuts. I sobbed—I swear, it took every bit of power I had not to be sobbing when I was with my daughters. Thank God they were in school so I had some time alone. I would just sob and sob and write. I never slept more than three hours at a time and I think the lack of sleep made me crazier. I just wrote and wrote and wrote. Poor guy—I wrote my son a letter every day and they must have been six pages long. He said, "I've never read this much before in my life, Mom."

When I look back at my life, the only thing I would change would be to find a way to keep from losing my son. I wouldn't even change getting pregnant in the first place. After he found me, I found myself sitting out in my garage smoking and writing and sobbing and thinking, "If only I had a handgun, I would make it stop." But then I thought of my youngest, who was only eight, and I would cork the wine. Regardless of how much hell I was in, I could not do that because I could never, ever hurt my kids like that. So I am still here.

It is the loss of that baby. When he came to see us, maybe a month into the reunion, I just remember standing there hugging him and just wanting to somehow have the power to crank the clock back twenty-three years. To do it over and get it right. It's just a horrible, horrible, horrible loss. I have this week-old granddaughter and I look at her and I just think of my son when he was that age. How could society think that was all right? He was not even entitled to be held by his own mother. It's just . . . it's all so wrong. It's wrong! There was no reason he should have been removed from his mother, none. I had never harmed a child and I haven't harmed one since. It was all about what people would think.

I remember telling the social worker that I just really loved him and that's why I wanted to keep him, and she said, "How can you be so selfish?" And I was raised . . . oh God, don't be selfish. The reality was I really wasn't being selfish, I was being a mother. To have her tell me that my natural feelings as a mother were selfish was just, my God, it was just wrong.

It really wasn't until maybe the last two years that I've been starting to put it back together. I remember standing in the kitchen at suppertime and just sobbing and my thirteen- and fifteen-year-old daughters put their arms around me and said, "Mom, you have to get help." It was just the most difficult thing I ever had to do because for me to ask for help was just incredibly difficult. But because they told me I needed to, I did. I called my doctor and it turns out his wife is a licensed psychologist, so I went to her for fifteen months. She insisted that my problem was my childhood, not losing my son. I insisted that it was losing him, but I think it was a combination of both. She just wanted to go on and on about my childhood. She insisted that it was about my mother, so her idea was I needed to draw a picture of my mother in a phone book and then beat the phone book with pieces of rubber hose she had. I really thought that was the dumbest thing I'd ever heard and I refused. I had no urge to hit my mother.

But she did help me see that I actually had only one choice, which means there was no choice. She also helped me see that my boyfriend made his decision when he took a hike. I mean, she helped me see the reality of it. I was really, really blaming myself: "How could I possibly have given away my own child?" So I have no regrets that I went to the psychologist. I guess it's helped me think, "Maybe I'm okay. It's maybe okay to be me."

It's just . . . my whole life has just been based on shame. I'm probably over halfway through it. I can't go through my life crying. I mean, it was so bad in the nineties I had scabs under my eyes from wiping them. You hear about people's lives being touched by adoption. It's no damn *touch*. I mean, that just drives me nuts. You're smashed by adoption. I mean, it alters the mothers' lives forever.

From everything I see, I think the general public believes that mothers who give their babies away are glad to be rid of them, they're glad to be rid of the problem. They think, "She didn't care about that kid. She just wanted him out of the way so that she could go on having a good time." I've heard people say that. It's like if you have a child and you're not married, you don't have those same maternal feelings that other mothers have? I have never, ever met a mother who felt that way. Never.

My father-in-law and I had the same birthday and we were quite tight. He told me that the week before my husband and I were married the priest had called to tell them that their son was marrying a woman who was a sinner, who had lived with another man and borne his child. They had also gotten an anonymous letter in the mail when our engagement was in the newspaper, telling them that their son was marrying a whore who had a kid. I said, "I want to see that letter." I figured I'd spot the handwriting. He said, "We read it, tore it up, and burned it in this ashtray." To me, they are quality people. I mean, never once did they ever mention a word to their son about who he was marrying. I mean, really, you can't meet better people than that.

If there's a silver lining in this, I think it's made my children a whole lot more compassionate than they would have been. None of them are ever quick to judge anyone.

But there is this dichotomy that I have because I shouldn't have been left in the care of my mother. I remember sitting at the table with my mom and my grandma telling her, "You have to stop beating her or I'm gonna find a way to get her away from you." Everyone knew it was bad, but nobody could quite stop it. My grandmother wanted to send me off to a private boarding school for high school. She raised chickens, sold the chickens, butchered them, sold eggs, and she was going to pay for it. My dad said, "Hell no, she's my kid and she's living with me." Now and then he would make an effort to make my mother stop: "Damn it, leave that kid alone!" And then he'd go out to the barn and do his chores and she'd beat the crap out of me. So when he would speak up, I would just cringe. When I was ten, I went outside and sat in the snow. I just decided I was going to sit outside until I was dead because I didn't want to live with her anymore. Somehow my dad noticed I was missing and came out there. "Get in the house, you moron!" he said. I said, "Okay," and I went back in.

She was just nuts. When I was in third grade she came in to tuck my sister in and tripped over one of her high-heeled shoes that my sister had been playing with. She picked it up and started beating me with it because it was my fault. In the morning I'm brushing my hair for school and it's all stuck together because it's bloody. So I wore my little cowboy scarf with a little horse on the back that I got from my uncle Louie, who lived in Arizona. I get to school and I'm supposed to take my scarf off and I said, "Oh no, I have a head cold. I have to keep it on." I didn't want my teacher to see the caked-on blood.

The abuse from my mother certainly prepared me to be a birth mother. Get out there and live that lie–"Life is okay"–when it isn't. So I was in basic training until the time came when I could enlist. And you know what? I really miss my mom. My brother and sister-in-law had her put in the nut ward of an Alzheimer's unit. She is in there with people who make noises that a lot of people have never heard. I can't get her out because I have power of nothing. I can't save her but I miss her–I really, really miss her. After my son found me she was very, very nice. We talked all about my childhood. She kept me up until four in the morning wanting to talk about it, and how sorry she was for being so horrible.

I just feel so strongly that our stories need to be told, most importantly to our babies. They had no choice whatsoever in this. I'm thrilled that the one choice my son did have—to find me—he made. I mean, both he and I agree that there will never—regardless of how long we live and how wonderful life is—there will never be anything in either of our lives that will top finding each other.

You asked about the pain of the reunion. My son didn't cause the pain when he came back. He has never been the cause of any of my pain. The pain was always there—it just came out in the reunion. I was still burying that. If it hadn't been the reunion, there could have been something else in my life that would have broken it loose. I've always thought from the instant I knew I was pregnant that he was innocent in all of this. He didn't choose to be born and he didn't cause my pain. Actually, by tripping it loose he's the reason that I have been able to heal as much as I have. I'm very grateful for that.

5

❧

The Family's Fears

My mother and my father were both one of eight or nine children, and each of them came from very poor families. But by the time I was in high school they were very affluent. My father was a banker and my mother played bridge, and they went on nice vacations and we had drapes that somebody came to our house and designed. You know, things like that which in my town were quite hoity-toity. I had nice clothes and proper dental care and all that stuff.

But when I got pregnant it was like slipping back a generation somehow. It was like slipping back in time. The climbing that they had done and their aspirations were suddenly under threat. *They* were going to be those people they looked down on. There was a clear social category for unwed mothers and that was the "you must not come from a very good home" category. I think it was impossible for my parents to get past those feelings and to see me as somebody who needed some help from them. They had no choice. They had to find a place for me to go where they didn't have to deal with the questions and the funny looks. It was just more than they could take.

—Deborah

W HEN I HEARD THE WOMEN recount their stories, one of the most shocking aspects of their experience was the way they were treated by their families. It's hard to imagine how the families could have been so harsh.

In order to understand the actions of these families and the intensity of the pressure to relinquish, it is helpful to take into account the enormous social pressure to conform that followed World War II. The 1950s are notorious as a decade of mass conformity, but it's revealing to look more closely at the social forces at work during those years. The postwar period was a time of remarkable new prosperity in which a significant number of American families joined the middle class—though that was true disproportionately for white families because of continuing racial discrimination. For those families who were moving up, whether white or black, there was a tremendous fear of losing the ground they had gained. Conforming to the middle-class values of the time was paramount. Many of the women I interviewed spoke about their parents' fears of being ruined if anyone learned they had an unmarried pregnant daughter. The parents' fears of being ostracized from their community or church ultimately led them to treat their daughters in precisely the same manner that they feared their neighbors would treat them.

> I told my mother and she started screaming at me. It was horrific. I was told to leave the house and not return. I was not allowed to make a phone call. I was not allowed to take any clothes, pack a suitcase, nothing. I don't remember where I went to use a phone, but I called the doctor I had babysat for and I went to their house. I stayed with them. I guess he pleaded with my mother and father to let me come home. He told them that I needed my family and that was where I belonged, and he was right. But they refused to take me back.
>
> —*Mary III*

Studies of relinquishment patterns suggest that unmarried pregnant women who chose to make their children available for adoption were generally from higher socioeconomic backgrounds and had higher educational aspirations than those who chose to parent.[1] Another characteristic cited was that women who surrendered their children were more likely to have parents who were "supportive of the placement decision."[2] The backgrounds of most of the women I interviewed are consistent with these findings, though I would use different language to describe the parents' sentiments. In most cases, especially those involving high-school or college students, parents not only supported the placement decision but *made* the decision. The vast majority of these parents *insisted* that their daughter surrender her child.

> I told my parents, "I can't do this." And they said, "You can't come here. You can't bring her here." My father said, "You'll have other children." People have asked me how I got through it, and I say, "I turned myself into a stone."
>
> *—Edith*

Most of the women I interviewed did not refer to the surrender of their child as a choice at all. Choice implies making a decision between at least two viable options, and, with few exceptions, these women felt they had no other option. Many were in their twenties but still would have needed some family support, either with babysitting while they worked or with an offer to live at home until they could get on their feet. Rather than offering help, many families threatened to ostracize their daughter if she kept her child. Most parents simply took over when they discovered their daughter was pregnant, and made arrangements for her to go away and relinquish the child. The women often likened their experience to being moved along a conveyor belt, with no discussion, no weighing of options, and no say in the decision. They felt that they were in no position to object, since they had already brought shame upon the family by becoming pregnant.

> My father took me to the family doctor and when we came back to the house and my father told my mother she fainted. They conferred with my boyfriend's parents as to what to do and the decision was made to send me to a home, because I was from a very middle-class type of family and my mother didn't want anybody to know about it. I had to drop out of school, because the schools didn't allow you to attend school pregnant in those days.
>
> We had to make up a story and I couldn't go anywhere. If my mother had to take me shopping we'd go out of town, someplace where we wouldn't run into anybody. My mother was always worried about what people would think and that was probably the

worst part of it for me. She was more worried about what people would think and specifically about what they would think about her. That affected all the decisions that were made. My mother decided that I was going to give the baby up; I didn't decide that.

—*Diane II*

One of the sentiments that was expressed by many of the women I interviewed was that their mothers felt betrayed by them, and that sense of betrayal seems to have fueled the intensity of the disgust and anger that so many parents, especially mothers, inflicted on their daughters.

In all those months I was sent away, my mother did not visit me. My father would drive an hour and take me out for the afternoon. We went for ice cream, we went for walks. He never looked at my belly and we never talked about it at all. I don't know what we talked about, but he was there for me.

—*Sheryl*

My mother was horrified. She called me a slut, a whore. "No wonder he followed you around like a dog in heat all the time." My dad looked at me and said, "Have you been with a man?," which was the terminology of the day. I could only nod my head: yes, daddy's little girl had been with a man. That was hard.

And it seemed like just a day or so after that, my mother came in and had me go to the bathroom, disrobe, and get into the bathtub, which was very humiliating in itself. She administered a douche, which was very painful. I didn't know anything about a douche. I found out later that what she had used was Lysol from the brown bottle, and I blocked that out of my mind for twenty-something years. One day my husband was cleaning and I smelled the Lysol and it took me back.

—*Pollie*

The rise in social status for so many families after the war and the concomitant pressures on these families to conform to middle-class standards were unprecedented. By the mid-1950s, almost 60 percent of the population enjoyed a middle-class income, as compared with 31 percent in the years before the Great Depression.[3] Government-guaranteed loans had allowed returning veterans to purchase single-family homes by financing up to 90 percent of their mortgage at low interest rates.[4] In 1947 alone, 800,000 GI's received home loans.[5] The difficulty was building homes fast enough to meet the demand. For sixteen consecutive years, from 1929 to 1945, new construction had not kept pace with the need for housing, and as GI's returned from the war and married, the demand intensified.[6] Private developers were poised to meet this need with assistance from the government. Developers received tax incentives and government guarantees that allowed them to build enormous suburban developments like Levittown, the Long Island community of seventeen thousand homes built by Levitt and Sons between 1947 and 1951.[7] Before the war about one third of homes had been built by their owners and another third by small contractors who built a handful of homes every year. But by the late 1950s two thirds of all houses built in the United States were erected by big builders who primarily created uniform suburban developments that were monotonous but affordable.[8] Mortgages on these new suburban homes often cost less per month than the cost of renting an apartment.[9] Housing starts went from 114,000 in 1944 to 1,692,000 in 1950.[10] Whereas only 40 percent of families had owned their own homes at the end of World War II, 60 percent were homeowners by 1960. Between 1950 and 1960, 18 million people moved to the suburbs.[11] All of these new homes needed furniture, appliances, a television, and often two cars, and all of that purchasing furthered the economic boom. Americans bought 20 million refrigerators, 11.6 million televisions, and 21.4 million cars in the four years that followed the end of the war.[12]

The percentage of the population that conformed to the postwar model of the perfect nuclear family was also far greater at this time than at any time in history. During the 1950s and 1960s, the percentage of the population that was married rose considerably and was higher by about 10 percent than it was before or has been since. In census reports from 1900 to 1940, the percentage of the population that was married moved up or down in relatively small increments and averaged about 58 percent. But in 1950 the figure rose to 66 percent and then climbed to 68 percent in 1960. After 1970, this percentage started to return to prewar levels and in 1980 the percentage of the population that was married was the same as in 1900: 54 percent.[13] In the U.S. Census for 2000, the percentage was also 54 percent.[14]

After the war the average age at which couples married also dropped. The median age at first marriage in the 1980s was the same as in 1890, roughly age 22 for women and 26 for men. However, between 1945 and 1960 the median age of marriage dropped to an average of 20.5 for women and 22.75 for men.[15] By 1950, almost 60 percent of women between 18 and 24 years of age were married.[16] Most couples had completed their families before they reached age 30, and they also had more children than in previous decades. Women who reached adulthood in the 1930s had an average of 2.4 children, whereas those who did so in the 1950s had 3.2 children.[17] The sum total of these changes added up to the baby boom, which by definition includes those born between 1946 and 1964. Even though marriage and child-rearing norms of the time came to be seen as characteristic of traditional American family life, in fact they were abnormal in comparison with marriage and childbearing patterns throughout the twentieth century.[18]

Writers and sociologists of the time began to identify a major shift in the American psyche. Sociologist David Riesman in his 1950 book, *The Lonely Crowd,* identified a transformation in social character—away from the "inner-directed" individualism that had been valued in the nineteenth century to "other-directedness"—and a shift from production to consumption.[19] William Whyte argued in his 1956 bestseller, *The Organization Man,* that white-collar men increasingly subordinated their independence and personal goals to conform to corporate demands so that they would belong to a group and fit in.[20] Both of these men argued that the suburbs were an extension of corporate life and that people willingly accepted their life of conformity as part of a package that included the creature comforts they now possessed.[21] It may well have been impossible for families to step out of line if they wanted to hold on to what they had. Between 1952 and 1956, although disposable income increased 21 percent, borrowing had increased 55 percent, and by the end of the 1950s almost half of families were deeply in debt and had less than two hundred dollars in liquid assets.[22]

> You have no idea what things were like in the sixties. Everything depended on your social status and what everybody said about you.

And if this befell you, you just got axed totally to the bottom of the pit somewhere, at least in my mother's eyes, and she had worked so hard to build up our status. I mean, it was just a sham. You have this perfect façade—one boy, one girl, achieve in school and all this kind of stuff. But meanwhile at home I'd go to my room to avoid shouting matches. I mean, basically the communication style in our family was to shout at each other. Yet we're the perfect family, right? I don't know, these are the ironies of the sixties.

I know there was no sympathy for me whatsoever. I think I did tell them that I was raped, although we didn't have the actual term "date rape" in that day. But it was still all about how I disgraced *her*. That's what it was all about.

—*Ann*

Those who were living the middle-class American dream in suburbia were geographically removed from those who had not benefited from the postwar boom. A prominent feature of the economy of this time was how disproportionately the benefits accrued to white families while economic prosperity lagged behind for African Americans. While millions of white families in the 1950s were purchasing new homes that were affordable because of government-backed developments and home loans, many African American families were being discriminated against through redlining policies that prevented them from moving into these new neighborhoods. William Levitt's contracts, for example, stipulated that residents must be Caucasian,[23] and Levitt was far from alone in preventing African Americans from moving into better neighborhoods. Even many returning African American GI's were excluded from securing loans for homes in desirable areas, and thus from building the home equity that contributed so significantly to the longer-term wealth and financial security of their white counterparts as real estate increased in value over the years.

One of the overriding characteristics of the social change during this period was, in fact, "white flight" from urban communities and multiethnic neighborhoods into the suburbs. Whyte referred to the suburbs as the new melting pot, because it was during this time that many white ethnic groups, such as Italian Americans, German Americans, Irish Americans, and American Jews began to be thought of as simply white.[24]

The lack of opportunity for many African Americans to join the expanding middle class may have played some role in the huge discrepancy between the numbers of children surrendered for adoption during these years by white women versus African American women. Between 1952 and 1972, whites surrendered at an average of ten times the rate of African Americans.[25] But the relationship between social status and surrender is only part of the picture. The maternity-home system, which expanded tremendously after the war to provide a place for girls to live out their pregnancies, primarily served a white clientele. Immediately after the war, many maternity homes had the same segregationist policies that were evident in other institutions of the time. In addition, those who were poor, both blacks and whites, may have been less able to travel to maternity homes in distant cities or to pay the fees that they required. Perhaps some rural and urban poor did not even known about the homes or were not referred to them as readily by doctors or social-service agencies. A Florence Crittenton Bulletin from 1952 reported that about a third of the forty-nine maternity homes at that time provided services for African American girls and three were "solely for Negro girls."[26] However, some of these homes were not the large maternity homes that white girls were sent to but boarding homes that were "under the supervision of Florence Crittenton staff" and could take in only a few girls at a time.[27] One of the women I interviewed was sent to such a home.

> My parents found out I was pregnant and then there was talk about me not having the baby. I said to them, "I won't submit to an abortion–I plan on having my baby." They decided that they were going to send me away, which was a big, big shock because I was so involved at school. I just loved being in the high-school band and my grades were important to me. But they did take me away. They called it a home for unwed mothers, but it was more like a foster home. They had foster children there and then they had one other young lady who came in after I did who was pregnant. The parents in the home were very nice people, but they were elderly people. It was a black home, of course. During that time–this was 1963–

everything was pretty much segregated here. My high school was all black. It was just prior to the schools integrating.

I grew up from very early childhood until about age fifteen in a housing project, and while in today's time when you think of a housing project you think of abject poverty, single parents, slum-like dwellings, there was none of that. When I grew up in the projects, we knew maybe two families where there was not a mother and a father in the home. You had two parents, you had working parents, and it was expected of you to finish high school and go to college. Being black, most of the people I knew went to college and became teachers.

To be a single, unwed mother was just something you didn't do. I knew two other young ladies who got pregnant when we were in high school. It was just something you didn't do. You were an outcast, so there wasn't a lot of help for you.

I think the main issue was shame, behaving outside the acceptable norms and bringing shame upon the family. I don't think women were perceived as being capable of raising children without the financial support of a male. But I can think of quite a number of extended families around where *couples* moved in with the grandmother and they all lived together and pooled resources. But single parenting I didn't see. I don't think it was looked upon too favorably.

Incidentally, my ex-husband is an adoptee. His mom was married to his father when he was born, but his father was abusive and he told her if she kept the baby he was leaving. So my husband was raised by a woman who knew his mom and said, "I'll raise your baby." He grew up with an adoptive mom, but he knew who his mother was. My children enjoyed a beautiful relationship with both women, both the natural and adoptive grandmothers. The secrecy and the lies weren't there.

—*Carole II*

One concern that was not raised directly by the African American women I interviewed, but was talked about by white women who gave birth to biracial babies in the 1960s, was the fear that adoption agencies would not be able to find a home for their baby and the child might end up languishing in the foster-care system. In fact, race is a factor in the placement of babies for adoption even today. Despite the high demand for adoptable babies in this country, and a 140 percent increase since 1995 in the number of foreign-born children adopted by Americans to meet this demand, some African American babies are sent to foreign countries to be adopted by couples in Canada, Germany, France, the Netherlands, Belgium, and England.[28]

During the 1950s and 1960s there was a great deal of turmoil for both white and African American families when a daughter was discovered to be pregnant. But unlike many middle-class white families of the time, fewer African American families disowned their daughters or insisted that they surrender. In the majority of cases, the baby was absorbed into the extended family or adopted informally. The reasons for this difference are complex and reflect the disparity between the experiences, and the social, cultural, and economic histories, of black versus white Americans. [29] Interestingly, today white surrender rates have dropped to match those of African American women, which have remained fairly constant over the years—at approximately 1.5 percent of premarital births. It is worth noting that the majority of the women I interviewed gave birth in the 1960s, when the white surrender rate was extremely high. In 1964, the percentage of white surrenders was about 40 percent,[30] almost twenty-seven times the rate for African Americans.

The stories of women that appear in this book reflect the difference in black and white surrender rates in that the vast majority of the women I interviewed are white and most were raised in blue-collar or white-collar middle-class homes. Only a small percentage described their families as either poor or affluent. A common belief at the time was that girls from affluent homes routinely obtained abortions out of the country or through doctors in their communities who charged a hefty sum. Those who desired and could afford an illegal abortion could often find one. It is estimated that between 250,000 and one million illegal abortions took place each year in the postwar years. These "back room" abortions were often highly dangerous and were responsible for 40 percent of all maternal deaths.[31] Some women who might have been able to afford these illegal procedures chose not to get such abortions because of that danger.

Another factor that intensified the pressure on individuals and families to conform after the war was the escalating fear of communism. This climate of fear and suspicion led to both legitimate inquiry and reckless persecution of people who were suspected of being Communist sympathizers. Many civil servants, actors, and writers lost their livelihood for holding views that were left of center.[32] The fear of internal subversive forces fueled an obsession with nonmarital sexual behavior and efforts to identify individuals thought to be sexual perverts who had infiltrated our government and were considered to be "as dangerous as actual communists."[33] Anyone with a sordid past or believed to be involved in unsanctioned sexual behavior was suspect. In the climate of cold war paranoia, "loose" women and homosexuals were especially suspect and thought to pose security risks since they were presumed to be weak by nature and therefore susceptible to blackmail.[34]

Women who did not subscribe to the prevailing domestic model were seen as a threat both to the family and to society. It was not at all uncommon for women perceived as loose to be seen as the responsible party when it came to a whole host of problems that required a male counterpart. During the war, loose women were blamed for spreading venereal disease. The government warned soldiers against seductive women who might be spies in disguise and against "good girls" whose morals had loosened due to wartime independence, and who threatened happy homes by luring men away from their wives and children.[35]

The nuclear family—typified by a male breadwinner and a wife who stayed home and devoted herself to the needs of her husband and children—was held up not only as the ideal but also as a patriotic endeavor.[36] Men and women who did not conform to this model "risked being perceived as perverted, immoral, unpatriotic, and pathological."[37] The belief being espoused was that the strength of our country depended on manly men whose lives were typified by marriage and procreation, and on womanly women who did not compete with men or otherwise emasculate them. This ideal woman was subservient, domestic, and sought fulfillment through her role as wife and mother to the next generation of children who would continue to fight the "Red Menace." The consensus was that happiness for both men and women depended on marriage. A survey from that time indicated that only 9 percent of those polled believed that a single person could be happy.[38]

After the war, women vacated, or were pushed out of, the high-paying jobs they had held and into low-paying or part-time jobs to make way for returning veterans. With the expanding economy, it was feasible for more men to earn a decent living, and a wife working outside the home came to be looked upon as evidence of a man's inability to support his family. Nevertheless, the number of working wives doubled between 1940 and 1960, and as consumption rose many families depended on mom's part-time income to meet the monthly bills and allow them to retain their middle-class lifestyle.[39] Despite the fact that many wives were working, their primary responsibility was taking care of the home and raising the children. Women who could not find fulfillment in canning, housework, and changing diapers were seen as neurotic.[40] Since child rearing was the mother's primary responsibility, it was also her fault if the children did not turn out right. Having a daughter who was pregnant was unequivocal proof of her failure and the family's social standing in the community could instantly plummet since it was commonly accepted that only bad or low-class families were plagued with such problems.

I feel that my mother was as much a victim of the times as I was. Later, when my daughter from my marriage was born, I saw a side of her that I didn't remember from when I was young. It must have been very, very hard for her but she did what she had to do. She did what society dictated. Years later, she told me that she was very much afraid that if anyone at work had found out that I was pregnant she would have lost her job.

She was a single parent before the term was coined. My father had abandoned the family when I was under four years old and he didn't provide any support. She did not admit to being divorced because there was such a social stigma attached to being divorced then. She told people that she was a widow. My mother and aunt made their home together. They were both clerical workers at the *Milwaukee Journal* and if my mother had lost her job it would have been a horrible economic situation for us.

She did what she had to do and it was hard for her, but she was from the generation that didn't show their emotions and certainly didn't talk. You don't talk about feelings. What are feelings? You do what you have to do. She was not a cold, heartless person, but it was just a different time.

—Annie

Polls from the mid-1950s indicate that housewives were not nearly as content in their marriages as they were supposed to be. In studies from that time, researchers concluded, "Women were twice as likely as men to report they were dissatisfied or regretted their marriages."[41] But given few high-paying jobs for women, a 26 percent decline in women's wages after the war,[42] and the stigma of divorce and single motherhood, many wives stayed put even if they were dissatisfied. The social pressures experienced by the mothers of this generation come through powerfully in many of the interviews I conducted.

From what I could figure, I don't think my mother ever really wanted to have kids. She said that when the war came—World War II—she dropped out of college and went to work and she's always resented that she didn't finish college and have a career and do more with her life. She was a very intelligent woman. She resented being home, being the housewife. She didn't like that role at all. She didn't like the cleaning, the whole thing. She said she was dissatisfied even up to the time of her death. Having five children was just too much for her. That wasn't what she wanted.

At that time women stayed in the home, they were the housewife, they didn't work outside of the home. There were no divorces at that time, either. It was a very rare thing when somebody got divorced, so a lot of families stayed together that shouldn't have. Women would get together and have their coffee klatches and talk about somebody's husband's running around with somebody else, and how unhappy they are, and this one's getting beat up. These days they never would have stayed together but they did at that time.

I think the wives leaned on their women friends a whole lot. I think that's why my mother didn't want to have her friends find out. She had a circle of maybe eight to ten women who hung together and did the Girl Scout thing. They were troop leaders and they visited all the time and I think they depended on each other for support. I think she felt that she wouldn't be accepted by them if they knew I was pregnant. She didn't want their pity. She wanted to be the one they came to. She was a very proud woman.

—Carol I

My mom married my dad in California in '42, and he shipped out overseas and he was gone until '44 or '45. During that time she worked in an airplane factory and lived by herself. She used to tell us how proud she was. They worked so hard—they wanted those airplanes to be the best for their boys, you know. She made friends. She was very happy. She saved her money. She had a good little nest egg by the time the war was over. Then my dad comes home from the war and they started their little farm. They farmed the land that my mom's dad and mother had cleared. They used her folks' barn and used her money to buy the land and the cows, but he told *her* what to do.

She went from being an independent woman to being somebody who was absolutely dictated to. She had to live in a house with no electricity and wash diapers by hand. A few years later, she tried to get a job at the hospital doing a little laundry work and he had a fit. She worked for one week while his mother stayed with us, but it wasn't good enough. He wouldn't let her work.

She had that independence and then all of a sudden it was all gone. Then he lost the farm and took the money that was left and bought a brand-new 1953 Oldsmobile with it. When she inherited more money from an aunt years later, that money bought a house and she lost that after the divorce because she couldn't keep it up.

It used to make me so angry that she was just like a lapdog. But it was the expectation of the fifties. You were supposed to be a good little housewife, you were to keep things clean, get the bed made, get snacks made for the kids—yet he could just tramp through the house with his muddy feet and that was okay. It had to have been a terrible shock for her to come back from her war job to that little dirt farm and try to make a go of it. She was absolutely stifled.

—Glory

My mom told me that she had been date-raped by my father and that's the reason they were married. I was that child, I was the product. It was in February in the woods of Wisconsin, and she screamed and tried to get out of the car and he said, "Fine, I'll just leave you here to freeze." He date-raped her in the car, and then he dropped her off at her farm. Two months later, she discovered she was pregnant.

She finally told her parents and her father tracked my dad down and then told my mom, "You are going to marry him because that's what you do. You're going to get married." She stayed married because she was Catholic and that's what you did. He was a savage drunk. We used to wake up in the middle of the night with him calling her unspeakable names. We just accepted that. He was our dad. He was nice to us and when he was sober he was fine. They even had some good times together.

When he died, at the showing before the funeral the family was all sitting there and Mom went to his casket and knelt down and just sobbed hysterically. I thought, "My God, why is she doing that?" She came and sat down next to me and I said, "Mom, why are you crying?" She said, "For fifty wasted years."

—Joyce II

One of the most compelling ways in which the image of the "perfect family" was established and reinforced was through the television shows of the time. Many of the most popular shows—*Leave It to Beaver* (1957–63), *Father Knows Best* (1954–63), *The Adventures of Ozzie & Harriet* (1952–66), and *The Donna Reed Show* (1958–66)—featured perfect nuclear families with nurturing dads, and moms who deferred to their husbands and did the housework in perfectly coiffed hairdos. An especially revealing feature of television shows of the time was the popularity of shows featuring widowed fathers, including *The Rifleman* (1958–63), *The Andy Griffith Show* (1961–68) (though Andy had quite a bit of help from Aunt Bea), *My Three Sons* (1960–72), and *Bonanza* (1959–73). Two programs featured father figures who raised orphans, a boy in *Fury* (1955–66) and a girl in *Bachelor Father* (1957–62). And in *Sky King* (1951–54) a fatherly uncle came "out of the clear-blue western sky" every week in his plane, *The Songbird*, to spend his days with his niece, Penny. Meanwhile, there were no popular shows of the time that featured single moms—not even widowed moms—even though in the aftermath of World War II many more widowed women than men were actually raising kids on their own. The anomaly is a powerful testimony to the social stigma of single motherhood.

Despite this stigma, many families did allow their daughters to keep their children, and even helped to raise them. Studies of the time show that women whose families did offer to help raise their child were, for the most part, from less economically advantaged families or from families that had had a previous experience with single pregnancy.[43] I did interview women whose families had offered to help but who elected to surrender nonetheless. In these cases, the women surrendered either because they did not want the child raised in the environment being offered, because they felt it was not economically feasible, or because they saw education as the only hope for a better life.

> I was a senior in high school and we had a really strong romance going on and it was really difficult because he was white and I'm black. There we were in Georgia, you know, trying to date. So all kinds of horrible, horrible things happened to us. I got pregnant coming up to Brown University to spend the weekend with him. He took me to see Dionne Warwick as a birthday present.
>
> I don't know when I started to feel like I wasn't in love with him enough to get married, but I was sensible. Something told me, "You better figure out a way to go to school." I really wanted an education. I had been in the Upward Bound program and it had given me just a little glimpse of what was out there. When I was growing up, it was all about being a maid and cleaning somebody else's house. You know, being married to a man who could treat you like a dog.

I was sick and tired of the ignorance I saw around me. I was tired of the men treating the women like crap. You couldn't even fight the system, because you didn't have the words. I decided I'm not going to be a part of this. My education was the only key I had. That's what they were saying all over the country. That's what Kennedy was saying, that's what Dr. King was saying.

My mother was the worst about it. She ragged me out a lot of times about giving my baby up. She would get mad and say, "I don't understand why you just couldn't bring her home. That's my grandbaby." I did say to her, "Because I don't want her to have the influence." I didn't want her to have the influence of my stepdaddy.

—Rose

My mother was the unwed mother. She was in a mother and babies' home in England for six months—three months while she was pregnant with me and three months afterward. About a month before I had my daughter, late in the evening when the younger kids were sleeping, my mom was sitting in the rocker and I was lying on the couch. And for the first time, she talked about my biological father. I think she was trying to relate to me by saying, "I know what you're going through." She told me how much I would have liked him, how he was such a nice man, how much she loved him, and how good-looking he was in his Canadian Air Force uniform. My mother loved uniforms. She told me how they danced. I was born in '46, after the war, but they had known each other during the war.

She told me that my grandmother had said she couldn't come home with me and she didn't know what she was going to do, but she knew she wasn't leaving the maternity home without me. Evidently, Grandma relented and we left the home when I was three months old.

After I delivered and came home from the hospital, I was lying in my bed crying and my mom came in and said, "What are you crying about?" And I said, "I want my baby. I love my baby." And

my mom said, "If you really loved her, you would have kept her."
I stopped crying and I never cried again. I never cried until 1999,
when I found my daughter. I didn't think I had the right to cry.

My mother and I never spoke of my daughter again, not one
word ever, ever again. For all those years I thought my mother was
wicked and horrible for saying that to me, but now I think she was
disappointed. I think she was disappointed because of what she
went through. She had me, and kept me. No matter how our lives
turned out—and my mother paid her price, marrying the man that
she did, and through that us kids suffered—but no matter the
childhood, I am so thankful that I was with my mother.

—*Christine*

Married couples who were not raising children seemed odd in the pro-
natal environment of the 1950s and 1960s. The desire to parent, and to conform to the normal social and family expectations of the time, imposed
substantial strain on couples who could not conceive. Such couples turned
to adoption in record numbers during those years, and the rising demand
for adoptable children intensified the pressure applied to young women to
surrender. One of the most common arguments made to unmarried pregnant women at the time was that the child would have a better life if they
surrendered it to a married couple who would have more to offer economically and could offer legitimacy to an otherwise illegitimate child. Many
women I interviewed recounted how maternity-home and adoption-agency
workers strenuously made this case to them.

The staff were very condescending and very judgmental. They
would say, "Your child will be better off without you. You're doing the right thing. There's a loving family out there." And I was
thinking, "Well, how come I can't be a loving mother?"

—*Cathy II*

The intense social pressures that families felt during the 1950s and 1960s
and the stigma associated with unwed pregnancy have waned dramatically
over the last forty years. In fact, young women who place children for adop-

tion now are more likely to be viewed by their peers as "selfish" and their actions thought of as "incomprehensible"[44]—the very same language used against young mothers who did *not* want to surrender their children forty years ago. For mothers who surrendered in the fifties and sixties, a more tolerant society today offers little solace. Instead, the change in views underscores the flexible nature of societal attitudes and the degree to which the women's lives were governed by the attitudes of their time. They are well aware that many who have grown up in subsequent generations—including their surrendered sons and daughters—cannot understand how mothers could have "given away" their own flesh and blood.

> Three years later and my life would have had a different outcome. Three years later, the first girls in the area were pregnant and staying in school. I mean, think about that—twelve hundred days later. You didn't have to go to an unwed mothers' home. You didn't have to give your baby up, and you didn't have to hide in shame. Twelve hundred days later.
>
> I was scared for my baby all those years. I never slept through the night. I never made it through a night without wondering how she was.
>
> —*Susan II*

JEANETTE

I was a senior in high school in a small town in Washington State. I'd had a boyfriend since the previous summer. He was captain of the football team and very athletic and, you know, I was one of the cute girls. I was Roman Catholic, and absolutely believed that I would burn in hell if I didn't lead a good life. However, we started having sex in the fall. The first time was after a football game where he had done very, very well, and after that it continued. I really cared for him. I liked his family and my family liked him. I told him I had missed my period, and we went to a doctor who I assume other football players took their girlfriends to. He gave me this little white pill and said that I should have my period soon. Well, I didn't. My boyfriend and I talked about it. He had a really good football scholarship to Washington State University and, of course, he couldn't be married. This was 1952.

I started wearing a girdle because I had to keep my stomach in. I was so sick that spring. I had a sister who lived in San Francisco and I wrote her a letter and said I was "in trouble." She knew exactly what I was talking about. The day after I graduated from high school, I went to live with her. I never told my mother, I never told my father, I never told anyone. Both of my parents died without knowing.

The previous year, in my little town of five thousand, there was a girl who had a baby and wasn't married. She kept that baby and it was a scandal. Their house was about five blocks from the high school. One morning we were sitting in class and we heard this terrible explosion. Their house had blown up. The baby was fine, but she was terribly burned on her legs and her arms. We all thought it was God's way of disapproving. I don't know if he disapproved of her getting pregnant or of her keeping the baby, but I thought about that incident constantly when I was pregnant.

Single people got pregnant, but almost everyone married. There's a saying the Irish have—something about six-month babies, I forget—but it was very common. We couldn't even say the word *pregnant.* My mother became pregnant when I was nine or ten years old. No one told me until she brought the baby home. The first time I heard the word *pregnant* out loud was when I was in nursing school.

While I was at my sister's I had one maternity dress and I remember it to this day. It was a yellow checked smock with a matching yellow skirt. I wore it every day. We didn't wear pants much in those days. I would write to my parents and say I was looking for a job. My boyfriend would write and he would send me a dollar bill once in a while. It was the only money I ever had. The apartment house had these little mailboxes. I didn't have a key, but I would peer in there to see if there was a letter from him. If there ever was, I would sit by that mailbox until my sister came home. Toward the end, he wasn't writing at all. I thought it was strange because the plan was that we were going to get together afterward.

The entire time I was pregnant, I actually separated myself from this baby. I had been told repeatedly, "Don't see that baby and it won't hurt. If you ever hold him, it will be very painful for you." But they brought him to my room. The nurse was standing in the doorway holding this baby and I screamed at her, "Get that baby out of here." That's a hard, hard memory— that I rejected him. They never brought him back again.

I was isolated from the other mothers at the hospital. Let me tell you how naïve I was. I had been in labor for so long and they kept doing rectals to see how dilated I was. And I was so sore that afterward I asked my sister, "Where does that baby come out anyhow?" I thought it must have come through the rectum.

I'd taken my high-school annual with me. There was one very nice nurse's aide. She was the kindest person I'll ever meet in my life because she never looked down on me for being pregnant. She would sit with me and I'd go through the annual and I'd show her my boyfriend, and me at the ball games cheerleading.

Immediately after I had that baby, I was angry—I got angry at everything. I was angry at my sister and we got into a terrible fight. I just wanted to go home. She kept telling me, "If you go home now, they're all going to know. Your stomach's all out of shape." My mother obviously suspected. When I went home, she had new clothes for me that were two sizes larger. My mother would have loved that little boy. But my mother was a blind-faith Catholic and sex was something that was never talked about. Never. It was like everything was the immaculate conception. Last year, my sister said she heard a rumor that Mom was pregnant when she got married. It kept gnawing at me, so I sent for a copy of her wedding license. Not only was she pregnant, she was seven months pregnant. She could have told me that. We would have loved her just as much.

I went home. I needed a job. I had been a fairly talented writer in school. I had won some contests. As a matter of fact, I won the state "I Speak for Democracy" contest. I got twenty-five dollars, which was huge in 1952. The whole basis of my essay was something like "Communism is like a cancer. It has its little claws and tentacles that reach out everywhere." My mother loved that. She said, "It was the line about the cancer that made you win." We absolutely thought that if we didn't kill the Russians first, they would drop a bomb on us. We were terrified of the bomb.

People who worked on the farms were getting jobs with General Electric, the government subcontractor for the Hanford Project, which was just thirty miles from my home. They extracted radioactive plutonium to make the atomic bomb, which, of course, was used to wipe out Nagasaki. I applied and got a job there. It was very isolated, way out in the sage brush. The workers would go out to these top-secret fields and do something with radiation. They had little badges they wore to see if they got too much exposure. My job was to put these badges in a machine to see how much radiation they'd received.

I'd been in the job for about four months and I was putting badges in the machine and my supervisor came in and said, "Jeanette, I don't know what this is about, but they want you down at AEC." That's Atomic Energy Commission. "You're to go now." In order to get to the job site, you took these shuttle buses that drove about forty-five minutes to an hour out to these Quonset huts. He said, "Take the shuttle bus into town and go to the office." I had no idea what this is about. I'm eighteen years old. There was an outer office with a gray-haired woman receptionist. I gave her my name and she said, "Have a seat. He will be right with you."

Shortly after, this young man—twenty-four, twenty-five years old, very handsome man with coal-black hair, white, white teeth, impeccably dressed in a blue suit—called me in and told me to sit down. He said, "Do you know why you're here?" I told him no. He said, "You weren't honest with us." And I said, "What do you mean?" He said, "In your application . . ." He said, "Do you know what we do here? This is top-secret work. We have to be very careful who we hire." And I'm trying to think, "What did I do?" He says, "On your job application you were asked if you've ever lived anywhere else for over four months? You have, haven't you?" And I said yes. And he said, "You went to San Francisco for five months and had a baby, didn't you?" And I said yes. "And you didn't tell us, did you?" I said no. He said, "You thought you could sneak away, have a baby, come back and lie about it on your application." He said, "Have you ever considered that if the Communists found that out, in order for you to keep that secret you would have to give them secrets about your job?" I was just sobbing, sobbing, sobbing. He convinced me that I could be coerced into giving up information so that the Communists would keep my secret. I put badges in a hole and wrote down numbers. I had a security clearance, but I didn't know anything. I didn't even understand what they were doing. But at the time, it made all the sense in the world to me. I thought, "My God, I could have overthrown the free world."

When I left through the outer office, the gray-haired woman wouldn't look at me, but she said, "He didn't have to do that. He didn't have to do that." I was sobbing all the way back on the bus. I knew right then that I would not be going around telling anyone about this baby, and I didn't for forty-three years. If I had not separated that baby from me when I was pregnant, I really separated him then.

I became a registered nurse. I got into a terrible marriage a few years later and had other children, but I never even mentioned this incident ever, ever, ever. I had visions, though. I had visions of a knock on the door and it would be him.

In the small town where I attended nursing school, the newspaper would list all of the births in the paper. The reporters would call every night. We had two boards—the real births and the "no information" births, which would not be listed in the paper. I thought those were terrible, terrible women. They were tramps. I never connected my pregnancy with anything that happened in my life, ever. The social structure at that time was so rigid that I couldn't acknowledge it. Eisenhower was president and we were in an ultraconservative era. The boys had just come home from the war and they were building houses, they were going to school on the GI Bill, and we were getting America back together again. I never really knew that the adoption movement was opening up, never paid any attention to it. It had nothing to do with me because I had never had a child. I never had a child.

In 1995, my kids are grown, they're out of the house, and my neighbor came over one evening. She was divorced and had two adult sons that she was having difficulty with. She started crying, and to make her feel less bad I told her about my son. I thought, "Oh, my God. I'm talking about it for the first time ever." She said, "Why don't you find him?" And I said, "I can't. What are you talking about?" And she said, "Just go find him."

She came back with a phone number for the Oregon Adoption Rights Association and I listened to their message. I'm thinking, "This is crazy," but I went to their meeting. I was sitting there with my mouth open. This woman is talking about her search. She said she knew that her daughter was in Iowa and she was going to see if she could find a yearbook picture. I said, "Why?" and she said, "Because I yearn for her." That was so alien to me. She said, "Why are you here?" And I said, "Because I'm curious. He might have died in Vietnam." I'm thinking, "What's this concept of yearning?"

When the searcher called me and said, "I've found your son," I wanted to argue with her: "That's not my *son*. No, no, no, no. It's *the baby*. It was always *that baby*." It was just the most remarkable thing to think, "This is my *son*."

I called him and said, "I have something very personal to talk to you about." He said, "You're my mother," and he started crying. We talked for about forty-five minutes and he said, "It wasn't good, you know, it wasn't good. My mother started drinking right away." He said, "I'm coming to see you on Thursday."

I fell in love with him instantly. Absolutely instantly. He stayed the weekend. He was planning to leave on Monday, but he left on Sunday and I'm glad he did. It was too much. It was more than I could bear. I didn't hear from him for two months and I went into an incredible depression. Then he called and said, "Well, I need to tell you something. When I saw you, I drove as far as Roseburg, pulled over at the rest stop, called my wife, and asked her for a divorce." He said, "It was a terrible marriage, but it was so liberating to meet you, I was able to do it."

The first two years of our relationship were very rocky. I've never figured out why, then one day it all came together. He asked me to come down and visit him and he asked if he could call me Mom. We've had the best reunion. I fell totally in love with him—every part of being in love. I was obsessed for four years; ten minutes didn't go by that I didn't think about him. He's a really nice guy. He was a commander with the county sheriff's department and he left to become the chief of police in another town. He just retired.

He had a terrible, terrible childhood. His adoptive mother drank herself to death when he was fourteen or fifteen. His father traveled and left him in charge. At eleven years old, he was buying the groceries and raising his younger siblings. I was just outraged at them. I thought adoption was wonderful. It never occurred to me that it wasn't. Why didn't they help me keep him, rather than help me give him away?

This is kind of unfair to my other children, but I think my life began at sixty when I found my son. For the first time ever, I was able to love someone in a way that I was not able to before. I started loving my raised children more—I *could* love them. The most shameful thing in my life was now sitting in front of me, talking to me. I never had to be ashamed of anything I did again. I went to my fiftieth high-school class reunion and I told them the story of having my son because I didn't ever want to hide him again. If there was anything shameful about it, it was giving my baby away to strangers, not having my baby. It was by far the biggest event in my life. It shaped my adulthood because I was a child when I had him. I couldn't get close to anyone, ever. I had self-esteem issues that were just incredible. I married down. I never stood up for myself. At one point, I probably drank too much and I could have been a better mother. I think I spent a lot of my life being unhappy.

Then there was the incredible joy of finding him, and the terrible sadness of having missed all those years. But it almost felt good to get into that grief and live it. I don't know if there's such a thing as joyful grief, but that's what I would call it. I would cry and sob and scream, but so glad I was finally grieving.

It's still very shameful to say you gave a baby away. One day at work I printed something out on the printer that had something to do with birth mothers and one of the nurses picked it up and said, "Jeanette, is there something you're not telling us?" So even though I never wanted to hide him, ever again, I still do. I had my seventieth birthday not too long ago, and it still colors my life.

RUTH

I was a sophomore at Boston University. I was dating a wonderful young man. We were falling in love and I was just very, very happy and really naïve, and got pregnant. I was shocked, but I was really happy about it. We had talked about getting married, and this just moved everything up.

My parents were not happy about it. My parents are Holocaust survivors, and I was raised very strictly. I remember the look on their faces when we told them. My daddy called me a whore, and it was very upsetting. My boyfriend's father never said anything. His mother was very, very upset—irrationally so. His mom had bouts of depression her whole life. She was just very upset. I think she felt I wasn't good enough for him. He came from a family of means, and I didn't. She realized we were going to get married and she tried to talk us out of it. The night before our wedding, she locked herself in the bathroom and refused to come out.

I was happy because I was marrying him and I was going to have a baby and in my soul I knew it was going to be a little girl, I just knew it. We continued with school. We got an incredible, horrible, wonderful apartment. I mean, it had bugs, but it was our apartment. We were so happy. His parents cut him off financially and he worked two jobs and went to school full time, and I worked one job and went to school full time.

His mom kept calling and giving us reasons why we should not keep the baby—that we didn't have insurance, that we were too young, that we didn't have careers. Those weekly phone calls turned into daily phone calls. She drove us nuts. I just tuned her out, but he couldn't. We were twenty years old and it's true we didn't have two nickels to rub together. He decided that his mom was probably right. I just kind of blocked out everything and went on my merry way, excited about my baby. Then he told me we couldn't keep the baby, that he wanted to give the baby away. I didn't even acknowledge it.

I went into labor and my husband took me to the hospital and they knocked me out; I don't think it was that unusual in those days. It was October 17, 1968. When I woke up, I said to the nurse, "I'd like to see my baby." She said, "You can't, your baby's been adopted out." I had no idea what the hell she was talking about. My husband told me it had been arranged, and that it would be the best thing for the baby because we really couldn't take care of her. So I never saw my baby. He took me home and I went to bed, and I didn't get out of bed.

The time came for me to sign the papers. My husband got me up, got me dressed, got me to the office, and told me to sign, and I did. We went home and that was it. Nobody talked about it. I was just supposed to go on with my life. Any feelings I had about that baby were kept inside because I had no one to talk to about it. Whenever I brought up the subject with my husband, he wouldn't discuss it with me. It just became a taboo thing. No one talked about it, ever. We finished school and graduated and I became a high-school English teacher.

My mother-in-law finally realized that he and I were good for each other. I think she thought that if we didn't have the baby we would break up, and it didn't happen. She got to know me, and she got to love me, and I got to love her. As a graduation present from college, she and my husband's father took us to Europe. She and I actually had such a ball. We laughed; we had the best time. When we came home from Europe, she killed herself. She was fifty years old.

Years went by, and every single day I thought about my baby. It was the worst pain that I ever had in my life. Every night when I went to bed I prayed that God would forgive me for the awful sin I had committed by allowing my baby to be taken from me. I felt like a horrible human being that I didn't stand up for her better, that I didn't tell everybody to go fuck off and keep my baby. I blamed myself.

Time went on, and I got pregnant again and I had my two daughters. I was thrilled when I had my children. With my first daughter, I was so overprotective because I thought God would take her away from me because I was so bad. He took away my other baby. They didn't know my secret. So the best thing that I ever did in my life was to go to a therapist, and this was a super therapist. He helped me figure out what to say to the kids. And one Christmas when my daughter came home from college we sat down and I told them. I was so scared to tell them because I thought they would hate me. My kids have always said I was the best mommy. And I thought that if they knew what I had done that they would hate me, but they didn't. We all sat and cried, and they all hugged me and said how much they loved me, and it was wonderful.

After that, I decided I would look for my baby. I wasn't sure how to go about it, but I got some great advice from my therapist. The first thing I did was call the adoption agency and ask for nonidentifying information. It was a religious agency, and it was an outstanding agency. In about a month, they sent me the papers. Oh, I was so glad to get them. They were a piece of my baby. I ran into the house with the mail and ripped them open and started looking at them. There was a paper in there and I read it, and it was just filled with nonsense and lies. It said that I had approached the adoption agency and that I had arranged for the adoption, that I had a social worker come out to my apartment many times and every time she did I reiterated that I did not want my baby. It said that on the day my baby was born the social worker came to the hospital and I was smiling, and my husband was sitting on the bed smiling, and I told the social worker that I had seen my baby and I still wanted to give her up.

I read that and I freaked. I screamed. I didn't know what to think. I called my husband screaming. And then I called the adoption agency and spoke to the director. I made no sense, I was just screaming. She put their therapist from the office on the phone and I screamed some more. Then I hung up and fell on the kitchen floor and just cried. My husband came home and I was still on the kitchen floor crying.

The next day I was calm, so I called the adoption agency. I realized what must have happened. My mother-in-law had gone to the adoption agency and arranged for the adoption, and my husband obviously knew about it. She got a social worker to write down these lies. I think that might be one of the reasons she killed herself, because of what she had done. She finally realized that she loved me, and I was a good girl, and I would have been a good mom to her grandchildren.

I called the adoption agency back and I said, "I want these papers taken out of the file. God forbid my daughter should go looking for me and read those papers. She'll think I never wanted her, that I didn't love her." They said, "You can't do that, it's part of the legal document." I said, "I want them out. I want them expunged. I'm going to find a lawyer, and I'm going to sue you, and I'm going to find the social worker who did this. If I have to rip her out of an old-age home, I will. So you go talk to your lawyers, and I'm going to go talk to mine." The next day, I was making my bed and the phone rang. It was the adoption agency—the paper had been expunged.

Through the therapist and the people he had me talk to, I found somebody who found my baby. She found my baby in one week. It was the most amazing thing. My baby was living in another state. She was a rabbi. I got the call when I was at work. There were people all around me and the woman who found my baby was giving me this information and I was writing it down, trying hard not to cry, because people are going by, back and forth around me. It was like I was alone in a wind tunnel. It was the most wonderful news.

I'm also a breast-cancer survivor, and that was another reason I wanted to find my baby. I wanted her to know, and tell her doctor, that her birth mother had cancer. So I wrote my daughter a letter. I wrote maybe sixty letters and ripped them up and started again, and ripped them up and started again, and cried over them. Finally, I had one that explained what had happened, and that I wanted her to know that I had had cancer. I stood in front of that mailbox for twenty minutes, and I finally mailed it.

My birth daughter got that letter when she was in the company of her mother, thank God. They were coming home from her wedding shower. I'm glad her mother was there. They cried together. And then I got a phone call from my daughter. I couldn't even talk. She said, "I just can't do this. I just can't do it." I said, "Okay, I understand, but there are three things that I want you to know before you hang up. One was that I always loved you, and I always wanted you. Another is that you have two sisters—they're your full sisters, and they're wonderful young women and I would love for you to know them. And the third is that it's very important that you speak to your doctor about the cancer, my cancer." She hung up and I thought that was it.

The next week I got a letter from her mom with pictures, and she looked just like my daughters. And her mom sent the most beautiful letter. Her mom is the most wonderful person, and the most generous person. The next week I got a letter from my daughter with more pictures. She explained that she was about to be married and she was going through a whole lot and that when she got back from her honeymoon perhaps she'd write. Her mother wrote me again just before the wedding and said, "When I walk our daughter down the aisle, you're going to be there with us." I tell you, her mom is just a peach.

Since then, my birth daughter and I e-mail every week. She's going to have a baby. We haven't met, we haven't talked since that first time on the telephone, but she e-mails, and she signs her letters "I love you." It's more than I could ever have asked. If I never meet her, I'll know that she's happy and healthy and has a fulfilling job, and is about to have a wonderful family, and that she has the best parents. I begged God every night that she would be happy and healthy and be with loving people, and God gave her to the best.

But for thirty-two years I really didn't live. After we gave the baby away I was in shock. For a long time, we didn't have a very good marriage and I thought I deserved that. Everything negative that happened in my life I thought I deserved, because I was a disappointment to my family, I dishonored my family. In my mind, I committed a sin. I felt I deserved unhappiness and I didn't deserve a good marriage. I was ashamed and I was angry, and I just felt like I let God down, and I let my baby down because I didn't do enough to keep her.

It was a combination of finding my baby and losing my breast to cancer that made me realize that it's important to live in the here and now. I have forgiven my mother-in-law. I think she did what she did out of love for her child. I have forgiven my mom, and my dad, and finally, after fifty-five years, I have forgiven myself.

I was really messed up emotionally for a long time. It wasn't until I went to the therapist that I allowed myself to have a better life. I have a really, really good marriage now. And I'm doing what I always wanted to do—going to school and studying things I love. I hope someday my birth daughter will meet me and tell me she doesn't hate me, because I'm still hoping for absolution from her, but I'm okay.

I am sure that there are some people who surrender their babies because it's really not feasible for them to be a parent, and they know that they're doing something good. They're giving their child to somebody who can really care for her. In that situation, it's an act of love that they should be proud of. In my situation, I never wanted to surrender my baby. My baby was taken from me. It's like somebody ripping out a piece of me for thirty-two years.

I think any woman who's had a child knows the depth of feeling she has for that child, and can imagine the pain you would go through if you lost that child. To not even be allowed to look at your child, to feel it inside of you and then have it gone into thin air—it leaves you feeling like a shell. You shut down all emotion, because if you don't it comes to the surface and then it just spills over. So you keep everything bottled up and you keep pushing it down, down, and it's just a horrible pain.

It's important for people to know, while we honor adoptive mothers—and they should be honored—that birth mothers must be honored, too. That baby is with them every breath they take, every second of their lives. Every prayer, that baby is with them forever.

6

⚓

Going Away

I was in beauty school in Florida and my mom picks me up and takes me back to Alabama and takes me to the doctor. The next recollection I have is being dumped at the Salvation Army Home for Unwed Mothers in Birmingham. It was an old, old, old house with big rooms. I was just put in a situation in which I had no control. It was almost like being put on a train or like being in a car wreck or something. Once you start skidding, that's it. I kind of skidded through it.

Anytime they approached the subject of the baby, it was "When you give up the baby" or "After you leave here." They were telling me that I could just forget all about this, go home, and pick up my life where I left off.

—Joyce I

T HE MATERNITY HOMES that many women were sent to in the 1950s and 1960s were modern incarnations of homes run by organizations that had been doing "rescue work" with women and girls since the late 1800s. Two of these organizations, the Salvation Army and the Florence Crittenton Mission, had initially defined their work more broadly as offering shelter and redemption to all sorts of "fallen women," including prostitutes, the homeless, and unwed mothers. During the first two decades of the twentieth century, the Christian women who ran the homes gradually narrowed their focus to residential facilities for unwed mothers. In part, this was due to their lack of success with prostitutes. By turning their attention to "first offenders," they hoped to find women who were more amenable to redemption and to intervene in their lives before they turned to prostitution for survival.[1]

Maternity homes continued to proliferate and in the years when the women I interviewed were sent away there were more than two hundred maternity homes in forty-four states run by the Florence Crittenton Association of America, the Salvation Army, Catholic Charities, and others. Despite the sizable number of facilities, by the 1960s they could not accommodate the growing number of single pregnant girls who needed a place to live out their pregnancies. A young woman who could not go into hiding as soon as she began showing often hid her pregnancy by wearing one of the massive Spandex girdles that were popular at the time, even among girls who needed them only to hold up their nylon hose. These girdles were invaluable in helping a girl preserve her reputation, since it was often impossible to enter a maternity home until the seventh month of pregnancy. Collectively, the homes could house only about 25,000 girls a year and as many as 35 percent of the applicants were turned away.[2]

Frequently, a young woman destined for a maternity home was sent to a "wage home" until space in the maternity home became available. Families in these homes took girls in and provided them with room and board, and occasionally a little spending money, in exchange for housekeeping and, ironically, childcare. This arrangement allowed a young woman to leave her family's home and community while she waited to enter the maternity home. It also meant she would earn her keep during the weeks or months she stayed with a family and thus the total cost of her exile was considerably lower than if she had stayed at a maternity home the entire time.

> A priest and family friend came out to the house and an arrangement was made where I was going to be whisked away. Nobody would know where I was. It was arranged through Catholic Charities. I would be living with a family. He would be my gynecologist and take care of the delivery of the baby and in return I would be the nanny, help the kids with their schoolwork, and do the laundry. I was given a room in the basement. While I was living there, everybody was told that I was living in Florida. The priest had a cousin who lived in Pompano Beach and I would write out

postcards—"I'm having a wonderful time. I'm doing this and that"—and he would mail them in an envelope to his cousin and they would be postmarked from Florida. So any correspondence I had was very controlled. My mother would come to see me on Saturdays and remind me that I shouldn't eat too much because I would put on weight. I was given a sun lamp to make sure that when this was all over I looked like I had spent the time in Florida.

—Kathi

They found what they call a wage home for me right away. I went and lived with a family that had eight children. You were their servant. I went to the Catholic Infant Home in St. Paul one or two days a week for school until I graduated. Other than that, I did laundry and cooked meals and took care of eight little kids. They had many pregnant girls stay at their home.

—Mary I

I was sent off to be a nanny for a family. The man was a physician, and they had three children—a five-year-old, a two-year-old, and a newborn baby. I was the nanny and did light housekeeping. They gave me a nice room in the basement and they liked me because I was their *girl.* It was the "in" thing in their neighborhood to have a girl. Word got around that we were virtually free help.

—Sheryl

Middle-class girls who did not go to a maternity home were often confined in their family's house, where their mothers could keep a watchful eye on the door and send them running to their room if anyone came knocking. Many older women, including college students and those working full time, simply continued to live on their own, while others went to live with relatives in distant towns. Some worked directly with adoption agencies and never spent time in a maternity home or told their parents they were pregnant. Sometimes the woman's parents never learned that a grandchild had been born until long after the event, if ever.

I was working in Washington, D.C., at the time for the telephone company. I went to talk to someone at Social Services and she made arrangements for me to go to a Florence Crittenton Home in my seventh month. All the while I'm going to work and getting bigger and bigger, so everybody at the telephone company knew my situation. In fact, I was in D.C. when Martin Luther King got shot and there was martial law in the city. I was working that day when the rioting started and we couldn't leave our building. There was one bed in the whole building and they were kind enough to let me sleep in it because I was six months pregnant. It was kind of eerie, you know, because troops were marching up and down the street. The National Guard was out and there were fires everywhere. We didn't know what was going to happen.

A month later, I was in the Florence Crittenton Home and during that time we were watching the presidential primaries in California and we saw Robert Kennedy get shot. So it was a traumatic time. My world was in turmoil but so was the rest of the world. It kind of put my problems in perspective. I started focusing on the people around me and that helped me to cope. I tried to help others who seemed to be emotionally distraught and it had a calming effect on me.

—Nellie

All I knew was that I had to somehow disappear. I didn't tell my parents. I just wrote and said I was going to go off to find a job, not to worry. My baby's father drove me to Cleveland and left me with some money that paid a little toward the Florence Crittenton Home. I was there from June through the birth of my baby, which was November 22, a date you can't forget because four years later, on the same date in 1963, John Kennedy was assassinated. So it makes that date even more melancholy because something very tragic in American history occurred on the same day.

—Carole I

The financial cost to a young woman or her family for the maternity home, the hospital, and a doctor's care was not insignificant. In 1951, the cost of a Salvation Army home was $50 per month, plus a $50 delivery charge.³ By the early 1960s, the cost of room and board alone could run over $100 per month. With an average stay of just over six weeks, and additional delivery charges, the total cost could easily exceed $200,⁴ or what today would be the equivalent of more than $1,200.⁵ Some maternity homes used a sliding scale and charged according to the parents' income. A few women reported paying nothing at all, though in some cases those who could not pay were admitted to homes contingent upon the surrender of the baby.⁶ Occasionally, the young man's family offered to pay part of the maternity-home expenses, but among the women I interviewed it was more common for the families of the young women to pay. Some families required their daughters to pay them back. Several women talked about the payments they continued to make to the home or to their parents long after their stay.

> After I came home from St. Mary's and got back on my feet, my mother told me straight out that I owed her for the money I would have contributed to the household income during the months that I didn't work. She actually wrote it out. She gave me a piece of paper that showed how many weeks, at half the pay that I would have gotten during that time. She said when I got a job I was going to have to pay her back. I even owed her for the months before I went into the maternity home, because I had quit work, obviously. See, back then you didn't work when you were pregnant. Plus, I owed Catholic Charities for the layette, the christening outfit, and the postnatal care. I remember it was a huge sum of money. I couldn't believe how much I owed everybody.
>
> I did get a job and I paid my mother back. It took a year and a half, and after that I started paying back Catholic Charities. Long after my daughter was adopted, I went in to make my final payment. Recently, I got my file from Catholic Charities and it's quite detailed about the whole sequence—from the first time I met with them through my stay at St. Mary's, and then every month after that until I paid off the final debt. But I just broke down and cried when I saw the last paragraph of all this documentation, the

last entry about me and the baby. It said I had finally come in to
pay the balance and I still had a chip on my shoulder.

                                                          —Sheila

The experience of living in the maternity home varied greatly among the
women I interviewed, but almost all talked about feeling afraid and abandoned when they were told they would be sent away. Many had never been
away from home and most were not given any information about what they
would find before they arrived. It is doubtful that the parents had much information to offer since most of them did not visit the homes in advance.

I was so scared. I wanted so badly for my parents to say, "You're
staying with us, you're our girl." I had this persona of a hippie but
I just wanted to be with my family. We drove to the maternity
home in Biddeford, Maine, on back roads. My mother and father
were so heartbroken. I was told on the way that I was supposed
to be in Old Orchard Beach working in a hotel as a chambermaid.
So while I was at the home I was to get a tan to continue the
cover-up.

I walked in and there were all of these strange pregnant people
and these nuns. And some of the nuns were harsh. Harsh. I had
committed a sin. It's not like today when you go through therapy,
for God's sakes. No. There was no therapy. When my parents
turned around and walked out the door, I felt abandoned—I felt so
alone. And I didn't understand it. I didn't understand how parents could do that.

                                                          —Lynne

I was sent away to a Florence Crittenton Home. I remember going
up a long drive to this Gothic castlelike building with big trees
and a winding drive. It had big, thick doors and when I entered
I saw two girls coming down the stairway and they just looked
so sad.

We had a little lounge on each floor and in the lounge we had
a little TV and what they called a hi-fi back then—this was in the

days before stereo. We had two records—one was Ray Charles's "Born to Lose" and the other was something about "... stuck up here, I want to go home. ..." I mean, real upbeat songs. Most of the girls didn't stay there as long as I did, but it was always full. It was just a revolving door.

—Pollie

Life at the maternity home generally included chores like washing dishes, helping in the kitchen, or cleaning toilets. Often tutors supplied by local school districts came to conduct classes in the homes, which enabled high-school girls to continue their education and avoid being held back. Recreational activities included instruction in pursuits that were appropriate for a young woman headed for a life of domesticity, such as sewing, knitting, or classes in arts and crafts.

Girls were usually asked to take an assumed first name when they entered the maternity home and they used this fake name with the other girls. This renaming—meant to protect a young woman's identity—could not have been very effective since the young women could obviously recognize each other. Perhaps it was meant to separate the young woman's pregnant identity from the identity she would resume when she left the home.

I was a sophomore in college, at Wheaton, and I was walking across campus and it was late at night in the fall. The street lamps were all lit and this girl is coming toward me and just under the light we saw each other's face and we both stopped in our tracks. It was a girl who had been at the home with me. That home was very confidential and nobody could say the other person's last name. But there she was. We hugged and we stood there under the lamp chattering away, but in hushed tones. We didn't want anybody to know we'd both given up our children. Nobody in our families knew except our mothers.

—Rose

Despite the rules, behind closed doors many of the girls divulged their real names, talked about boyfriends and families, and speculated about what giving birth would be like. Some homes organized outings or allowed the girls to walk freely in the neighborhood. Occasionally, the girls were required to put on wedding bands when they left the building. Since they often traveled in groups, it is doubtful that this charade was very effective.

The homes were sometimes quite strict when it came to communication with the outside world. The women were permitted visits from their parents, though some families did not visit, call, or write their daughters the entire time they were there. In some cases, letters in and out were read and censored and phone calls could be made only to individuals who were on an approved list. If there was a list, it usually did not include the father of the baby. This lack of communication generally ensured that there would be no opportunity to work out a resolution that included the young man if the girl had held out hope of doing so when she entered.

> I was not allowed to call the father of my child. Even when we would write letters they would read them. They would either cut out things they didn't like in them or they would cross through what they didn't like. If the letter really upset them, they would throw it away in front of us or tear it up. That goes for anything coming in or anything going out. They read everything. They censored everything. You were not allowed to call the father of the baby. You were not allowed to call friends. You were only allowed to call your parents or anybody else who was on the approved list.
>
> —Karen I

> My parents are both dead now and I actually found the letters I wrote them while I was away. They are hard to read because I was still so naïve and such a goody-goody. I was trying to protect them, trying to give them this picture of a normal life with my continual, Shirley Temple kind of "I'm having a great day, the baby is kicking, everything is wonderful," like it was a normal thing. "I'm going to ceramics class, I'm working on a very nice plate." I mean, I was living in an institution, for Christ's sake. They locked us in at night. It wasn't a normal life at all.
>
> —Deborah

Some women did not see the maternity home as a negative experience. They were relieved to be out from under the scrutiny of their parents and the community. A few recalled having helpful counseling sessions that enabled them to come to terms with the experience they were going through.

> I was sent to Buffalo to live with my aunt and uncle and then went into a maternity home the last six weeks. Many of the girls came from other parts of the country so nobody would know that they were there. They just came and went in the night. They appeared and then they left, and you never heard from them or had any contact afterward.
>
> But they had some excellent social workers there who really, really cared about us. From what I understand, after you give up a child your physical and your mental psyche just wants to get pregnant again. They worked very, very hard to make sure that did not happen. They were very concerned and spoke about our emotions afterward and how to handle it.
>
> —*Jill*

> I think if I hadn't been in this Florence Crittenton Home it would have been entirely different. My parents never talked about emotional issues. The group counseling enabled me at a very young age to sort of talk to myself and to ask myself the necessary questions to be able to make the decision: Will I be able to live with this? I knew I could go totally off the deep end, having to make such a decision, if I wasn't 100 percent sure that I could live with it.
>
> —*Pamela I*

Many women established strong friendships during their stays, though most did not keep in touch after they left.

> You're going to laugh at this, but what I remember most about this home was that it was right next to a black church and on Sunday mornings they sang and I had never heard anything like that in my life. I was a singer. As a matter of fact, I met the father of my

child in the chorus at the University of Toledo. But a memory I have to this day is looking down from this building and seeing the church and the movement of the bodies, and the singing.

I also remember going en masse with all these other pregnant girls to the museum. I was embarrassed to be going out with the other girls because it was so obvious to other people what the situation was. I was probably mixed with more varieties of girls than I had ever known growing up in a little town in Ohio where everybody was white Anglo-Saxon Protestant. My mother, who was Catholic, was looked upon as someone different. So it was broadening to be with such a variety of girls.

I remember two or three girls in particular. One got pregnant by her high-school coach and another worked in a motel and I think she got pregnant by one of the men who were staying there. I thought that was pretty shameful. One was a wonderful girl and we corresponded for years after. I don't believe she ever had any other children. I had to go back to Cleveland for a checkup and she lived there. Her family had me stay at their home; they were lovely people. She was very bright and she became a reporter for one of the Cleveland newspapers. Whoever got that little child must have been very lucky.

—Carole I

For most of the women I interviewed, however, especially those who were younger, being sent to a maternity home was a traumatic experience. They had been banished from their schools and homes, they were soon to give birth to a child, and rather than being surrounded by caring family members they were living in institutions among strangers. Although many felt camaraderie with the other young women who were there, they also felt that the environment was cold and demeaning and that the disapproval of those who looked after them was palpable.

The philosophy and mission of maternity homes had changed considerably since the early 1900s, when the maternity-home movement began. The religious women who first ran the homes saw themselves as sympathetic sisters who were there for women who had no other place to turn.[7] The home was a place of refuge and spiritual reform for women who had, in their eyes, been seduced and abandoned. Motherhood, they believed, would increase a woman's chances of living a good and proper life. During this time, babies were not separated from their mothers except under extreme circumstances, as when women "cannot be helped or compelled to meet their obligation as parents."[8] The homes generally encouraged bonding through breast-feeding and they helped the women find employment—usually as domestic servants— which would enable them both to care for their child and to work.[9] Well into the early 1940s, some homes still encouraged, if not required, the mother to breast-feed her baby to ensure that a bond developed between mother and child.[10]

But by the end of World War II a sea change had occurred in the mission and philosophy of the homes. Maternity homes of the 1950s and 1960s were, to a great extent, a place to sequester pregnant girls until they could give birth and surrender their child for adoption. If a young woman was unsure of or uninterested in relinquishment, the staff attempted to convince her that it was her best, and perhaps only, option. Though maternity homes were the only place a girl in trouble could turn for help outside of her family, by the 1950s they best served her interest if her interest was in giving her child up for adoption at the end of her stay.

The change in philosophy was highly contested among those who ran the homes and did not come about uniformly. To a great extent the views at individual homes changed as the staff changed. Between the turn of the century and the 1940s, the women who had founded the homes were supplanted by professional social workers who reshaped the understanding of nonmarital pregnancy.

In the first two decades of the twentieth century, social work evolved into a genuine profession, and those who helped professionalize the field were eager to differentiate themselves from charity workers and reformers, whom they saw as overly sentimental and old-fashioned.[11] These professionals formulated what they considered to be more rigorous approaches to social problems, rather than basing their practices on religious perspectives. As the professionals took positions at maternity homes and began to work alongside religious reformers, philosophical clashes resulted. Social workers claimed expertise. As trained professionals, they considered themselves better equipped to diagnose the problems associated with illegitimacy. While their religious predecessors had generally attributed out-of-wedlock pregnancy to the social circumstances of the women's lives and to outside social forces, the new breed of social worker focused on the women themselves. Over many years, they posited a number of theories about why single women became pregnant, all of which were predicated on the problems inherent in the women themselves.

In the early 1900s, most social workers argued that women who became pregnant out of wedlock were "feebleminded"; their pregnancy was proof of their feeblemindedness. This made them seem especially dangerous to society because it was believed that these women were not only likely to be repeat offenders, but that they would produce offspring of low intelligence. These concerns were amplified by social reformers who were already proclaiming that the country was in the midst of moral decay and that the family was breaking down, as evidenced by lower birthrates among the "better classes" of people. They believed that unwed mothers were both the product of bad homes and the cause of broken homes. During this time the concern over nonmarital pregnancy was so great that many "feebleminded" unwed mothers were either institutionalized or sterilized.[12]

Classifying all unwed mothers as feebleminded, however, proved impossible. Social workers themselves had to acknowledge that many of the women who became pregnant were "normally intelligent and relatively well-balanced young women."[13] So a new category was identified, that of the "delinquent."[14] This type of woman had a parallel in the male population. But where delinquency in the male was identified by criminal behavior, female delinquency was defined in sexual terms. The young women who fell into this category were largely seen as those belonging to the working class. By the 1920s, many single women were working in factories, offices, and department stores.[15] They enjoyed a degree of independence and opportunities to fraternize with men. Their sexual lives did not always conform to middle-class standards and in those cases were labeled "sexually deviant." This behavior, incidentally, was soon to invade the ranks of the middle class.

Despite the widespread characterizations of unwed mothers as either feebleminded breeders or sex delinquents, letters and internal correspondence from Florence Crittenton homes operating in the 1940s offer evidence to the contrary, and the personnel at the homes were still generally supportive of and empathetic to the girls in their charge. A concrete example of such support was found in the application materials for the Kate Waller Barrett Scholarship, which was sponsored by the Crittenton homes in the early 1940s. These scholarship funds were described in materials printed by the Florence Crittenton Mission as being available to "a girl who wishes to continue her education to enable her to care for her child."[16] The application required support letters from the superintendent of the home and if the application was successful, the agreement stipulated that the staff at the Crittenton Home would assume responsibility for the care of the child, if necessary, while the mother attended school.[17]

One such application, from a girl I will call Bea, was submitted by the superintendent of an Arizona maternity home after the deadline had passed. The scholarship committee wrote back to say that the home would have to resubmit the application the following year. The staff continued to write letters on behalf of the young woman, lent her money from their treasury to pay tuition, and pursued the matter until funds were secured. The application, with support letters, provides a vivid portrait both of the young woman and of the staff's perception of her.

Bea's application was accompanied by a letter from the principal of her high school that described her as graduating in "the upper bracket of her class . . . and rated by faculty as being outstanding, dependable and trustworthy, and one most likely to succeed in her undertakings."[18] The superintendent of the Crittenton Home wrote:

> *Bea has worked with our Graduate nurse and has shown a liking and aptitude for the nursing profession. Bea is a girl with a very pleasing personality, nice even disposition; soft spoken and reserved of manner. She has always been desirous of becoming a nurse and we feel that with these mentioned qualities and the fact that she takes "telling" nicely she will do well in this her chosen work. For the present we are keeping Bea's baby boy, who is a dear little fellow, until other plans can be worked out for him. It gives us pleasure to recommend Bea for this scholarship and we shall await your reply anxiously.[19]*

In November of 1941, Bea received her scholarship and wrote the following letter of thanks:

Dear Mrs.—

Since this is the Thanksgiving season, I thought it would be very appropriate for me to write and tell you what a great part your help has been and all the thanks I have to give this year.

Your Scholarship of $50.00 has enabled me to stay here at St. Mary's and continue my training where otherwise I don't see how I could possibly have stayed.

My work here is so very interesting—such good work—I've made very good grades and as I am Catholic the setting here is very much to my liking. We have a very lovely hospital two miles out from the city. Sister —, our directress of Nurses, has been very kind to me, and shows a great deal of interest in me and my little baby boy.

My baby is in Phoenix now and once in a while I get to see him. He's growing so fast and I'm so proud of him. I guess I'm just a little awed by him and of course there isn't anything I wouldn't do to enable him to have every advantage I think he deserves.

Mrs.— of the Florence Crittenton Home in Phoenix has been a great factor in helping me get back on my feet again. She's so kind and thoughtful. You can't imagine how wonderful I was treated at the Home. Mrs.— was always there to offer comfort or advice whenever it was needed—surely no other person could do her work quite so wonderfully as she.

Then after I left there the Scholarship Fund helped me into St. Mary's and here I am, trying earnestly to get back on my feet and more so I can support my little boy and prove myself worthy of all the trust that has been placed in me.

Once more I wish to express my thanks to you and all you've done for me and believe me a day never goes by that I do not say a little prayer of thanks for such wonderful friends as you.

Sincerely,

Bea[20]

Another young woman from Youngstown, Ohio, upon learning that she has received a scholarship, writes:

I wish to thank you for helping me fulfill my life ambition to become a nurse. This will also mean I can keep my baby, and otherwise my family didn't want me to. Now, because of what you have done to help me, they have agreed to keep her for me until it is possible for me to take her.[21]

The kind of support and compassion demonstrated by maternity-home staff in these letters seems to have all but evaporated in the years after World War II. The ongoing struggles between those who aligned themselves with the sentiments of maternity-home founders and those who adopted newer professional strategies came to a symbolic if not an actual end in 1947, when the National Florence Crittenton Mission abandoned its policy of keeping mother and child together.[22]

As the philosophical differences narrowed in the 1940s and social workers coalesced toward agreement on the best course of action for unwed mothers and their babies, efforts to identify the cause of out-of-wedlock pregnancy took a new turn. With the dramatic rise in premarital pregnancies after the war, and as greater numbers of middle-class women became pregnant, it became increasingly implausible to label all of those women as either feebleminded or sexual delinquents. Social workers noted that many of these new unmarried mothers were middle-class girls from good families. A Crittenton social worker wrote about these girls that the "sizeable numbers further confound us by rendering our former stereotypes less tenable. Immigration, low mentality, and hyper sexuality can no longer be comfortably applied when the phenomenon has invaded our own social class—when the unwed mother must be classified to include the nice girl next door, the physician's or pastor's daughter."[23]

Social workers turned to the growing field of psychiatry for their answer and, as early as the 1940s, began to classify middle-class girls who became pregnant as neurotic: the unwed mother was a neurotic woman who had a subconscious desire to become pregnant. This theory dominated much of the diagnosis and treatment of unwed mothers in the decades that followed the war. Though social workers had been quick to condemn working girls as sex deviants, this new explanation was more appealing in explaining middle-class pregnancy because it downplayed the issue of sexual drive. By identifying the young woman's goal as pregnancy, rather than sex, the diagnosis of deviance could be bypassed.[24] Though a young woman's peers, family, and community may still have attributed her pregnancy to loose morals or an overactive sex life, professionals determined that the problem was in her mind.

One of the outcomes of this new professional diagnosis was the justification of the separation of mother and child: a neurotic woman was seen as unfit to be a mother. Given the stigma of illegitimacy in the 1950s and 1960s, many middle-class parents were quick to agree that the solution to the problem was relinquishment and adoption. Following this course, their daughter would be given a second chance. Her pregnancy would effectively be erased from her history and she could expect to go back to a normal life, as if it had never happened. Without her child she would be able to marry a decent man and have *other* children. She would not have to live with her mistake. Adoption also came to be understood as being in the best interest of the child. Rather than growing up with the stigma of illegitimacy and an unfit, neurotic mother, the child would be raised by a stable, well-adjusted, married couple.

And though some maternity-home workers were still empathetic to young women who did not want to surrender their baby for adoption, in the postwar years this breed of social worker was rapidly becoming extinct. Internal struggles at the maternity homes continued even into the 1950s, and are evident in correspondence between the leadership of the Florence Crittenton Association of America and the newly hired staff of individual homes. In a letter dated December 23, 1952, Robert Barrett, the chairman of the Florence Crittenton Mission, expresses his concern over a move to shorten the minimum length of a girl's stay in the maternity home postpartum. The purpose of a mother and child's returning to the home after birth was, Barrett asserts, to give the mother time to be with her baby before making a final decision to surrender. He writes:

> *Personally I feel very badly that a girl in our Homes shall not be given every opportunity and help to keep her baby if she wants to. Often a girl who has made up her mind to give up her baby feels different after the baby comes and her mother's instinct is aroused. Not to give her that chance seems a*

cruel and unnatural proceeding. I am not sure but I feel it would be better
for the girl if she tries to take her baby and fails and has to give it up later.[25]

The new policies were shaped by the experts—primarily psychiatrists, social workers, and medical professionals—and promoted by social organizations that had the power and means to disseminate the ideas. The women
whose babies were being placed for adoption were not in any position to influence the policies made on their behalf. Shame is a very effective way to
silence individuals, and those who are less socially or economically powerful are rarely in a position to influence the decisions that affect them.

The message was: this is the good thing to do for your baby. It would
be really irresponsible to keep it. I was hooked up with a nice Jewish
adoption agency in New York, so it was: "Your baby could have the
best. How would you dare to cheat your baby of this good life?"

I know a little about the good life now because I have contact
with my birth son. It's stupid to tell young people that. Do they
know that what the baby's going to have is good? I mean, how can
you say what? I'm a psychologist now. Could I interview somebody and tell you what kind of parent they're going to be? But that
was the spiel. I'd say I was brainwashed. It's interesting when they
talk about cults and people feeling dependent on leaders, and abusive relationships. I mean, I think this had some of those qualities.

It wasn't like lecturing; it was a culture. It was a culture where
you were desperate. You were ashamed and desperate. You needed
these people and the culture was that you gave up your baby to a
life that was better than you could give it. I feel like, what was
wrong with me? I mean, I could have done it. I think I was numb
or something. You know how when you're sick sometimes you
feel like all your energy is going toward healing your body and
you don't have energy for anything else? I think all my energy was
going toward that baby and keeping my body okay.

I don't know, I must have been crazier than I thought. I really
believed that it would hurt my baby to be with me. They somehow

convinced me that all the bullshit of a fancy house and degrees—I have a doctorate myself and I think it's bullshit. I don't think it makes a good mother, I don't think it makes a good father, I don't think it makes a good person. It's stupid. But somehow or other in that vulnerable position, being pregnant and being dependent, somehow it all came together and I just let that baby go.

It feels like a real violation to me. I was so beaten down that I believed—or maybe out of fear I made myself believe—that I was doing a good thing for this kid. I think the shame is I can't correct it and I just really did the wrong thing. Really the wrong thing.

We have changed our idea of mothering. Now you're supposed to have enough money to have two homes and four cars and send your kid to graduate school. Where in the world does this come from? I mean, I see people in therapy who want to be stay-at-home parents when they grow up because both of their highly educated parents have not been around.

I think the whole idea that there's only one way for children to be raised—that we nice, white Americans know the way, and it's married—is a joke, because 50 percent of those idiots who were saying that are divorced now.

—Judith I

In theory, it was not the social worker but the mother who made the ultimate decision whether to parent or relinquish. A Florence Crittenton brochure from 1952 reads, "The mother is under no compulsion, either to leave her baby with us, or to take him with her. There is no priority for either." But it also states that "although the mother should perhaps make the choice, not always is she well qualified to make this last decision." And though maternity homes were thought to be safe havens and "the goal of all these efforts combined is to induct into society a mother and child, each well started on the road to successful living,"[26] in reality this goal was often not fully realized.

Rather than young women being given a realistic picture of the responsibilities and costs of raising a child and allowing them to weigh that information against the resources available to them so they could participate in making an informed decision, they were rendered powerless. And though it might be easy to empathize with a social worker's efforts to try to persuade a young woman of few resources to be realistic about raising a baby, especially if she lacked family support and did not understand the difficulty and sacrifice involved in raising a child as a single parent, the persuasive techniques were often quite forceful. The degree of pressure put on the women to surrender sometimes crossed the line from persuasion to outright coercion. Many of the women I interviewed recalled high-pressure campaigns waged by the maternity-home staff.

> I remember the woman at the adoption agency, a very pleasant woman, smiling, always smiling, and using comforting tones. She had dark hair. She sat there and said that I had nothing to offer a baby. I had no education, I had no job, I had no money. Oh, God, they really knew how to work you. Talk about no support, it was how far can we beat you down while we're smiling?
>
> The social worker was telling me, "No man is going to want to marry you, no man is going to want another man's baby." She proceeded to tell me that the adoptive parents they would find for "the baby" would be college educated, degreed, they would be much older, they would own their own home, have high incomes. They would be able to give "the baby" everything that I could not.
>
> They told me I was unfit because I wasn't married. I didn't have this, I didn't have that. Well, it turns out her adoptive parents were just a couple of years older, and neither one had a college education. Nothing against them, but the adoption agency lied to me. They also divorced when she was fourteen. I'm with the same man for thirty-eight years. Financially, her adoptive family was better off than we were, but other than that it wasn't anything like what the agency promised.
>
> —*Christine*

The argument that others would be "better" parents presumed, of course, that the mother's own economic standing would not improve anytime soon, if ever, through further education, job or career training, marriage, or family support. It also presumed that the adopting couple's status would not deteriorate through divorce or job loss. Essentially, the gap in economic and marital status between the mother and adoptive family was seen as fixed, whereas only a decade earlier the mother's circumstances had been viewed as temporary and improvable, and steps were taken to help her become self-reliant.

In the postwar years, most of the homes aimed simply to ensure that the physical needs of the women were met until they could give birth and relinquish the baby. And despite the momentous life change that they were about to go through, most were sent to the hospital knowing nothing about childbirth; nor were they counseled about the impending separation. Most were completely unprepared for the emotions that would follow their transition from pregnant girls to mothers.

> None of those girls in the home have given birth. So they're all in their little rosy illusions about everything. They might talk about their parents or their school or their boyfriends or whatever, but they don't know what's coming. They have no clue what's coming. So other than giving each other comfort—that we're not the only ones in the world who are pregnant and not married, which was a good thing—there wasn't any discussion about the things we should've been talking about. Just mostly happy little wasting-time kind of stuff.
>
> —Ann

> The most profound thing I remember is the nun at St. Andre's telling me that it was God's will. It was God's will. We were fulfilling the needs and the hearts of women who couldn't have children. And therefore God chose us to bear these children for these women who couldn't have any. I was so susceptible to this thinking: I must accept God's will. I could have more children, you see, so therefore what's one child to be given away? I would see this child in heaven.
>
> —Lynne

Of course, the pregnant women who went into hiding were not of one mind; nor were the staff of the institutions they entered. A few women reported that they were counseled in a respectful manner and came to their own decision. But the majority of the women I interviewed did not make a *decision* to surrender. Many women, even those in their twenties, followed the only path that was available to them—the one prescribed by society, social workers, and parents. After all they had been through, and all they had put their parents through, they felt that, more than anything, they needed to regain their family's acceptance. Some women decidedly did not want to surrender but were unable to devise a plan that would allow them to care for their baby without some temporary assistance. Many of the women who wanted to parent would have been capable of doing so with a modest amount of support, the kind offered to Bea only a decade or so earlier. But by the mid-1960s professionals were no longer offering this kind of support, and more than 80 percent of those who entered maternity homes surrendered.[27]

> In my mind, all I knew was that if I was ever going to get home and be back in my family's good graces I had to get this finished. I think we were too young to really realize that this child was going to be a little person until the day came and it *was* a little person. That always makes me cry. They were very unfeeling about it. I really felt we were being punished and they did a pretty good job of it.
>
> *—Mary I*

Whether the women were resistant or compliant, the supposed transformation—the wiping away of the past in preparation for a stable marriage and legitimate childbearing—was often not successful. Rather than leaving the system with a clean slate, free of their past, many were burdened with feelings of low self-esteem and unworthiness, and laden with secrets, shame, loss, and grief.

> I've battled depression ever since that time. I kind of overcome it. I'm successful. But I think of my life as before and after, sort of like B.C. and A.D. I think of who I was and who I am. Dealing with the emotion and the pain of it. Dealing with the loneliness I've always felt. Grief is exhausting. And I grieved. I think that sorrow

and sadness come about not just from the act of surrender but also from the lies.

—Lynne

The practice of telling young women that they would be able to give birth, surrender their child, and move on as if it never happened caused many irreparable harm. Rather than being prepared during their residency either for mothering or for the feelings that would follow relinquishment, the women were made to feel like something was wrong with them for loving and mourning the loss of their child. Not only did this practice not acknowledge their motherhood, it did not respect their dignity.

> Throughout my pregnancy I always thought that I could put this behind me. I thought, "I am growing a baby for a family that could not have children. They will be the best parents in the world. They will love him and take care of him." And I always thought my purpose of getting pregnant was to give a child to a family that could not have one. I thought, "I'm going to put it behind me, like it didn't happen." Like I had a lobotomy and I could cut off the memory. That didn't happen.
>
> I had moments when I wanted to cancel this interview because I'm reliving this. Why do I want to bring this up fresh in my mind? I thought, "Okay, I'm going to do my two, three hours and then I'm going to push it back again and go ahead." But I'm lying to myself now, just like I lied to myself then. I didn't deal with my pregnancy. I *never* dealt with the fact that I was growing a baby that I would have to relinquish.
>
> *—Sheryl*

KAREN 1

It was 1965 and I was just beginning my senior year of high school. This was the beginning of our second year together. I found out that his family was moving. His dad was in the Navy, and they were moving to Norfolk, Virginia. I was devastated. We were very close.

His family did move. We had kept in touch by phone, but two months later he called and said, "We got tickets to a Lovin' Spoonful concert." He was missing me as much as I was missing him. So his brother's girlfriend and I got on the Greyhound bus, all dressed up in our suits and miniheels, and traveled four hours to Norfolk. They picked us up at the bus station and we went to the Lovin' Spoonful concert, which was my first-ever music concert, and it was great. "Do You Believe in Magic" and "Summer in the City"—it was great.

So two kids caring very deeply about each other—it was just the right environment for something like sex and pregnancy to occur, and it did. Everything seemed fine until a month later, when I missed my period. I never had before. I thought it was just the stress of being without my boyfriend and trying to adjust to being a senior. But then I started gaining weight and I missed my second period. I still tried to deny it. I couldn't fit into my clothes. I was wearing Villager dresses at the time, and those penny loafers that were called Weejuns. You know, back then you couldn't wear anything but dresses or skirts to school and they had to be at the middle of your knee or you got sent home.

So I would wear my dresses unzipped in the back, with the same cardigan sweater over my dress, to school every day. And I could remember being so terrified. I mean just stark terror, knowing that I can't keep doing this—trying to fit into my clothes, using safety pins whenever I could. And I was seeing the change in the mirror of just getting bigger and bigger. And thinking, "Oh my God, I have to address this." I was terrified to tell my mom.

My dad and I were very close; he's always been my best friend. I had never called him at work; he worked at the Pentagon. I went to the pay phone and I called my dad and I said, "I'm in trouble," which of course, you know what those three words mean. That phrase is all you have to say. And he said, "That's okay, we will figure it out. I'll be home and we will talk."

So I came home and he came into my bedroom and he sat down on the side of my bed and said, "How far are you?" and I said, "Probably four or five months." And he said, "I wish you had told me sooner. We could have given you a pill." I don't know what kind of pill, but I remember thinking, "Oh, I'm so glad I don't get a pill." And then he said, "That's okay, I'll talk to your mom and I'll let you know what we decide. I love you. It's okay. Everything is going to be okay."

I got up the next morning and I'm listening to the AM station on my transistor radio and I'll never forget—"I'm So Lonesome I Could Cry," by B. J. Thomas, was playing. I mean, to this day that song stops me in my tracks. I'm lying in bed and I'm hearing my mother sobbing outside my door, and I'm thinking, "Oh God, the shit has hit the fan. Now I have to face my mom."

The only thing I remember after that is going to Sears and her buying me two maternity dresses and then she took me to a doctor who gave me my first internal exam, which was absolutely mortifying. And the next thing that I remember is that my mom is telling me to pack my suitcase, that I'm going to live with *people* in D.C. I had no idea this was coming. Apparently, this was a wage home. The maternity home didn't have enough room in it for the numbers of girls who were pregnant. So they had to farm out girls somewhere else to hide their pregnancy until they were seven months. Then we could be admitted.

So she drove me down to D.C. and pulled up in front of this brownstone. And she walked me in and I remember it being very dark. I don't remember meeting the people who lived there. My mother walked me up the steep stairs to the attic. My head brushed the ceiling of the room that was to be my bedroom. All there was up there was a single bed with just a mattress and the frame, a small four-drawer plain dresser, and an old bathroom with a claw-foot tub and a shower curtain that went around it in an oval. It scared me, because I wasn't used to anything like that.

I was to live there and answer to these people every day as to what they wanted me to do for them. I very much remember being asked to serve cocktails to their friends when they had their parties, and feeling like I was the conversation piece. I was their little unwed mother, serving them cocktails. I was seventeen years old. I was so depressed. I mean, I remember crying every night—it seemed like all night—listening to my radio. That was the only friend I had—my radio and all those songs that were out then. You know, like "Monday Monday," by the Mamas and the Papas. There is this one part in "Monday Monday"—"How could you leave and not take me?"—that just gives me chills to hear that verse because that's exactly how I felt. They just took me and dumped me off. I didn't know where I was, how long I'd be there, who these people were, or what they were going to make me do. I felt totally abandoned and rejected and defective and just lived in terror every day.

I told my mom in a phone call, "I'm going to leave and run away and you're never going to see me again if you don't come and get me out of here." They almost immediately took me out of there and put me in Virginia with a family that was much younger. I think the man worked on Capitol Hill as a representative. But they were very good to me in comparison, that was like going from hell to heaven overnight. They had two small children and I was to be the nanny to their children. I remember her sewing very simple shift dresses for me to wear.

Both of these families took me to the maternity home on a daily basis so that I could finish my senior year of school. They had a classroom at the maternity home. Then I was admitted when I began my seventh month. My mom came and got me from the house in Virginia and drove me to the maternity facility. It had three floors. I was on the second floor. The elevator door opened into the living-room area, which they called the congregation room, and it had green vinyl furniture with metal, cold metal arms.

I remember in the mornings going down to the bathroom in my slippers and it would just echo. Carrying my toothbrush in my hand. Early in the morning or late at night, you could hear girls crying in their rooms. We were only allowed to use our first name and last initial. We were not allowed to ask any questions of each other, like where did you go to school, are you from this area, tell us about your experience. We were strictly told, "Mind your own business. Don't ask questions. Don't get to know the other girls. You're here for a reason. Keep to yourself." So we did.

When we did hang out together, we would go down to the main office and sign out and put on our fake wedding rings and walk down the hill. We would either go to a movie or we would walk down another block to a little grocery store. I remember only seeing one movie while I was there and that was *Born Free*, which I find very ironic.

Those of us who were nearing the time of giving birth would go down on a weekly basis to see the doctor, whoever was there. We would see a different one every time we went. I don't know if they were interns from a local hospital or what the situation was. We were never given any information on what it was like to be pregnant, what to expect from month to month. We were given no instruction or classes regarding childbirth or labor and delivery. The only thing I remember hearing from some of the girls were the signs of labor coming, like your water breaking.

And of course therapy—which was really nonexistent—was just meeting with a caseworker once a week, if that. The whole time we would spend with them they would be talking about, "Well, are you going to arts-and-crafts class? What did you do there? Did you make any ceramics? Have you taken any classes on knitting? Are you feeling okay?"

Then they would say things about the baby. It's always "the baby," never "your baby." And they were not talking about adoption except to say, "This experience will end. You will forget that you were here. You will forget that you went through this. It will all be in the past. Given time, it will fade. You will get over it. You know what you did was wrong? You know that you are really not worthy of keeping your own child? You can't provide a home for that child. You can't provide anything that child needs. That child needs a mother and a father, and the things that they can give that child."

I remember feeling almost not deserving of having or keeping my child, but also feeling I don't have the right to be a mom. I don't have the right to be a mother. So, we really heard that on almost a daily basis and the other girls were believing them and reinforcing to each other: "You know, they said you will forget about this and it will be okay. We aren't going to remember and, after all, we are not supposed to think of ourselves, we are supposed to think of *the baby*. You're supposed to think of what's best for *the baby*."

When I went into labor, I was lying on that vinyl couch in the living room, watching *Bewitched* on TV. It was eight o'clock in the evening and my water broke. I was terrified and I got hysterical. I went to the phone. I called home and talked to my mom. I was crying because I was so terrified. And she said, "I can't talk right now, stop being a baby," and she hung up the phone.

I was still crying, and another girl went and got the housemother. She put me in a cab and got in and we went to the hospital. When we got there she said, "All right, go in and give them your first name and last initial and tell them you are from the home." I went in by myself. The nurse put me in a wheelchair and took me upstairs in an elevator and got me undressed. She gave me an enema, which I never had before. I didn't know why. She prepped me, which included being shaved. I had no idea why that was being done, either. The nurse came over and gave me some kind of shot, then next thing I remember I was out cold. I don't remember anything until after my daughter was born at two-thirty in the morning.

I said, "Where is my baby?" And she pulled this bassinet into the room. That's when I learned I had a girl and that she had been born eight pounds one ounce. I didn't get to hold her until they released me. They put me in a wheelchair and took me out to the front door. There was a cab waiting for me. I got into the cab and it had a housemother in it and they handed me my baby. We drove back to the maternity home, but this time when they pulled in they went to the building off to the side of the dormitory, which was the hospital building. It was totally off-limits to the girls who had not had their babies. So, once a girl disappeared in the middle of the night, we never saw her again. They were kept strictly in that hospital building.

It was like a ward where they would have, I think, six or eight beds with white iron headboards. I was on the far wall. Next to the bed was a white porcelain table with a drawer and at the end of each bed was a chair with a vinyl seat. It was very institutional. At a certain time, they would have us pull our chairs out into a circle and then they would bring our babies out for us to feed. Then they would take the baby back into the nursery. I stayed there with my baby for ten days, not knowing what day I was leaving or when she was leaving.

On the tenth day, my mom and aunt came in the morning. My aunt brought a baptism gown and the nurse brought my daughter in and I dressed her in the gown. My mom said we were going to take her down the street and have her baptized. There was a little chapel, a Catholic chapel called Our Lady of Victory. We went back to the maternity home and my mom and my aunt went somewhere.

About an hour later a woman came back and said, "Come with me." They took me down the hall to this room that was empty except for a rocking chair. Then she came back with my baby and handed her to me and said, "You have an hour to say goodbye." I put her on my lap and kind of unwrapped her blanket to look at her, and kissed her feet and put her up on my shoulder. I can feel her there. I can still feel her there.

I told her how much I loved her and all about her dad and how much he loved me. I told her that he was a good guy. I told her I hoped she would understand and forgive because I didn't have any choice. I had to do what they told me to do. I had nowhere to go. I had no one to help me. I just *begged* her to forgive me. And it just seemed like minutes later that woman came back.

I remember thinking, "How often does she do this? How can she do this?" She said, "I have to take her now." I just sat in there for a long time, rocking and rocking and rocking and rocking. I don't even know how long I was in there. Then I walked back and packed up my suitcase. The nurse said, "Your mother will be here soon. Go out the front door." And there was my mom. So I walked down the stairs, got in the car, and drove home.

It was just really weird being home, because I wasn't even the same person anymore. I was so changed by that. I was expected to go back and be this teenager and live under their rules. I was a mom, but I wasn't allowed to be the mom. All I did was just lie in bed because I think I was just in shock. I just knew something is really wrong here. I was just so empty.

They would call, and they would call to say, "Come in and sign the papers." "I can't do that, I can't do that now. Yes, okay, soon." At some point, I did go in and sign those papers because I knew that I had no choice. There was no way I was going to be able to keep her. They said, "Well, you would have to pay all the expenses if you keep your daughter." I didn't have any money. I was still living at home.

The social worker came over to me with these papers and put them down on the table. I remember there was just a pen and the papers on the table and she flipped it back to the last page and said, "Sign here and date it," and

I did. I guess I was just too naïve even to know that I should read it and try to understand what it said. I am just astounded that I got no explanation. Nothing happened in front of a judge, no lawyer was there at all, it was just the two of us. So I signed. I remember walking out the door and that door just slamming at my back like I'd just been thrown away.

So I went home and tried to get on with my life, like they said I would. I was going to forget. I got married two years later and had my second daughter. I had married an abusive man. We moved often and I really just fought to survive throughout that eleven-year marriage. I remember always pulling out the pictures that I had when I was alone and just crying over the pictures of the baby, thinking, "Where are you? Who are you? Are you okay?" And being so worried about was she alive or dead? Is she hurting?

Then I had another child, three years after having my second, and still struggling with the abuse of my marriage, until we moved to New Mexico and I left him. I understand that it's pretty common for mothers who have lost a child to adoption to marry an abusive man because we feel pretty worthless. I got divorced and moved back to the northern Virginia area where most of my extended family lived at the time. I got remarried in '84 and told my husband, or my soon-to-be husband, about my experience and he was very accepting.

It's really tragic. We were not told any of our rights. We were not told we had the right to keep our own baby. We were not helped to keep our baby. There was a conflict of interest in the agencies' not providing us with legal counsel. The social workers should have been required to tell us what was available to us, so we could make an informed decision. We were never told anything except adoption—it was the only option offered to us. We weren't told that we could get child support from the fathers. We weren't told that we could apply for welfare or Aid to Families with Dependent Children, which was available then. There was a lack of informed consent.

All of our rights were abused. Ignored and abused. The rights that people take for granted today, we were denied. We didn't know because we were young, and we trusted our parents, and we trusted authority. We trusted our elders and we were taught to respect them. They would tell us what was best. So we figured if that's what was best, then that was what we needed to do. They've injured and damaged millions of people.

My parents didn't come to my aid. I felt very abandoned by them, physically and emotionally. I wanted them to say to me, "If you want to keep your baby, you can come home with your baby." They never said that. They never said, "You can keep your baby and you and her father can live with us until you can get on your feet." *His* parents never said that. No offers were made to help me keep my child!

I just didn't know how I could do it all by myself with no offers of help. If her father had said, "I will send you money. Keep her. Take her home. . . ." I never thought, "I am just going to keep my baby and to hell with them all!" I didn't feel that power and I think that's because I was so ashamed and so full of guilt and not knowing what else I could do. I just knew that my parents paid a lot of money for me to be there. And I think that supported my thinking at the time, which was "How can I go against them after what they've suffered because I made a decision, a judgment, that I should not have made, which was having sex when I was not married. And how can I put them through more agony and more expense and more work?"

You're just so beaten down by being in that place and being told, "You can't, you can't, you can't." And "You *aren't* a mother, you don't *deserve* to be a mother, and you can *never* be a mother and you *can't* provide anything." It was just overwhelming. The odds were all overwhelming because nobody was offering a hand. No one.

The whole point was to just keep us scared all the time and feeling guilt all the time. And compliant, you know? "You do this and you can *go home.*" It makes me very, very angry today to think about that manipulation. You know? It was evil. To me, it was evil. To think that these people could play God like that with people's lives. And determine who can have a child and who can't.

Nobody ever said, "What do you want, Karen? What do *you* want? Do you want to keep *your* baby?" Even though our bodies were telling us that baby was ours, they were counteracting all of those normal, natural feelings with "No, no, no. Don't even think of that because it's not *your* child. It's these people's child over here. It's been *promised* to them." *They* were always real to us. This baby was going go to *them* and they *deserved* it. "They can't *have* children. You should be *happy* you're giving your child to someone so wonderful who has so much to offer that child. You should be *grateful* for that. You should be grateful we're solving your problem. You made this mistake. You caused this *problem* for everyone." Not just for my parents but for *everyone*. "You've put an enormous amount of people out because of your illegal sex. And now you must do the right thing and give the baby to these people over here who are married. And let it have a father and a mother that can give it everything you can't give it."

There was such emotional and mental damage done by all of that. And it has intensified with every passing year, you know. It just got worse and worse and worse. I am very overprotective of my children because I am afraid that they, too, will disappear, you know? And like when they were born, expecting somebody to come in and take them from me, you know? Not being able to have them away from my sight because somebody could just take them. Always trying to make everything right for them, because I was not a worthy, decent person. I was defective and I was substandard and I have spent thirty-six years of my life trying to be the perfect mother, the perfect person, the perfect woman, the perfect employee, and the perfect wife.

I have nightmares and flashbacks that catch me totally off-guard. I mean, even a song would just freeze me in my tracks. You're haunted by it. I don't know how you ever get over that feeling. The only way to heal from this is to be accepted by your child and for the public to know the truth of what really happened. And understand it's *the truth*. Instead of always pushing adoption as this loving, wonderful, rescuing thing. Yes, that may be the case for people who adopt. *It is not the case for us.* You never are whole. Never. It's a hugely damaging thing. It's an enormously injuring, painful, fracturing amputation of *families*. And the closest thing to healing you can find is your child being willing to know you and love you. And being accepted in their life, where you should have been all along and were denied.

We were not criminals. We're mothers. The difference was I was not an *authenticated* mother. I was an illegal mother. I was a denied mother. And I had to come home and live my life after being robbed of my child. It's as if I was an unwilling accomplice to the kidnapping of my own child. So you have to live with the trauma of losing your child and then you have to live with the trauma of knowing you didn't stop it. How do you do that?

PAM

The father of my son was my first love. I met him in junior high and I figured out I was pregnant early on in the ninth grade. Carnation Instant Breakfast was popular back then and that's what I used to have every morning before I would go off to school. Well, this one particular morning I had had vanilla. My mom and dad had just gotten brand-new carpeting and all of a sudden I got sick all over my mother's new carpet. I didn't feel like I had the flu; I just erupted. My mother asked, "Do you feel sick?" "No." The next morning, like clockwork, it happens again, so my mother's kind of looking at me sideways.

From then on, I would take the Carnation Instant Breakfast and I would dump it in the toilet. My mom got a little wise to me. She'd say, "Do you have something you want to tell me?" I would play innocent and say, "I don't know what you are talking about." She asked, "Are you pregnant?" In all honesty, my mom was a very sweet person. She really wanted to know, not because she wanted to clobber me but because she wanted to help me. But I thought, "No. If I tell her, I won't get to see *him* anymore and my life will be destroyed."

I'm not exactly sure how I thought I was going to pull all of this off, but I intended to. My boyfriend had given me this big brown faux fur coat for Christmas, this kind of big, bulky thing. They were very popular then. The one he gave me was too big, but *he* gave it to me. As it turns out, this coat would become extremely important for several reasons—it was the coat we cuddled in, and it became my uniform once I realized I was pregnant.

Being fourteen, we decided that we were going to get married. We got jobs and started saving our money. He worked two paper routes. He had a Sting-Ray bicycle that he would ride me on the back of and we would throw newspapers and make collections. I took up jobs doing all kinds of little things. We thought we were set. We bought a little tiny color TV, we bought booties, we bought outfits, we were looking into health insurance. We were just going to show everybody how grown-up we were because we intended to raise our child.

We thought we were pulling it off and nobody knew. PE class was becoming problematic, though, because you dressed and showered with everybody. I got pretty good at lolly-gagging so I could get dressed without people really noticing, but eventually rumors started going around the school. It's getting warmer and I'm still wearing this brown coat and my clothes are getting a little tight.

So, one day I'm getting dressed and the gym teacher came up. There was a nickname for her but I won't say what it was. Anyway, she confronted me: "Hey, you pregnant?" There were a couple of other girls in the locker room, so I didn't turn around. I thought if I respond to it, it's like I'm admitting guilt. So I pretended I didn't know who she was talking to, even though I was the only one in that aisle. So she reaches out, grabs my shoulder, spins me around, and says, "I'm talking to you." I said, "I don't know what you are talking about. Don't put your hands on me." She didn't like that comment, so she pushed me and I lunged forward and pushed her back and said, "Don't you touch me," and she came up swinging. She couldn't get me down. I was this quiet little blond-haired, blue-eyed simpleton who never opened her mouth, and all of a sudden she's got a problem, because I was fighting for my life.

So another two weeks go by, and I start to develop a little itchy rash and I'm really worried. The German measles were going around and I thought, "Oh my God, I've got German measles." So I go to the counselor and asked if she has a minute. I said, "I have this friend who thinks that she is pregnant and could have been exposed to German measles. How far along does that person . . . ?" I maybe got a few more sentences out, but not many more, and she said, "We are going to the nurse's office." I'm thinking, "You idiot, why did you say anything?" But I was really frightened for the baby. She tells the doctor that she thinks I am pregnant and I laugh and say, "I don't know what she's talking about. I don't know what's the matter with her." He opens my coat and with every muscle in my body I am trying to pull that baby in. Then he put his hand against my stomach and my son decided to do a jig. The doctor got an almost gray, serious look on his face and said,

"You're pregnant, and you're quite a ways along." I was still saying, "No, I'm not. I don't know what you are talking about. I haven't done anything. This has got to be Immaculate Conception."

God, I can see it, like a videotape in my head. They are looking at me, saying, "Listen, we know you're pregnant. You've been exposed to the German measles. You have to tell your parents. We will give you this weekend. Either you tell them before you return to school on Monday or we will tell them." I don't think I've ever felt more trapped, more frightened, in my life—ever. I've got to go home and deal with my parents. My father was in the air force and he was also an educator. I had a lot of respect for my father, but I was very afraid of him. I think more than anything else, I didn't want to disappoint my parents.

My dad worked late hours and was going for his doctorate at UCLA, so my mom and my sister and I would have dinner alone a lot. That evening, my mother was sitting on the couch watching the news and my sister and I were doing dishes. I said to my sister, "I have a problem. I think I'm pregnant." My sister got a huge smile on her face, turned on her heels, walked out of the kitchen, barely got through the door, and hollers to Mom, "Pam's pregnant!" And I heard my mother start to sob.

I stood in that kitchen looking at the back door and trying to decide whether I was going to run. Then my mother said, "Pam, come here." I went in and she had that look that I never wanted to see. She was devastated, absolutely devastated. She said, "Is this true?" I said, "Yes." And she started to cry. She said, "I asked you. I asked you, why didn't you tell me?" And I couldn't answer the question. My mom was just destroyed. I destroyed my mother.

My sister was quite pleased with herself. I felt horribly betrayed—probably about the way my mother felt, to be honest with you. My mother felt betrayed by me, and I felt betrayed by my sister. But the longest wait was waiting for my father to return home. I lay in bed with the covers across me. I heard his car drive up and then I heard him come in the front door and say hello to my mother, very cheerful. My mother said, "We have to talk." My father had a routine of getting orange juice and vanilla ice cream when he came home and that's what he did. Then he sat down in his chair and it had these leather straps underneath that made a certain sound, and I knew as soon as he was in that chair the discussion was going to take place. My father said, "It can't be that bad. What's the matter?" And my mother said, "Pam's pregnant." There was absolute silence. Just absolute silence. My dad got up and I don't know where he went. I was expecting him to come in my room but he didn't.

The next morning, I could tell my mother had cried all night—her eyes were very red and tired and gaunt looking. My father had the kind of look on his face—I mean, it would have been easier to have someone just take a gun and shoot me. The afternoon comes and we hold a big discussion. They are discussing what *we* are going to do, *me* not being part of the *we*. I was to see the doctor and then we would have another meeting. I thought, "Well, they don't know I have a job lined up and all this money saved. They don't know that I bought a television and baby clothes, and that my boyfriend and I love each other and we're going to get married." So I wrote out a plan and felt very prepared for the next discussion, but nobody ever asked for my opinion. I never got to open my mouth. The decision was made. It was so surreal to have people talking about you like you're not even in the room, like your life doesn't matter, like the baby was a mistake. He didn't feel like a mistake to me; he never felt like a mistake.

I continued going to school for a period of time until it became more difficult to hide it. The faculty decided that I was becoming disruptive to the schooling process and a bad example. It was determined that I would leave school. "I was not welcome there" was what I was told.

My parents decided that the best thing for me was to be sent away to a Florence Crittenton Home. They packed my suitcase and late one night they took me away. I'd never been away from home, never spent a night over at anybody's house, never gone to camp, never anything. They walked me up the steps to this place that was not in a very good neighborhood, my dad handed me my suitcase, and they turned around and left. I'm sure my parents thought they were doing the right thing because there was this booklet that talked about the wonderful meals, and the education, and the beautiful dayroom with its bright colors. I know what my parents *thought* they were bringing me to, but that's not where my parents left me.

I didn't understand it at the time, but in the military they do a thing where they train you to comply with the rules by tearing you down and breaking your spirit so you will conform, and then little by little they build you into what they want you to be. That's what they did there. I was gonna try and get through this and get out. That was my goal. I wasn't gonna let anybody there know me.

The next day I had to have my physical—kind of like an entry physical, I guess. I go to the infirmary, where there is a nurse and a doctor and I am told to take my clothes off. Nobody hands you a gown, nothing. I mean, my father didn't even see me without my clothes on and they wanted me to undress in front of this strange man. It was the first time I ever had a speculum used on me, and it hurt. I kept trying to move back and the nurse was holding me down by the shoulders and telling me to relax. I wasn't relaxing. Finally, the doctor said, "Listen, you got yourself into this. If you would have kept your legs together, we wouldn't be doing this now." I remember our eyes locked and he was smiling. I don't think he liked women, I really don't, but I'm sure he looked good in his community because he was volunteering his time with all these bad girls.

And it's funny. While I was locked up, I would call the father and he was going on with his life. He was having his summer and was, you know, worried about whether he would get a new tape or album. People had gossiped about him but they were still allowed to hang out with him. Before I left home, nobody was allowed to be around me.

Occasionally, the house got to go out as a gaggle of pregnant females. The neighborhood we were in, like I said, was not a good neighborhood. When we would take the van to go places, the neighbor's kids would throw things at us—rotten fruit, eggs—and eggs hurt. When you get hit in the face with an egg, that hurts, and sometimes it would actually break the skin. They would never let us go back in the house to change. I remember one time they took us to the beach to walk the boardwalk and we had gotten pelted pretty good. So here we are, a gaggle of pregnant girls marked with this stuff, and it smelled. I was thinking to myself, "You know, they tell us not to make a spectacle of ourselves, to maintain our dignity, but they go out of their way to make sure we're humiliated."

We had to write thank-you notes to whoever dared to drive the van. One time we couldn't even get out the front door, there was so much being thrown, so everybody retreated, including the person who was going to drive the van. I remember the driver crying; it had never happened to him before. The lady who was with him just kept saying, "Oh, this is normal, this is normal." And he kept saying, "These poor girls, these poor girls." She said, "Well, they just have to accept it." She wasn't trying to be hateful, she really wasn't; she was being matter-of-fact. A lot of the treatment there was matter-of-fact. That driver never came back, by the way.

We had different volunteers all the time. I called them do-gooders. There were those who wanted to elevate themselves in the community, and those who cared. I avoided all of them, especially the ones who cared. Looking back, I was becoming extremely hard. You couldn't afford to have somebody care about you because you weren't really allowed to care about yourself. I didn't want people feeling sorry for me. I just wanted to survive.

I have to say they fed us very well. They took excellent care of us from the food standpoint. The lady who worked in the kitchen was an African American woman. She used to call us marshmallows on toothpicks. Her jokes were always about being a Negro. She didn't like the term "black." I blush very easily, I'm very fair, and when she would say that, my ears and my face would light up, she just loved getting that kind of a reaction from me. I learned to like to cook as a result of watching her. When she cooked she was taking care of us, she was loving us all. It didn't matter if you were a twenty-five-year-old woman having a baby or you were a girl as young as fourteen, she congratulated each and every one of us after we had had our babies. Nobody else did that. She'd tell us what a good job we did. I've always thought of hearth and home as being such a positive thing. That comes from her. I don't know if I ever told her—hopefully, she knows—but that was the best part of my day, being in the kitchen with her.

When they wheeled me into the delivery room, my mom and dad were standing in the hallway. My dad was giving me a kind of pep talk and my mom had a smile on her face, but she just looked like she wanted to cry. She's looking at this little girl holding a stuffed animal on her way to deliver a baby. I can't even begin to imagine. My baby was born and he was perfect, he was beautiful. My doctor gave me a blue badge that said "It's a Boy," so I had my stuffed dog and this badge. I asked my parents, "Have you seen him? Have you seen him?" My father wouldn't answer, but my mom went to see him and she told me that he was tiny and had very long sideburns.

It was funny because this was in Los Angeles and a famous movie star's wife delivered that same day. Her room was directly across from mine and there were flowers . . . I've never seen so many flowers in my life. All these people were going in and out, and there were photographers, and it was like watching a fairy tale. I'm across the hall and there is nothing. My room is very sterile, very green, no flowers, no pictures, no congratulations. I would watch what was happening and my mom said, "Well, you know, when you get married and have a baby you'll have your turn, too." Everybody was talking about this brand-new life, and I thought, "My son's a brand-new life."

They made the mistake of bringing my baby to me; I wasn't supposed to see him. When the nurse came in, I said, "What are you doing?" And she said, "I'm bringing your baby so you can feed him." I struggled with what the right thing to do was, and I thought, "I'm not gonna tell her." I thought it would be the only time that I would ever see him. I unwrapped him and counted his toes, and I looked at his belly. When he would breathe his whole tummy would move. His little face was so tiny and he had the tiniest little fingernails, but his feet were just like his dad's. I said, "You've got Fred Flintstone feet, just like your daddy."

I got to see him every day, three or four times a day. When I was able to start walking, I would go and sit outside the nursery. All the fathers were going, "That's my boy, that's my boy," and they had my baby and another one way off in a corner, like they were diseased or something. There was no name tag, nothing at the foot like the other ones. I felt so horrible, like I had done this to him. I had caused him to be ostracized. That's when it sank in that I didn't deserve him. I couldn't do this to him for the rest of his life. He didn't do anything wrong, I did.

It came time to sign the papers. I hadn't seen him for weeks and weeks and they brought him in. He was so little. He had a preemie outfit on with a short-sleeved shirt and his fingers barely stuck out past the edge of the sleeves. I was ecstatic seeing him, but my heart was breaking because I knew it was going to be the last time. I kept thinking, "If he is in trouble, how am I going to know? How will I help him?" It's very hard to explain—part of me had enough indoctrination to believe I was not a mother. They make that very clear: "You're not a mother. You are too young. You are a bad person. You got pregnant and you aren't married. You are not entitled to this baby.

You're gonna give this baby a chance in life." Part of me accepted that wisdom, but then there was the other part of me that had feelings that I wasn't supposed to have.

So they walked off with the papers and the baby. I walked off believing that my son was going to go to the kind of environment I had asked for and that he would have his history. They had asked me to write out in longhand what my requests were and I gave it a lot of thought. My son was a mixed-heritage baby: he was half Swedish and half Mexican. I wanted him, if possible, to have a combination family, and if not, a Hispanic family. I can still remember the lady sitting at the desk and nodding her head as if she was listening and understood what I wanted and taking me seriously. I wrote down my information and the father's information, my Social Security number, where I lived, my parents' names, and I was secure in the knowledge that if he needed anything—if he needed a kidney or blood or anything—I'd be there for him. I put it all in the envelope and sealed it. She took that envelope and was very careful with it. The agreement was they were going to give that piece of paper to my child. It would become part of his file and on his eighteenth birthday it would be made available to him. When people make promises to you and you don't have a way of verifying, it gives people a lot of latitude to do or not do what they've promised. She promised me, and that was my promise to my child: "You get to know your history—you're not someone that I'm ashamed of, you're not bad, you did nothing wrong." I told him I loved him with all my heart, I did the best I could, I wished I could be with him, and I would think about him every day that I drew breath.

I came home and no one ever said a word. Not "Are you okay? Do you want to talk about it? Do you miss your son? Are you heartbroken? Do you worry? Do you wonder if he is alive?" They never asked, probably because they were afraid of the answer. When I would think about him, I felt like I was violating the trust, the deal. He wasn't mine anymore; I didn't have that right.

I went back to school, but I never fit in again with the kids. I was never a teenager, never went to a prom, never went to a dance, never went to a football game, never had counseling, never got out of line. I worked about sixty hours a week. I went to school full time. I was an adult.

I married at eighteen and I had a son. I did it the right way but I was petrified when it came time to go home from the hospital. I was afraid they were gonna take him from me. My husband knew I had given a child up, but he still couldn't understand what was the matter with me. I didn't want anybody to see me walking out of the hospital with this baby. We got into the car and my mom said, "What's wrong?" I said, "I'm afraid that someone's gonna come take the baby." I was waiting for the police to come. Giving up my first son had left such an imprint. It was trapped in my brain . . . I was not allowed to be a mother.

Society expects you to continue with your life, be a productive human being, don't think about it, don't dwell on it, don't feel sorry for yourself. You did it to yourself. But you are conscious every single day that there is a little person out there. They are trapped as a little person in your head because the last picture that you have of them is of a helpless baby. I can't tell you how many times my next son would have a first—his first tooth, the first time he rode a tricycle, the first anything—and my mind would go to my other son. What were his firsts like? Is he happy? Did I do the right thing? I must have done the right thing. Everybody said I was doing the right thing.

I've spent thirty-four years thinking, "If I had a choice, would I have done it differently?" I wanted college for him, I wanted him to have a mother and a father, I wanted him to have all the things that normal kids have, and it was very clear to me that society and the people around me would make that impossible. As an adult, you find out you did have a choice: you could have kept that baby. Would I have done it differently? I don't know. I wish I could have done it differently. That's what my heart says. I would have given anything to have been able to do it differently.

My sons from my marriage are the absolute apple of my eye—my whole world, everything. I became a school nurse so I could be at their school when they were there, and off when they were off. I mean, it was a little bit neurotic, to be honest with you. My boys grew up knowing my first son's father. He was a part of their lives for about twelve years, so they always knew about their older brother. I would say, "I don't have the right to look for this baby but he has the information, so don't be surprised if someday he shows up on the front porch. He's as welcome in my home and my heart as you guys are. We are a family."

I'm sure there are women who suppress the experience, but I don't think it ever goes away. There is not a day since I was fifteen years old that I haven't thought about him. I will live with this for the rest of my life. Criminals sometimes get a life sentence and that's what I feel like I got. I think that's what people don't understand. The expectation is that you will get over it. I will never have peace. I will never have peace.

7

Birth and Surrender

Many times I've thought about the difference between the labors and deliveries of my two daughters. Such a difference, and it was only because I had "Mrs." in front of my name. That's all. I was the same person. I was still with the same jerk guy. I was not rich. I still did not have a degree. The only thing that had changed was "Mrs." That was it, and they treated me like a human being.

After the birth of my first child I had nothing, not even a piece of paper. You walked out of the hospital with whatever memories you had and the stretch marks on you body, that's it. There was no piece of paper. Nothing. It was as if it never happened.

—*Christine*

WHEN A YOUNG WOMAN in a maternity home went into labor, she was often sent to the hospital in a cab. Sometimes a housemother or a nun accompanied her as far as the hospital door but they rarely stayed. There was little hand-holding through labor and certainly no family celebration after the birth of the baby. Most of the girls labored alone. The majority knew little about what to expect physically or emotionally from childbirth. They had no idea what labor or delivery would be like and were stunned when nurses came to prep them by shaving their pubic hair and giving them an enema, a common practice at the time. It was an incredibly frightening and lonely experience and in some cases cruel and dehumanizing.

I was not in any way prepared for labor, delivery, or for how I would emotionally feel. Nobody told me that the doctor had given orders that I was not to see the baby. I was beside myself, screaming at them, "Let me see my baby! Let me hold him!" To stop me from screaming, they finally let me touch my son's cheek. I had no idea how intensely I would want to touch that baby. I just wasn't prepared for how desperately I wanted to hold that child and just feel him and cradle him.

—Glory

They took me into the labor room and I labored for hours and hours. They put me in a room, turned off the light, closed the door and left me to labor by myself. I just wanted somebody there with me because I was so frightened. I was young and I was in so much pain. I remember praying to God: "Please let this be over. I'm sorry, I'll never do this again." You barter all these things, being Catholic—or being human, actually. I was allowed to hold her just once. They didn't want you to bond at all with the baby. Some women chose not to see their babies. I just could never imagine that. I wanted to see that face. I'll never forget it as long as I live. You never forget that face.

—Carolyn I

Some of the young mothers were given the choice earlier in their pregnancy to see or hold their babies once they were born. Others were advised not to, or were told that it was against the policy of the maternity home, agency, or hospital.

Another part of the agreement with the doctor was that I would never see this child. From the time I felt the first bit of labor, I would immediately be put out so that I would have no memory of labor, delivery, or anything. And that was supposed to make it easier for me. I begged them to please let me see my baby, so they told me I could see the baby for a minute. I walked down to the nursery and they pulled up the shade and they moved the crib, not right in front of the window but where I could see it. I said, "Oh, my God, she is the most beautiful . . ." She was regal looking, is the word. And it was just the fastest minute because then they said, "You have to go back to your room now," and somebody pulled the shade.

—Kathi

In some cases, parents tried to persuade their daughter not to have any contact with her child. A few women declined on their own because they felt it would be too difficult to see their child and then let go. Some saw their newborn baby only through the glass of the nursery window.

My father had said, "Don't look at the baby." But I went to that nursery and I said, "Which one is mine?" He was in the back and he was crying, screaming. I could see his arms whaling and I had the biggest urge to run into that nursery and pick him up. But my father told me not to hold the baby, not to look at the baby, because it never happened. It never happened. I didn't have a baby.

—Sheryl

Institutions that limited or forbade contact worried that it would initiate a bond that would make surrender more difficult, implicitly disregarding the fact that a bond had already developed during the preceding nine months.

All through my pregnancy, when I was seeing the counselor at the agency she encouraged, "Don't get attached. Don't think of it as your baby." After my daughter found me, that was one of the first things she asked me. She said, "Do you think you bonded with me?" How could I *not*? How can you carry a child for nine months and not bond? It's not humanly possible.

—Connie III

In some instances, the mother and baby returned to the maternity home together and stayed anywhere from a few days to several weeks. The maternity homes that followed this procedure had special hospital wards for postpartum women. In these cases, the new mothers were kept in a separate area, away from the girls who were waiting to deliver. They often had daily contact with their babies and were permitted to bottle-, but not breast-feed, them. A few were even allowed to take their baby to a local chapel for christening.

But the most common practice seems to have been for mother and baby to part company at the hospital. An adoption-agency worker would pick up the baby from the hospital and take him to a foster home, where he would stay for a specified time period, after which the adoptive parents were permitted to take him home. In the late 1940s and early 1950s, babies were often kept in these foster homes for two or three months. Today, there is often no waiting period at all.

> I was unprepared for the last time that I would hold this baby girl. The nurse made a big deal out of clipping our wristbands. My wristband got clipped and taken and the baby's wristband got clipped and it was like the umbilical cord being cut. I was hysterical. I didn't want to let go of the baby. I was just a mess. You know, it makes you wonder. All the support that they gave prior to this, there should have been a little support then, that's when I needed support.
>
> —*Pamela I*

> I had to stay in the hospital for an extra two days and the adoption agency came to get my son. They didn't know I was still there. I remember coming out of my room and I see this woman carrying my son down the hall. And I said, "Where are you going with him?" And she looked at me and said, "Why?" And I said, "Because that's my son!" And she went, "I'm so sorry. I'm from the adoption agency." I still remember, I grabbed on to the blanket and I lay on the floor pulling at it. I still have dreams about it.
>
> —*Charlenea*

> They let me hold the baby once. It was a little boy. I guess it was a couple of days after that, a woman from social services came to take the baby and she asked me if I wanted to carry him out to the car. That was a big mistake. I shouldn't have done that, but I

wanted to. I guess I did something really stupid, I don't know. But when he was in the car I just let out the most bloodcurdling scream. I thought, "Wow. That's kind of scary," but I guess I wanted him to hear that in his subconscious . . . to know that I didn't want to do it.

—Nellie

I was in a ward with a couple of other women from the maternity home, and they brought the babies to us. In those days, you stayed in the hospital for four or five days. It was an otherworldly experience. I can't quite explain it. There we were, five or six of us, in the same situation. I know when the babies were brought to us that was precious, precious time. I remember I'd glance at another woman across the way without talking. I'm sure we all felt the same way. Then it was time to leave.

I went back to the maternity home and that's when the grief started. I just couldn't stop crying. I called my sister-in-law and brother and I begged them to come get me because I was just a mess and I couldn't stay in this impersonal, humiliating situation. I couldn't bear it. I was deeply, deeply mourning and no place to go with it. I continued to see the social worker and she gave me a little bit of time, then she pressed me to sign the adoption surrender.

—Rachael

I have heard many people, both men and women, describe the monumental change that occurred the moment they held their newborn child. Some describe it as an overwhelming love for their baby that they had not anticipated and were totally unprepared for. The circumstances of the pregnancy—whether planned or unplanned, or even inconvenient at that point in their lives—were of little consequence once their child was born. I have also heard adoptive parents describe similar feelings about the moment a baby was put in their arms. Yet even today, few seem to perceive that these emotions must also be present in mothers whose babies will be adopted, whatever the circumstances. It is as if their unmarried status, or their intention to relinquish, has rendered them incapable of love or motherly instincts. There has been no widespread recognition that mothers who surrender children for adoption experience grief or suffer a real loss.

> The nurse came in with this little pink bundle and she said, "Do you want to see your baby girl?" And the minute that the nurse puts the baby in your arms, everything changes. Because now you're holding your own baby and it's like something changes in your whole body. And now you don't want to give this little baby back.
> —*Karen II*

Some women recalled the love and attachment they had for their baby during their pregnancy. They sang and talked to their baby and all along dreaded the separation that was to come. Others remained more detached and accepted the advice of authority figures who told them not to think of the baby as their own. Until they gave birth, the baby was not truly real to them. These women were even less prepared and were completely taken aback by the intense feelings of love they had for their child at birth and the overwhelming desire to hold and touch their baby. A few described being in an almost total state of denial about what was happening to them. Some remained in a closed-off emotional state until many years later, when they met their child.

> It's funny. The whole time I was carrying my daughter, I told myself that I wasn't her real mother. I really believed that. I knew that I was carrying her but, you know, that was the party line, that's what they told you. The social workers said that you were carrying the child for someone else. And I really went along with that in my head. I guess in a way I was less tormented because most birth mothers didn't have that kind of detachment. They knew that they were their child's mother. They knew what they were losing, and I was just totally out to lunch in that department. Until my daughter was born. I realized at that moment, that's not the way it works. She was my daughter. I realized that fully, in every way, she was my daughter.
>
> You don't talk about those things with your social worker. You talk about what you're going to do afterward. Although I must say

that my social worker was a good person, she was a young person,
she had never given birth. It's funny to me that they have social
workers for pregnant teens who have never given birth themselves, because giving birth changes you and there's no way to tell
a person what that is like.

—Ann

Although it is difficult for any woman to be wholly prepared for birth, it
is hard to fathom the lack of counseling given to these women about the feelings they would have after the birth of their child and possibly over a lifetime.
The social workers watched many young women go through this transition
and it seems cruel not to have prepared them either emotionally or logistically
by exploring every option open to them before the baby was born. After the
birth, when the reality of motherhood had sunk in, many of these women
were desperate to formulate a plan other than relinquishment. But there was
no system of advocacy for a woman who knew she wanted to mother from the
beginning, nor any effective recourse for those who came to that realization after their babies were born. Many women were presented with papers in the
hospital while they were still recovering from childbirth and were authorita-
tively instructed to sign. Some did not even understand what they were signing. Often these papers gave temporary or joint custody to the adoption
agency, and once the child was in the agency's care the mother had a more difficult time, both legally and emotionally, halting the process. Though each
state did have a set period of time during which the mother could revoke consent, as they still do, many women who announced that they had changed
their minds or who asked about having more time to decide were not informed of their legal rights but rather were told it was too late. The only staff
person most of them had to turn to was the caseworker, and most of these
were strong advocates for surrendering.

Nobody talked about legal rights in those days. They told you the
baby was adopted right away. They didn't tell you it takes a while,
and they didn't tell you that you could legally change your mind.
You didn't have an attorney, you didn't know what your legal
rights were, and they lied to you. I don't know if it would have

made a difference. It's real hard to say years later. But there was a miscarriage of justice there. You *do* have rights.

—Diane II

Women who wanted to parent were often subjected to a humiliating competition of sorts with the prospective adoptive parents. It was routine for agency workers to provide trumped-up descriptions of the adoptive families. Many women were told their child would go to a family where the husband was a doctor and the wife was a housewife. It was suggested that if the mother loved her child she should not deny him or her this wonderful opportunity. The agencies, of course, did not foresee these mothers reuniting with their children twenty, thirty, or forty years later, and learning that the profile of the adoptive parents had been untrue. Many women I interviewed have met their child's parents and some have built wonderful relationships. They feel that, given the circumstances, they could not have wished for a better family or outcome for their child. Others, however, were unequivocally not pleased by what they found.

> When you give up a child, you certainly hope that they get better than what you could have done. My daughter certainly did not get better than what I could have done, even as a child myself. The original adoptive parents had adopted one child prior and then adopted my daughter within a short period of time. Within a couple of months after adopting her, the husband left the wife with the two kids. Apparently, the wife had some mental-health issues and so at some point she was institutionalized and the kids were put in foster care. My daughter remembers her grandparents being integral in making sure that they got food and were bathed and stuff, even before the mother was institutionalized. She remembers how her grandmother took care of them, because sometimes her mother just couldn't.
>
> *—Wendy*

The "better life" argument was made all the more compelling by the fact that so many couples were clamoring to adopt in the years following World

War II; for every healthy baby available for adoption, it is estimated that there were ten couples waiting to adopt. As word reached the public that unwanted babies were available and in need of homes, millions of couples flooded adoption agencies with applications. The number of nonfamily adoptions per year went from approximately 8,000 in 1937 to over 70,000 in 1965.[1]

With so many couples in competition for babies, social workers could be selective. Agency workers vetted prospective couples and placed children in homes for a trial period, usually six months to one year, to ensure that both parties were adjusting to the new arrangement before the adoption was finalized. During this temporary-placement period, social workers conducted home visits to make sure the baby was thriving. If the prospective adoptive parents changed their minds before the adoption was finalized, the child could be returned to the agency.

Interest in adoption had increased, in part, because of the availability of newborns rather than older children. But couples of this era did not make the decision to adopt in a vacuum. Social acceptance of adoption needed to be cultivated. Adoption had not been a common way to build a family in previous generations. Families needed assurance that babies available through adoption agencies were healthy babies of normal intelligence who were otherwise unwanted. Social acceptance was predicated on the idea that these babies were unwanted. This belief eliminated a potential moral dilemma, especially for adoptive families: most couples, no matter how much they wanted a child, would not want to be involved in taking a child away from a mother against her will. But given the secrecy and the social stigma of the time, adoptive parents were never exposed to the story of the pain and grief felt by so many of the mothers. And as more and more couples adopted, social acceptance grew apace. People read stories about Hollywood stars like George Burns and Gracie Allen and Roy Rogers and Dale Evans adopting children. Popular magazines promoted adoption by publishing articles that further confirmed the practice as an admirable and joyful way to build a family.

The February 19, 1951, cover story in *Life* magazine provides an example of the dissemination of these ideas on a massive scale, and of the reassuring language used to describe the experience of adoption.[2] What is interesting about this article is that it also purports to tell the story of the surrendering mother.

The cover of the magazine displayed a full-bleed photograph of a child's face with a title to the left, "The Adoption of Linda Joy." Inside the magazine, readers encountered a seven-page picture story that included thirty-two pictures, extensive captions, and a narrative that offered statistics and answers to concerns that might be on the minds of prospective adoptive families. The pictures and text chronicled the entire process, from the paperwork required of the adoptive family to the follow-up home visits.

A sequence of five images with captions is meant to tell the story of the eighteen-year-old unwed mother who gave birth to Linda. In the first image, a noticeably pregnant woman is standing outside a building, suitcase in hand, looking at a plaque that reads WOMANS HOME. The caption explains that after traveling 175 miles by bus, she has arrived at the Salvation Army Home in Los Angeles to have her baby. It then shows her meeting with her caseworker at the maternity home and the caption explains that at the maternity home the expectant mother "while awaiting her baby, decides she cannot keep it." She says, "It hurts, but I have a long life ahead of me." The third image shows her with her newborn in the hospital after delivery and explains that during her stay in the home "the case worker came regularly to help her decide baby's future." The fourth depicts her kissing the baby's face as she says good-bye. The caption reads, "She says goodbye to baby five days after birth. Unlike many unwed mothers, who are too chagrined to care, she took deep interest in the baby, liked to dress her." The caption under the fifth and final image about the mother explains that "she has a few weeks to change her mind and keep her." The only other reference to surrendering mothers is included in the beginning of the main story, in a passage warning potential adopters to avoid black marketers, "who charged as much as $5,000 to close the gap between couples who wanted babies and the mothers who wanted to get rid of them." The circulation of *Life* magazine at the time this article was published was more than five million.

A close reading of the feature reveals much about a series of assumptions that came to be commonly held during this time. First, the pregnant woman arrives alone "by bus." She has not been driven to the home by her family or boyfriend, who may later have a change of heart and come to claim her and the baby. Second, she has reached this decision on her own and has based it on the fact that she has "a long life ahead," which clearly suggests that she does not want to burden herself with a child at this point in her life. Third, she acknowledges that "it hurts, but . . ." The simple phrase "It hurts" does not adequately convey a life-defining decision or indicate any real depth of feeling. Fourth, the caseworker "helped" but does not pressure her about her decision. Fifth, "unlike many unwed mothers" she has a "deep interest" in the baby. In other words, many other unwed mothers do not have a deep interest in their babies. Evidence of her "deep interest" is that she likes to dress the baby. This observation makes her seem shallow and immature. If the only evidence of the mother's "deep interest" in the baby is dressing her, perhaps she likens motherhood to playing with dolls. Sixth, the story indicates that she has an opportunity to "change her mind." This phrase reinforces the predominant view that the decision made by unwed mothers at the time was a personal one, that they simply made a calculated choice to keep or not to keep their child.

The scenario presented suggests that the mother made an uncomplicated decision that was not influenced by outside forces such as social, economic, or family pressures. It is presented as a matter of her deciding whether she prefers to parent or not. She is given time to change her mind and the implication is that if she does not keep her child she will ultimately belong to the same category as the other mothers mentioned, who "wanted to get rid of" their babies.

So convincing was this popularized story, and so silenced were the women about how they really felt, that this basic scenario is still widely accepted by the public and by many adoptees, who feel they were unwanted by a mother who abandoned them because she had a lot of living left to do and they were a burden. The reality was that the mothers often found themselves up against people who knew just how uninformed they were. Carol, one of the women I interviewed, returned to her home state after giving birth in California to learn that the father of her child wanted to reconcile and marry. She wrote her caseworker to ask if, under the circumstances, it might be possible for them to get their child back. The caseworker's written response offers insight into the professional thinking of the time. In the 1960s, many states still did not place a baby with an adoptive family until he or she was two to three months old, and when Carol contacted her caseworker her child was still in temporary foster care. The caseworker stressed that in *her* opinion Carol had made the right decision the first time and that it was still the best decision for *everyone.*

Despite the fact that Carol was writing because circumstances had changed, the social worker continued to affirm the "decision" Carol made earlier when her situation was entirely different. She mentions nothing to Carol about her rights or about procedures for revoking consent. The caseworker writes:

> *I believe that it is still the right decision for [the baby], for you, as well as for [your husband-to-be]. [The baby] will have a wonderful, stable family who will love her and be able to give her everything—emotional and financial security. You and [your husband-to-be] need time to adjust to each other, build a stable relationship and then start building your family.*

Interestingly, the letter was typed and dated but not mailed immediately. Carol contacted the caseworker once again and she finally responded by writing a little handwritten note at the bottom of the original typed letter, congratulating Carol on her upcoming marriage. By the time the letter was actually sent to Carol, her daughter had been placed with an adoptive family.

Given the gravity and consequences of the legal transfer of a human being between natural and adoptive parents, it is surprising that a mother is permitted to relinquish all rights to her child without separate and impartial legal counsel. There was no requirement for social workers to inform the women of services available to them through county, state, or federal agencies. Surrendering mothers were not given clear, written information about time limits for revoking consent, which vary from state to state and change year to year as laws are revised. They were not given copies of any of the papers they signed, so they were unable to review them afterward. Social workers are still not required to provide women with information about state and federal resources that might enable them to keep their child.

Many of the women I interviewed describe being emotionally shut down when they signed away their child. They had papers placed in front of them, they were told to sign them, and they did.

I remember the social worker's face and I remember going into the nursery. I don't remember having feelings on that day about anything. I just went in and somebody blah-blah-blahed some words to me, but I don't know what they said. They threw the papers in front of me, I signed them, and I walked out. I didn't read them. I don't know what the woman said to me. I'm sure she was telling me what was in them. I mean, logic dictates that she was trying to explain it to me, but I don't remember what she said. I just signed the papers and I left. My family didn't talk about it. It never came up again. On Mother's Day, my mother gave me a sweater and a skirt with a Mother's Day card. She didn't say anything to me; it was just sitting on my bed.

—Maggie

Any of my conversations I had with the social worker before giving birth were basically trying to help me understand why I couldn't keep my son. Afterward, I had to go to the district court in Augusta and sign the papers. The judge was not friendly; he was being very businesslike. He put the papers in front of me to sign and I just kind of stood there. Finally I said, "What happens if I don't sign?" He got very angry with me and said that I'd already cost the poor, honest, hardworking taxpayers enough time and trouble and if I didn't sign the papers he would declare me incompetent, and how would I like my son to know that about me?

—Connie I

Young women in the 1950s and 1960s had little experience with being assertive. But regardless of whether they tried to fight the system or accepted their fate, they discovered that moving on and forgetting was impossible. The full emotional weight of the surrender affected some immediately. For others, it came later. Feelings of loss and grief were compounded by a sense that they had been lied to. Some thought that they had been duped out of their child. The damage in many cases was lifelong. These women had not just surrendered a child. They had surrendered control over the most important decision they might ever make to people who they felt did not necessarily have their best interest at heart. The shame was no longer about being single and pregnant. The shame was that they had given away, or not fought hard enough to keep, their child.

> One of the questions that come up when you go to court and relinquish is they ask you if you have been coerced in any way, and I thought it was the height of hypocrisy. Of course, you're coerced. You're coerced by your parents, who said, "Don't come home again if you plan to keep that child. We're not going to help you." You're coerced by everyone around you because of the shame and the lack of acceptance by society and your community. You're not acknowledged as a fit mother because you had sex before marriage.
>
> The judge congratulated me on how courageous I was. I was furious that he would tell me it was about courage. It was about defeat. It was totally about shame and defeat.
>
> —*Sue*

> I stayed in the hospital about two days afterward and then it was this very strange *Twilight Zone* sort of time. I had to go back to the maternity home to collect my things, knowing what I knew. I couldn't say anything. They're all happy, happy, happy, chatter, chatter, chatter, and I've just experienced this loss. How could you tell people that? So I just became voiceless. I couldn't speak it. I really just kind of shut down.
>
> I went back to Penn State. I started school again in four days. I finished school and then I was on to happily ever after. But I wasn't happy anymore. I mean, I realized there was something really wrong.
>
> —*Ann*

There is a general sense that all mothers who consider relinquishing a child for adoption today have myriad options and are much more empowered than the mothers I interviewed. To a great extent, this is true. The social stigma of single motherhood has lessened. In fact, an increasing number of single women now *adopt* children. Families are less likely to condemn their daughters, and agencies point to the ability of women to pick parents for their child from snapshot albums made by hopeful adoptive parents, whom the surrendering mother often meets. Through "open adoptions," mothers are able to either remain in contact with their child or receive periodic updates from the adoptive parents—though the mother's continued participation is not always guaranteed by law. Certainly these changes are improvements over the lack of options and the social stigma experienced by many of the mothers I interviewed. But on the other side, surrendering mothers have lost significant ground in one important aspect of the process.

In many states, the two time spans most critical to surrendering mothers have been drastically shortened. The first is the duration between birth and signing consent, and the second is the period of time after signing during which the mother may revoke her consent. In nineteen states a mother can sign a consent to relinquish the rights to her child within twenty-four hours of birth, and in six of those states the consent is irrevocable upon signing.[3] If the stories herein are any indication, this seems hardly enough time for a mother to come to grips with the reality of the life she has created—something that is impossible to do beforehand—and to make a deliberate and irreversible decision to relinquish her child.

MARGARET

I had a fairly normal life. I had nice parents who loved me. My uncle lived with us and my grandmother was around a lot. I had good friends. It was a normal Catholic high school girl's life. When I came home from school, I would take care of my four younger brothers and sisters and cook their dinner. I had been going with my boyfriend for a little over two years and he would come over rather frequently. He had ideas what we should do in that time period. I wasn't always as thrilled as he was, but you know, I always said, "Five minutes of bad sex changed my life."

I don't remember my father finding out. I do remember him coming upstairs. Now, my father was very Catholic. My mother was not Catholic. He didn't use birth control. We went to church if there was a blizzard or if there was snow up to our waists, we went to church. And he said, "Is it too late for us to do something about this?" I was just shocked and horrified that my father, this *Catholic*, was willing to bend the rules. And I said, "That is not something I'm willing to do."

So the next thing I knew my father came to me and said, "You will be going to St. Anne's infant and maternity home and you will be giving your baby up for adoption." There was no room for discussion. I wasn't in any position to argue with them about what I was going to do and not do.

Many other birth mothers will talk about the maternity home as this evil place, but really and truly St. Anne's was a place where I was given a home, a shelter. I had freedom. I mean, there were lots of other girls like me. We could go out; we just had to let people know where we were going. We would sign out and sign back in. We went to the movies. We went shopping. The only thing they wanted you to do was to get up and go to Mass. But I was asking God to help me, so I didn't mind getting up at five-thirty to go to Mass.

One morning I woke at two o'clock with this horrible stomachache. I went to the bathroom, you know, kind of drowsy, and all of a sudden it dawned on me this wasn't a stomachache; I was in labor. The nun came and she put my girlfriend and me in a station wagon. We went tearing through the streets in the middle of the night. Nobody called my parents. We got to the emergency room and they examined me, and they said, "The head's down, you're four centimeters dilated, so we're going to admit you." And the nun said, "Okay. Well, we are leaving now." I turned around and thought, "What do you mean, you're leaving and taking my girlfriend with you?" But they did. They left.

In those days being prepped to have a baby, especially for a girl who was seventeen years old, was humiliating. There was an enema and the shaving. They weren't very compassionate to St. Anne's girls, I don't think. And, you know, you just labored by yourself.

The last thing I remember was the mask coming down on my face. I woke up and I said, "Where's my baby?" And I started feeling for my stomach. I started screaming that they'd taken my baby and screaming and screaming, trying to climb out over the railing, fighting. They said, "No, no, no. If you promise to stay here, within five minutes we'll have your baby to you." And they brought him in to me in a gray warming box, and I can remember falling asleep with my hand around the gray box. When I saw him, I fell absolutely in love. I can remember what he felt like, what he looked like, what he smelled like.

I wasn't supposed to see him at all. They said, "You shouldn't see him, because you're going to forget and have other children." They said, "Write down on this side of the paper what you can give your baby. Write down on the other side what the adoptive parents have to offer." So you had to write that down. I said, "I don't know." And they said, "Well, just picture what he's going to look like. You know, he'll not have the nice clothes that the other children are going to have and on the playground, they'll call him a bastard." And I believed that. I remember writing down they had money, they had a father, they had a house, and they had clothes and food. And on my side I only put down love. That's all I did have.

What's shocking to me is sitting with other birth mothers and hearing them tell the same story. I thought, "My God, there must have been a textbook." You looked up how to get babies away from the mother, and this is how to do it. There must have been, because we were all told the same thing.

Even the story about the playground. I've heard it from other people and I'm thinking, "Oh my God. It was a script. It affected me so much, and here it was just a script."

So while I'm in the hospital I'm saying to God, "Please let me keep this baby." And I can remember, it was a Saturday, my parents coming to the doorway and I said, "Have you seen him? Isn't he beautiful?" My mom said, "You can't see him. You're not allowed." And there was a nurse standing on the other side of me at the head of the bed and I can remember her saying, "She can see him whenever she wants. She's that baby's mother." That nurse didn't give me enough self-confidence to keep my child, but with those two sentences she gave me the foundation on which to rebuild my sense of self. She probably didn't remember me after that shift, but she became one of the most important women in my life. Just by her compassion and two sentences, you know?

When I returned to the maternity home they said, "You've only been gone from school five weeks, so you can go back to your school and say you had appendicitis, or if you're uncomfortable you may continue to come to school at St. Anne's, but your son will be here in the nursery and you have to agree not to see him." And I said, "I'll agree to that. I'd like to continue at St. Anne's. I'm too embarrassed to go back," which wasn't quite true. So I got to spend six weeks with him.

Because I was being individually tutored, my school hours were nine to one. So I got there at seven and I'd see him until nine. Then I'd see him after school from one to five. I went to Mass every morning, and I never truly believed my mother or grandmother or God would let him go away from me. On Saturdays I never saw him but Sundays from two to four they put all the babies by the window and the potential adoptive parents could go and look at the different babies. And I would go to look at my own child.

Somewhere in there I had to go sign the papers. I walked to Catholic Charities and they put the papers in front of me, and I said, "Can I have some more time? I'm trying to find a way." They said, "You can't have any more time. He's costing your family six dollars a day in the nursery," which sounds like a little bit of money today, but then it was a lot of money. And they said, "Haven't you caused enough trouble? If you sign the papers, the bills will be done." So I had to sign because I had already caused enough trouble.

I signed the papers and they never told me I had thirty days to change my mind. Thursday was Holy Thursday, and when I came back Monday he was gone. I finished school and that was the end of it for a few years. My parents wanted me to come back and just be their little girl again, like it had never happened.

I dated a couple of boys in between and then met the man who's now my husband, and ended up getting pregnant again. I know I was trying to replace my baby. When I had my first child with my husband, she was a girl. I was thrilled because I didn't want another boy at that time. I ended up having another baby a year later. Then we used some birth control for a couple of years and then I had a son and then two more daughters. And it never dawned on me why I was having these children, so many of them so quickly. So my husband and I had five children and somewhere along there I said, "Forget it. Having these kids isn't filling up this hole."

I thought about him every day. He was just mine, a part of me that I didn't share with anyone else. The part of me that was his mother remained seventeen and the rest of me continued to grow, to be a wife and mother, eventually a nursing student. I was in therapy for a while for a little bit of depression, and they said, "You have an overactive maternal instinct. You need to become a nurse," so that's what I did. I never mentioned, in this depression and everything, that I'd given a baby up for adoption—never mentioned it.

I went on with my life. In 1976, I saw a little ad for Concerned United Birthparents. I cut it out and carried it in my wallet. We didn't have the, whatever it was, thirty dollars, it cost to join, but for five dollars you could join a registry. So I joined the registry. Every birthday my mother gave me twenty dollars and my grandmother gave me twenty dollars, and I combined it for my ALMA [Adoptees' Liberty Movement Association] membership so I'd get the newsletter with all the stories of reunion in it. And that went on for quite a few years, just using the birthday money for that. My husband knew and every birthday I'd get very quiet, every March 6, very quiet. He was very nice to me on that day, no matter what else was going on in our life. If he was ticked off about something else, he was nice on March 6.

On my son's twenty-fifth birthday, I drove home from work crying the whole way because I knew I just couldn't deal with it anymore. I sent in money for my CUB membership and a woman called me right away and said, "Hi, I'm from Concerned United Birthparents." And I sat down and cried. I couldn't stop crying because I was talking to somebody who understood my seventeen-year-old self. She knew. She knew what my life was like. I know her well now and she's very different from me, but I will never forget her because she was there during that time period.

Finally, I went and asked Catholic Charities to help me find him. They sent me to their lawyer. He told me, "You're the first person that's ever done this. I don't understand what you want." I said, "I want to have contact with my son." And he said, "Well, we have to protect the baby." I said, "What baby? There isn't a baby. He's twenty-five now." He kept insisting there was this *baby* and they had to protect this *baby*. And I said, "He's older now than I was when you took him from me."

They had me fill out this whole form, this legal-size paper with questions, to prove I was fit to know him before they would search for him. Then they said they would look for him and they would contact his adoptive parents and ask their permission to see if I could contact him. And I said, "He's an adult, he's not a baby. There *is* no baby." Well, I was getting more and more frustrated, and they were going to charge me fifteen hundred dollars. A professional searcher was going to cost me two thousand dollars. We're talking about a time when my husband and I didn't have much money. But I just couldn't give them the power. They were making me feel like I did back then. The Catholic Charities social worker was incredibly nasty, telling me, "You didn't even want to see him then, why do you want to contact him now?" I said, "Obviously, you don't know what happened."

I decided to go with a searcher. My mother gave me a thousand dollars. Today, I realize she was really struggling financially at that time and couldn't afford it. And I borrowed a thousand dollars from the hospital. I gave my information to a contact person for the searcher. The next day I was walking down the hallway in Labor and Delivery, and they called me to the phone. I was the childbirth educator, so I had been answering the phone multiple times and I can remember thinking, "I'm on my way to lunch, I'll call them back after lunch," but I thought, "No, just go get it done." So I said hello and the searcher said, "His name is——." And I fell apart.

I had gone back to work at the hospital in Labor and Delivery as a ward clerk. I had to be where my son was. And later I worked as a nurse in Labor and Delivery and as the assistant head nurse there. After they tore the hospital down and changed it, I no longer wanted to be there because I couldn't go to the room where he was born.

I had to be with people giving birth. After finding my son, that has kind of diminished. I left OB five years ago to become a case manager. And now I'm director of case management and it's funny because I often feel I'm an impostor. I've got this position and I'm thinking, "One day they're going to find out I don't really belong here." It's really funny to be like that, so there's still something inside that makes me feel I'm not good enough. But it's changing, slowly.

Those social workers kept telling me I wasn't good enough to parent my son, and made me believe I wasn't good enough to parent anybody. I've held my children way too tight and that's why they've struggled as teenagers. My daughter is going to be thirty-five and she lives on my street. They've all had trouble separating. I cannot let anybody go. I mean, I'm still sending Christmas cards to people I've met on the street or something. I cannot lose anybody.

Self-confidence is an issue, self-esteem, I should say, rather than confidence. And I think the reason I'm heavy is because I was portrayed as a loose girl, so I'm always making sure that no man will want me. For me, it's always been: God didn't let me keep my baby. God took my son, because he didn't stop it.

When I found my son, I very much wanted him to be my baby again, and I went through a very difficult emotional period of trying to go back and get the part of me that was seventeen and incorporate it into my forty-two-year-old self, now fifty-four—to make that part of me old.

We make decisions for people that we really shouldn't make because we feel they're not living as we think they should live. Social workers made the decision that I wasn't good enough to parent my son, because I wouldn't have been parenting up to their standards. Maybe I wouldn't, but I could have done it. I could have parented my son. I was parenting within two years, anyway, and did a decent job of it.

To look at the surrender papers now is shocking. It's just like you're handing over your car or something, you know. To see your own signature thirty years later is just very, very painful. I loved him, and I would have sacrificed some of the things that I wanted in order to be his mother. They had no right to make that decision for me and for him. They robbed us of twenty-five years together.

You know, my mom became ill the last years of her life. But Mom didn't want to go to the nursing home. She was completely bedridden and lived alone until she died. And the way she did it was she lived on my street, and my brother lives on my street. And I have another brother and another sister and we all took turns taking care of her. It was a sacrifice for all of us, but we did it because we're family and that's what families do. Well, we were a family then, too, and they should have done it. They owed it to me because I was a member of their family. Not because I was good, bad, or whatever, but because I belonged to them.

LESLIE

My boyfriend had his first sexual experience the summer before we started going out. He kept telling me stories about Sheila, who had put out the summer before, and how wonderful it was when you finally had sex. I managed to stay a virgin all the way through my senior year. I was dangerously close, I might add, but I stayed a virgin until the night of my senior prom.

So the summer after graduation was my summer of being sexual. We had sex—and I use that term loosely—maybe six to ten times. In August of 1965, I had gotten tickets to the Beatles' concert in Atlanta and we went out parking afterward and had sex and when we came back to the house I said, "Something's happening in my stomach. I feel like it's the Fourth of July in there. What if I'm pregnant?" I'm not even sure I thought of it before that—denial is a wonderful thing when you're seventeen years old.

He went off to college, and I went to a local junior college and within six weeks I was throwing up in the morning. We were talking back and forth on the phone: "What are we going to do?" "I don't know. What are we going to do?" Finally he said, "I'll come home next weekend and tell my dad and we'll get married." I was madly in love with him and it was a huge relief that he wanted to marry me, but I also felt this tremendous ambivalence. I'm thinking, "I'm only seventeen years old. How am I going to get married and raise a baby?" So, to be honest, I really had a mixed reaction.

I told my parents and it was horrific. I remember being so scared and shaking because I had always been the good girl. Of course, in that day, everything had to look right for the neighbors. It was such a huge thing. When we pulled up in the driveway after a date, if we sat in the car more than two or three minutes the front-porch light started to flick on and off because "What would the neighbors think you were doing out there in the car?"

The closest maternity home was in Mobile, Alabama, about a hundred miles away. My mother couldn't get me out of town fast enough. But before I left she told me that my grandmother had to get married. I was so grateful that she told me. That was a little present she gave me: "You're not alone."

I don't really remember the drive over. I know it was just my mother who took me. The maternity home was this huge old brick, three-story building that looked very institutional. I was terrified. I thought it was going to be like reform school. I was so scared the other girls would be hoods—that's what we called kids with their sleeves rolled up and a pack of cigarettes, and possibly a switchblade, in their bobby socks. But when we walked in I could hear giggling. I was totally stunned when I started meeting the girls. They looked just like me—they were college students, high-school students, cheerleaders—the nicest of the nice girls. I was put in a room with four or five others and one of them was a little girl the nuns called Little Bit. She was thirteen years old and she wasn't any bigger than a minute. The whole time that I was in that room she cried herself to sleep every night; she was homesick.

At the maternity home the party line was: "If you really love your baby, you will give it up. You're doing a wonderful thing for a couple who can't have children. The baby would be called a bastard on the playground. It would be so selfish of you to keep your baby." And as long as you were going along with the party line, then you were with the group. But if you ever wavered or had second thoughts that you weren't going to be able to go through with the adoption, you immediately got separated from the pack so you wouldn't contaminate the thinking of the rest of the girls.

I look back now and think, "Oh my God, that's mind control, that's brainwashing." But at the time it just seemed normal, like if someone did something wrong they got put into solitary confinement. I would do anything they said. If they had told me "Go to the third floor and jump off the roof and that's how you'll regain your parents' approval," then that's exactly what I would have done. I had to get their approval back.

My mother gave me her wedding band from her first marriage so I could wear it when I went out in public, which she basically wished I would never do unless I put a bag over my head. We'd go out in little clumpets. I'm sure everybody in the world knew we were from the maternity home but we'd all walk around with our wedding bands on like we were just as normal as could be. My favorite nun was a big, tomboyish woman from the Midwest. We all loved her and you knew that she loved you. On one of our outings, we went to the Humane Society and got Sister two puppies. I don't know how she managed, but she convinced the nunnery that we needed the puppies on the premises and they kept them.

There was another nun who was the counseling nun and she wasn't more than twenty-five years old and she would come once a week. She was a social-worker nun. That was my first inkling that maybe if I survived this I could help somebody else. Maybe I could be a social worker and be a compassionate ear to somebody else who was going through difficulties.

I was terrified to give birth. I'd never been in a hospital. The sister took me over and pulled up in front of the hospital and let me out. At seventeen, I went in and admitted myself. They wouldn't allow your parents to come until the baby was born; I don't know why. I had to labor in the hall. I couldn't be in the labor room because all the women in that room were married. Finally, they pulled the gurney into a room and gave me something and the lights went out. I remember absolutely nothing about his birth. The next thing I remember was my parents standing over the side of my bed. They were smiling and crying and I said, "What did I have?" And they said, "A little boy."

When I came back to the maternity home I got to visit with my baby every day. I would feed him and rock him and when I would look at him . . . there in my lap, staring back at me, was the birth father and me. I could see both of us in that child, plain as day. Losing my relationship with the father was hard, too, because, seventeen or not, that was my first love, and when you have a child with someone you have a connection for life.

I remember little snippets of having to go to the courthouse to sign the papers to relinquish my son. My mom says she went along, but I don't have any recollection of that. I had to sit in what was like a witness stand and the judge was behind the big desk with this gavel. I remember him saying over and over, "Do you understand you can never go back on this? This is irrevocable. Once you sign these papers, you can never see your child or have any contact with your child, do you understand that?" He reiterated it in two or three different ways but I was so scared. I was in the frozen, good-girl mode. I'm sure I signed the papers, but I don't remember. I got to visit with him one last time and when I was holding him his little eyelids were flickering and he was smiling and Sister said he was dreaming of angels.

I never got any copies of the papers that I signed. I asked my mom years later if she had any papers put away, but she didn't get copies, either. I do remember coming back from the court hearing and squeezing myself into one of the beautiful dresses that I had made at the home. I remember being all mixed up, being sad, but kind of excited to get out, and terrified to see my friends—all those emotions were mixed in there together.

The first few weeks at home, I cried all the time. I'd lock myself in the bathroom or go to my room. I cried all night but I didn't let anybody hear me because I felt like I was being bad. I wasn't doing what they said I was supposed to do, which was "Get over it. Move on with your life and put it behind you." I thought, "Crap, I can't even do *this* right." I remember standing at my bedroom window at night, looking for my boyfriend's car to drive by. I would just stand and look out that window.

Finally, I talked my parents into letting me see my boyfriend one last time so I could tell him about the baby. We went out and oh, it was heaven on earth. I could *talk* about it. We cried together, and I told him what the baby looked like. He said, "We can go get him back," and I had to keep telling him, "You don't get it. There's nothing we can do. I signed him away."

I had a much lower profile once I was back home. I made preparations to go away to college. My mother found this little Catholic all girls' school for me in northern Alabama. I wouldn't have to worry about who knew and who didn't, so there was some relief in that. I had been gregarious in high school and had lots of friends. But when I went to this school and tried going to a few mixers with the boys I was just all in knots inside. I couldn't make conversation and I couldn't wait for the bus to come and take the boys back to their school.

Then in January I got a phone call from a fellow I hadn't heard from in probably two years. He was my boyfriend from the ninth grade until my junior year. He was getting shipped to Vietnam. He and another friend from high school had enlisted in the buddy system. They were going to 'Nam and they wanted to blow it out before they left, before they got their hair cut off, so they came for the weekend. I fixed his friend up with my best friend and we drove to Birmingham and got two rooms in the seediest motel you ever saw. The idea was the two girls were staying in one room and the two guys in the other. We were going to get drunk, but we were going to go to bed in our respective rooms, which I think, in fact, we did.

I remember drinking Rebel Yell and Coke and I got so drunk I didn't know my name. I have snippets of memory, but I don't remember a whole lot of the evening. I was with people I really enjoyed but I was anxious, so I got drunk. That voice in my head was going, "Do they know? Do they know?" One of the snippets I remember is being on the floor of the motel room with him on top of me, making out. I think the other couple had gone off to the other room. I remember thinking, "The only reason he came to see me is because he heard about me. I'm sure that's it. He heard I put out." Then thinking, "What does it matter, I'm not a virgin anyway? What does it matter?" I woke up in the morning in my room with my girlfriend in the next bed. We were all hung-over to beat the band and they took us back up to school and left. I hoped I hadn't had sex with him, but six weeks later I got up one morning and I threw up. I knew immediately I was pregnant again. I just felt frozen. I literally started shutting down.

When my mom came to pick me up at the end of the semester, I slept on and off in the backseat of the car. I remember lying back there thinking, "What am I going to do? What am I going to do? What is wrong with me?" I mean, you could forgive someone a first pregnancy. How in the world could you ever tell anybody you did this again? You can't. So I ate like a mad woman. I gained seventy pounds. Lucky for me, it was the era of tent dresses and muumuus, so I made myself dresses and I ate everything that wasn't nailed down. Mother would lecture me, "You're gaining weight. You used to be such a pretty girl."

I drank a whole bottle of castor oil to induce labor. And a few times when my mother and grandmother went out together I stood at the top of the stairs and threw myself down. All that happened was I got black and blue. Over the course of the summer, I would go out to visit my sister, who lived a few miles away, and there was a really sharp curve in the road and I remember thinking, "I really have to kill myself because I can't tell anybody and I can't go through this again." One time I got up to about a hundred and twenty on that curve and then it occurred to me, "They'll do an autopsy and they'll know I'm pregnant. God, I can't even get out of this life without anybody knowing."

Then one Saturday I was at work and I didn't feel good, so I went home around lunchtime. I just had these horrible cramps. I thought, "Maybe I'm going to have a miscarriage. I'll have a miscarriage and nobody will ever know." I was upstairs in my room and my grandmother was downstairs. She was a big football fan and she was cussing at the television: "God damn you! Get a touchdown." I was upstairs holding on to the bedpost because my stomach hurt. A little later, I went into the bathroom. I got into this crouch position over the bath mat and I gave birth to my son. He looked at me and I looked at him and neither of us made a sound. I pulled towels down from the rack and wrapped us up and drifted in and out of sleep.

My mom came home from work and said, "Are you okay in there?" And I said, "No, I'm not." I had locked the door, which was never allowed in my family. No locked doors. She said, "Let me in." And I said, "I will, but I have to tell you something first." She said, "Okay." I said, "There's a baby in here with me." And she said, "Okay, just let me in." Years later she told me she thought I'd kidnapped a baby because after I gave birth . . . every time I saw a baby I started to cry. She thought I had slipped a cog and kidnapped somebody's baby. Of course, when she opened the door she saw that there was blood and he was still gooey and we were still attached by the umbilical cord.

She called our family doctor and the minute they took him away from me he started crying and he never stopped. They took him down to my mother's room and he cried and he cried and he cried. I was in my room putting a pillow over my head, trying to get the sound away. I was so full of shame I couldn't look anybody in the eye. I still struggle with that at age fifty-six. I begged my mom not to tell my grandmother and she said, "Leslie, we've got to, there's a baby here." The doctor said, "You know, I have to register this baby as a live birth." I remember my mother being horrified because she knew somebody who worked in the vital-records center. He said, "I love you, honey, but I'm not going to lose my license over this."

My son cried that entire night and it was just more than I could bear. The doctor's wife called the next morning to see how we were and my mother told her that it had been pretty rough so she said, "I'll come take the baby until you can take it to the agency."

I delivered on a Saturday and I was back in school the next Monday, wrapped in foam rubber so nobody could see how quickly I lost the weight. My parents wrapped me in layers and every few weeks we would take a little more off. I remember my world turned gray—the light sources just shut off. I just felt like I was in a dim, dim world. I begged my mother to take me to a psychiatrist, which she did in a few weeks. We had to go to the next town because then you would never let your license plate be seen at the office of a psychiatrist. He saw me twice. On the second visit, he gave me some anti-depressant medication. I started to take it and my mother saw it and flushed it down the toilet, because that was the era of, you know, "Bite a nail, honey." So that was the sum total of my therapy.

I finished that year of school. I had my little sports car and worked in the Villager store to get more Villager clothing, and I went off to the University of Georgia the following year, but my life was never the same. I joined a sorority and I distinctly remember one day we were all out on the sidewalk during rush, jumping up and down like a bunch of fools. I felt like a total nitwit. I'm thinking, "These girls don't know what they're in for in life." I just felt like I was playing this humongous charade, a charade I continued.

I never told anybody about it. I sealed it off. I laughingly called myself the born-again virgin because the country was now having a sexual revolution. It was Vietnam, hippiedom, and everybody was having sex like bunnies, real out in the open. Not this girl. I just kept putting on a lot of weight. I stayed very heavy. I had one or two boyfriends but if it would begin to get serious I'd either eat more or get rid of him. I didn't have sex again until I was about twenty-three and believe you me, I had been on the birth-control pill for several months prior.

As an adult, I got my buns into therapy. I worked hard at it but I never told anybody outside of therapy that I was a birth mother. I had a best friend who was a supervisor and a mentor and one night she told me that she had surrendered a child and I said, "Well, sit down . . ." and that was the first person that I'd ever told I'd had *two* children.

The first time I said it in a room full of people was when I was in my late thirties, in group therapy. I always felt like people would be so totally re-pulsed by me that they would run from the room. After all, I didn't just do it once, I did it twice. But I got nothing but compassion from the group and I was so stunned by their response that I couldn't walk out of the room. My legs were like jelly. Two other therapists had to help me to the car.

It's been a very slow journey. Every time I tell, I get better and nobody's left the room yet. That started me down the path of talking about it more openly. My husband and I had twins after we'd been married a couple of years. We went through in vitro. I thought I was going to die if I didn't have a child that I could raise, yet I kept picking all these lousy relationships. I finally found my husband and I knew he was a good, solid guy. People always ask, "Did he know about this before you got married?" I'd say, "You've got to be kidding. That was part of the litmus test."

After I gave birth to the twins and settled down into a routine, depression started creeping in. Every stage they went through, I realized the stages that I had missed with my sons—when they talked, when they walked, when they cut teeth. It just became so real. I got more and more depressed and I was having a hard time getting close to my twins. I would have panic feelings that something was going to happen and I was going to lose them. If there was a kidnapping or any harm came to a child, I'd start crying and shaking and I had to turn off the TV. I mean, it was a little over the top. I was so frightened of losing them that I kept an emotional distance. So I got back into therapy and I worked on learning how to attach.

Then I had a dream that I was driving down the street—the same type of curve where I thought about killing myself—and there were two little toddler boys sitting by the side of the road. I thought, "Oh, my God. They're going to get hit." So I stopped the car and I put them in the backseat and I said, "I've got to find their mother." I relayed this dream in my group and a woman said, "So when are you going to look for the boys?"

I started reading everything I could get my hands on and I called Concerned United Birthparents and talked to my district person. I remember saying, "But you don't get it. You don't get it. I had *two* kids." She said, "Honey, we have workshops for women who gave up two and three. There's a conference in a few months in California. You've got to come." I said, "There are other people who gave up two children?"

I went to my first CUB conference. I don't know where we got the money but I got on this plane and I'm looking at everyone thinking, "Could she be a birth mother? Could she be a birth mother?" I forgot to ask what they did at these conferences. A van picked me up and another birth mother's son was driving. The other guy in the front seat turns around and says, "What do you do at these retreats?" And I said, "You know, I haven't a clue. I've never been to one. I didn't even ask." And the son of the birth mother piped up and said, "They cry a lot. They cry and they cry and they cry." And on the way back I said, "Boy, were you right."

But instant friendships were formed and it was like I came out of a deep freeze. I felt like Rip Van Winkle. God, where had I been? I'd been through the women's movement and I got militant about everything except this. I began to see it as an incredible women's issue. My husband has always said he put one woman on the plane and an entirely different one came back.

I became the chief social worker for one of the hospitals in town. Those were the days of hospitalizing teenagers who acted out for really long periods of time. In the beginning of the eighties, it started to go the other way—twenty-eight-day treatment for substance abuse—but before that people could be in the hospital for three to six months. I was the head of this unit and one of the things I kept noticing about the admissions was how many of the teenagers were adopted. I thought, "My God, could I have done more damage than I thought?" There was nothing in my college training about adoption. Adoption was what happened at the agency. It was an event. It wasn't a physiological anything. I hadn't learned anything about it. I think it's in the best interest of the public to learn a whole lot more about the consequences of adoption. There are repercussions for this little societal experiment—for all of us. You don't just pick a baby up from one place and graft him onto another. It doesn't work that way. This false view that society has of adoption is still costing an awful lot of people a lifetime of pain and regret.

They thought they were protecting people. They were protecting adoptees with all the secretiveness. They were protecting adoptive parents from any disruption, and they thought they were protecting a girl's reputation. That was all a part of the secrecy. But it made it all the more shameful and it ended up hurting people. We were all kept apart by the system and it was very unhealthy.

Sometimes when I meet birth mothers who fought tooth and nail for their babies I feel so ashamed of myself, that I didn't have the fight. How does a woman separate from her own flesh? Only by dissociating—I don't think there's any other way you can do it. I met one woman who wouldn't sign the papers and she was put in a mental institution by her parents and kept there for a year until she signed. I thought, "Oh, why couldn't I have been that one?"

8

⊥

The Aftermath

I guess once I got married I felt more normal but still, it's kind of like being in a black hole somewhere. It's as if part of you went away when that happened. A really big part of you went away and you pretend that it didn't. You don't know who you are anymore. It's like suddenly you got cut in half. So what you really end up being is half a person who pretends she's whole. Even though I got married twice, I had two kids, and I have a very successful business, nothing takes away that black hole. Because you're always lying, you're always pretending. You're not true to who you really are.

—Ann

SURRENDERING A CHILD for adoption has been described by many of the women I interviewed as the event that defined their identity and therefore influenced every major decision they made thereafter. Since most of these women surrendered when they were between the ages of sixteen and twenty-three, the event shaped their entire adult lives. It affected the timing of, or ability to pursue, their educational goals, their choice of a career, their decision about having subsequent children, their parenting style, and their relationships with parents, friends, and partners.

Women who said they never entertained the idea of parenting at the time of their surrender often described the same lifelong grief as those who fought to bring their baby home. Their grief has been exacerbated, and in some cases become chronic, because they were not permitted to talk about or properly grieve their loss. Not only was the surrender of their child not recognized as a loss; the implication was they should be grateful that others had taken care of their problem.

> It was never to be mentioned, it was never to be grieved, it was just to be denied. Then little by little, I started picking up with life, but I think I was filled with rage. I have to say, it was the most altering event of my whole life—a defining moment, a defining time. I believe that the way that I led my life, let's say the first ten years after, was reckless, was without regard for myself, my health, well-being, anything, because I had no value. And it was probably without regard for other people as well, because it was difficult for me to respect other people, it was difficult for me to trust.
>
> I'm sure people looked at my life and thought I had everything all together. I have a lot of aunts and uncles and I can remember being called nice little Kathi and thinking, "If you only knew." I felt like I was a demon. It wasn't until I went into therapy that I ever reached the point of feeling I deserved to be valued; it was all about deserving. People do not have a clue what people's lives are like from appearances. Appearances are just the greatest illusion. I think if somebody feels they're all alone, that's one of the worst feelings.
>
> *—Kathi*

Studies that have examined the grief of relinquishing mothers have identified a sense of loss that is unique and often prolonged. In one such study, the grief was likened to the separation loss[1] experienced by a parent whose child is missing, or by a person who is told their loved one is missing in action. Unlike the grief over the death of a child, which is permanent and for which there is an established grieving process, the loss of a child through adoption has no clear end and no social affirmation that grief is even an appropriate response.[2]

> Afterward I was very introverted. I could not have a close friend because I felt like such a fraud. How could I consider myself a close friend without them knowing about this? And, of course, I wasn't supposed to tell anyone. I was a good girl and was going to

do what I was told. It just makes you feel like a lesser person, because you've done this horrible thing, this unspeakable thing. I
just kind of withdrew. It's like the person that you are was put on
hold and you're somebody else, you're flawed.

*   —Connie III*

Anger, guilt, and depression are normal grief responses to a major loss.
And though grief may never go away, it generally subsides with time. For relinquishing mothers, however, the grief may actually intensify over time.[3]
One study has shown that high levels of unresolved grief in women were
found to correlate with the "lack of opportunity to express feelings about the
loss, the lack of finality of the loss (the child continues to exist), the perception of coercion, and the resulting guilt and shame over the surrender."[4]

Before I went into that place I was always very happy, liked
everybody, would talk to everybody, was a class officer in high
school, a cheerleader. I was *that* kind of a person. I came out of
there a different person. It changed me. It really changed my personality. I got very sad. I was very withdrawn.

I went back to school after that happened and everybody
would say to me, "What's your problem? What's the matter with
you? Did someone die in your family?" Well, having a child, giving it up for adoption is like having a death in the family. The only
difference is you can't publicly be sad; you gotta be sad by yourself. I think it hardened me. I was really nasty to people. I was mad
at the world. I was mad at my parents, I was mad at everybody,
even if they had nothing to do with it.

*   —Cathy II*

The National Mental Health Association has issued a list of the best ways
to cope with a major loss, like the death of a loved one.[5] The list suggests that
the grieving person should "seek out people who understand your feelings of
loss; tell others how you feel; take care of your physical health and be aware
of the danger of developing a dependence on medication or alcohol; make
an effort to live in the present and not dwell on the past; try to take time to

adjust to your loss by waiting to make major changes such as moving, remarrying, changing jobs or having another child; seek outside help when grief seems like it is too much to bear; and be patient because it can take months or years to absorb a major loss." Without proper guidance or counseling, most of the women I interviewed took action that was precisely the opposite of these recommendations, some of it on the advice of professionals.

> I got married. I thought, "I better get myself off the streets. This is not going well." I was just living this lie, this lie, this lie. "Do you have children?" "No." It's like being Judas every time. You're denouncing who you are, who they are. You just feel terrible. I married this man under false pretenses. Did he ever know I had children? Absolutely not. I didn't tell him.
>
> I had a wedding, the wedding that my sister wanted. Everything was a lie. I didn't want a wedding, but he was Italian and Catholic, and you had to have a wedding. Oh, God. Then he says, "We can have children." I looked at him, like, "Are you insane?" The last thing I ever wanted to be was pregnant. I said, "I'm too young to get pregnant." That's what I told him. I was twenty, twenty-one at the time. He was an airline pilot, I was a stewardess. I said, "Well, maybe in five years, I don't know." But the whole idea was so repellent to me. It was all mixed up with this grief and this guilt. No, I just couldn't.
>
> So I'm married and everything is so perfect. We go on a Hawaiian honeymoon—everything is just so, so, nice. We lived on forty acres of land, we built this beautiful house, we had so much money. Every weekend we were going over to my parents' house and having steak dinners and barbecues. I remember one of these Sundays as we pulled into my parents' suburban neighborhood I just started hitting my head against the seat of the car. I was just going a little crazy. It was all the things I couldn't say. It was July. The birth month. So July was always horrible, horrible, horrible. Even if my mind didn't remember, my body remembered. This really lives in your body.
>
> —*Diane IV*

The symptoms described by the women I interviewed are precisely the same as those of the surrendering mothers chronicled in professional studies of their grief. Many women had experienced several—and some nearly all—of the following symptoms: depression; damaged self-esteem; persistent guilt, shame, and self-loathing over "giving away" their child; an enduring sense of emptiness and loss that is not erased by having other children; persistent loneliness or sadness; difficulty with intimacy, attachment, or emotional closeness; lack of trust; anger; severe headaches or physical illnesses that cannot be explained or diagnosed; and occasionally posttraumatic stress disorder, characterized by extreme anxiety, panic attacks, flashbacks, and nightmares.[6]

After I surrendered my child, I had a conviction that I was a horrible person. I was a horrible, horrible person and I acted like one for many years, too. I know people from that time told me that they were actually afraid of me because I was so bitchy and sarcastic and kind of radiating hostility and anger. I have a very cutting tongue. Over the years, it's been much modified. I'm a much kinder, gentler person than I was then. I wasn't worth much for a long time. My husband was a huge dose of reality. He was a good friend. He knew everything about me. I mean, he knew *everything* and he still liked me. I lost a lot of my bitchiness with him.

I thought I made the intelligent decision. I made a *rational* decision that I'm still convinced was the best thing for her. I can't imagine what our lives would have been like. In some ways, it was probably pretty frigging self-serving. I wasn't strong enough to face the idea of raising a child on my own. I came from middle-class, normal, suburban Americana. It was not acceptable under any circumstances to be a single mother, and I wasn't tough enough to face all that. But the pain never goes away. It just never does.

My identity somehow got wrapped up in having the longest hair and the coolest guitar player in town. I was so frigging proud of that hair. Yeah, I was way cool. I dressed really well and supported an entire band on my salary. People wrote songs about me. That was my identity. I didn't have any sense of myself at all. So whatever I attached myself to, that was my worth. I didn't know who the hell I was. I knew that I was not a good person, though. *That*, I *knew*.

—Nancy III

Although these women were released from the hospital without any documents related to the birth of their baby, some did manage to hang on to artifacts from their days in the hospital, or to acquire pictures that provided a tangible link to their child.

> I remember going home and then trying to start my life over, with all the secrets and hush-hush and all that. I cried every night with the diaper I took. I had this diaper and I could still smell her. They took pictures of my daughter and I couldn't wait to get them because I just wanted to have *something*. I cried and I waited for the pictures to come from the hospital, but they never came.
>
> *—Carolyn I*

> I got a picture of him in the mail. You know, they have photographers that go to the nurseries and take pictures of the newborns. Well, I got the picture. I kept it for probably ten years. I had it in a little brown frame in my drawer, hidden away. Every once in a while, I'd take it out. I always cried and cried. Finally, when we lived on the farm in the seventies, I burned it. Oh, how I wish I hadn't. I thought it would somehow get rid of the pain, but it didn't.
>
> *—Glory*

> I had a little black-and-white photograph of my daughter, and on the front of the little folder it said "First Picture of Life," and it had little gold stars and little angels on it. I would only allow myself to look at the photograph on her birthday every year. I would take it out and it would take me quite a while before I could even open the little cover, so I knew the cover with the little stars very well. I would study that cover and try to compose myself enough to look at the picture.

You go on with your life but you know out there in the world is a piece of you floating around. I'm not a religious person, but I would pray to trees or stars, or the moon, or whoever is in control, to please make her safe.

—Pamela I

Women often experienced extreme sadness on the anniversary of their baby's birth. The birth of subsequent children was also a powerful reminder, triggering not only memories of the earlier birth but also fears that this new baby might also be taken from them.

For a while I was abusing alcohol, especially during the month of June, because my daughter was born in June and I couldn't face any part of that month. I would cry most of the month and feel miserable. My youngest daughter had no idea what bad, bad thing happened to me in June, but she knew that June was the month you couldn't talk to me. When she got a little older, I told her about her sister and she understood. Out of all of my kids, my youngest girl is very, very sensitive to other people's feelings.

—Bonnie

I always wondered where my little girl was, if she was being fed and loved and held and cuddled. Every birthday I would say to myself, "Happy birthday, Kelly Maureen. Mommy loves you." My calendars were always marked in really, really tiny print. I always thought that maybe when she turned eighteen she might want to find her mother. Or maybe when she was twenty-one or twenty-five. Those were the years I figured. Nothing happened, but you never stop thinking.

I remember after she turned eighteen I started going through the brides' section in the newspaper every Sunday. She could have been anywhere in the world, but I'm checking every Sunday. Eight years, I'm looking in the newspaper for anyone that looks like me. Anybody that happened to have the name Kelly—because I didn't know they changed the name—and every blonde, I've got to read the whole thing and check it out with a magnifying glass. That's just what I did on Sundays.

—Karen II

I wanted more children so bad. I got pregnant and that's when it all started coming back to me. That's when everything started. That's when I couldn't run away from it anymore. She was due almost the exact same time of the year that my first one was born. It was, like, I had my baby back. I just held on to her. I was in heaven for a month, but then I had to go back to work because my husband didn't have a job. I couldn't handle it. That was the beginning of the end of my marriage. That was the beginning of me becoming aware of what I'd gone through. I had to put her in day care and it was devastating for me. It felt like I had given her up. It felt like I had abandoned her. It was terrible.

I knew nothing. I've never met another birth mom in my life. I still know nothing except that when my baby was three days old they took her away. That's all I know. It's like my blood runs cold when I think about it.

—Suzanne

One of the most common consequences of relinquishment for the women I interviewed was difficulty in forming healthy relationships with men. The low self-esteem, anger, resentment, and lack of trust they felt made it difficult. Some women dated, and some married men who treated them badly. They felt so worthless that they believed they didn't deserve a decent guy. Others married the first man who showed any interest in them because they were eager to normalize their life and, in some cases, have another baby as soon as possible.

I never told my husband about my experience with having a baby and giving him up for adoption. We were married for fourteen years. We had two children—two girls. The only thing that was wrong with the marriage was he drank and it got worse as the years went on. He lost a couple of jobs, cracked up a lot of cars. In the back of my mind I was thinking, "My God, I can't believe I live with this." But also, "Well, this is what I deserve." I'd say to myself, "You know, you're no great shakes. Look at your past." It was always, "Well, this is what I deserve." I mean, how could I even expect to have anything better than this?

—Maureen II

The only other relationship I ever had with anybody that I was serious about turned out to be a bad person. I didn't think I deserved a nice guy. That relationship was my last opportunity to be with somebody that I loved enough to have a child with. So I decided I was never going to have kids and I found a doctor and went in and had a tubal ligation when I was thirty.

You feel different than everybody else. That never went away. I mean, if you're normal, at some point you meet the right guy, your parents plan this big wedding and you have a family. I knew I wasn't going to be able to have a "normal" relationship. Most guys want to have kids at some point. Maybe that gave me permission to do what I did, I don't know. But the men that I was meeting were not appropriate husband material at all. I worked for a halfway house and met real criminals; I dated real criminals. It didn't occur to me that I should be dating a banker or a lawyer or somebody like that. You can't expect anything from a drug addict, so they never disappointed me. All the other men in my life were big disappointments. The semiserious types, who had regular jobs, always disappointed me. Only afterward did I realize that this is a self-esteem issue.

—Diane II

Another profound impact of surrender was evident in the women's subsequent response to babies. There seemed to be no middle ground. Some women had a very strong desire to have another child immediately and were conscious of trying to replace the baby they had lost. Others said they could not stand to be around babies.

I met a young man when I rented a television set. He was working part time as the television-rental person, so we went out. I suppose I would have dated anybody at that point—a frog, a hamster, whatever, anything breathing and warm. We ended up having a very quick romance and marriage. I married this guy after knowing him for four or five months. Looking back, I wanted another baby. That was all it was, that was the focus of my life.

I was married for three years and I told him it wasn't working, that I didn't want to be married anymore, probably because I couldn't get pregnant with him. I had to go find someone else, which I did do in short order. An old high-school boyfriend was home from the army. He was kind and nice. I thought I was madly in love. We met up and lickety-split, we got married. About a month after we were married, I got pregnant.

I was the happiest person in the whole world. It was unbelievable. I savored every little ounce of that pregnancy. I was in absolute heaven. When it came time to have this baby, I was in such heaven that I had no labor pain. My endorphins were so active from my psychological state that I didn't feel a thing. They put that baby on my chest and . . . this is the one that I could keep. The whole thing was ecstasy for me. It was joyous. It was heaven. It was totally, totally, totally wonderful, absolutely, spectacularly wonderful, and filled up that hole inside me a tiny bit, but not completely.

My level of devotion to this baby, I think, sealed the fate of my marriage. I loved my husband, everything was fine, but way down deep inside of me, I needed that baby, I didn't need a husband. He must have sensed that on some level. We were married for eleven years and then he found somebody else. I remember him asking me early on who was more important to me, the baby or him, and of course I said, "The baby." I made some lousy decisions about men, that's for sure. I should have just gone the turkey-baster route—had artificial insemination and gotten my baby that way. And that's the truth.

—Pamela I

Although many women were anxious to get pregnant again, others were decidedly not. For about 30 percent of the women I interviewed, the child they surrendered was their only child. A similar high percentage has been found in other studies of surrendering mothers.[7] Four of the mothers I interviewed resorted to extreme measures to avoid having more babies: they surgically ended their ability to have children before they were in their mid-thirties.

> I couldn't stand to be around children, couldn't stand it. I didn't want to look at babies or be around babies. If my friends had babies, I vanished. It was too painful. It was just too much. I would pooh-pooh it, you know, like it was an undesirable thing to do. That was my self-defense.
>
> After I left my ex-husband, there was a thirteen-year period before I lived with another man and that's the man I'm married to now. During that time, they wanted me to go off birth control, so I had my tubes tied. I couldn't allow myself to have a normal relationship and have a family of my own. So there's a huge thing that is irretrievably gone. I will never have that experience of being a mother. I gave that up when I gave her up.
>
> *—Nancy III*

The women cited a variety of other reasons for not giving birth again, such as early menopause or cervical cancer. Still others did not form the stable relationships that might have increased their chances of parenting. Some women did try to get pregnant again but experienced secondary infertility, which is defined as "the inability to become pregnant, or to carry a pregnancy to term, following the birth of one or more biological children."[8] Secondary infertility is a condition thought to be common among surrendering mothers and it is often mentioned anecdotally as the primary reason that such a high percentage of these mothers never had other children. However, among those I interviewed, unexplained infertility was no more prevalent than the conscious decision to remain childless. Some women did not have other children because they felt they would be dishonoring the baby they relinquished if they raised another child. Of those I interviewed, five who did not give birth to other children either adopted a child or raised a foster child.

> When I was around twenty-nine, I met my first husband. I wanted a family, I think that was the number-one reason I got married. I found out I couldn't have any more children. I went through whatever was available for fertility testing at the time and they could never find a reason. There was nothing medically wrong. I did find out in therapy later that oftentimes that happens as a result of trauma.
>
> —*Kathi*

> After I gave up my baby girl, I don't know how to explain it but it's almost like you go about your business day after day, and you do what you have to do, but your heart is so broken. I never had any other children. I know this isn't going to make sense to a lot of people, but in my mind I *had* my baby and I gave her up. I really wasn't . . . worthy. Maybe it's because I gave her away, I don't know—I just felt I should not have any other children. That's the way I looked at it. I had my chance.
>
> —*Karen II*

Most of the women who did have subsequent children described themselves as overprotective mothers. They worried constantly that something was going to happen to their children. Some of the women talked about the difficulty they had in forming strong attachments because they feared their children would be taken from them or would die. They stayed emotionally distant in order to protect themselves from another loss.

> My three children from my marriage suffered because I didn't allow them to do anything. I kind of broke their spirits because I was so overprotective. I didn't allow them to do so many things, because I was just so sure they would die.
>
> When my first child from my marriage was born, I was terribly afraid. I was a nervous wreck. I was just so uptight . . . just the fear.

I was calling the doctor almost every day. I just *knew* this baby was going to die because God was going to punish me for what I did. As a human being, it is wrong to give your flesh and blood away. I never, ever felt relinquishment was the right thing. So I knew God was going to punish me and he was going to do it with my secondborn. I was a little more relaxed with my third, and then more so with my fourth child. But with all three of the kids I raised I was never really affectionate. I just felt somehow somebody was going to take them from me or something was going to happen to them.

—*Christine*

It did affect my relationship with my subsequent children in this way. When I had the first child that I raised, five years later—I don't know, it's like because you've learned this pattern of keeping yourself distanced it's not so easy to break that pattern. So part of me always held myself away. Part of me always holds some part of myself away in every intimate relationship. I've really had a pretty hard time with intimacy, because it doesn't feel safe. I really have to force myself to be intimate with people I love. I really have to make a conscious decision. It doesn't come naturally.

—*Ann*

Quite a few women reported that they had problems with intimacy in general. Some women felt they were afraid of closeness in all of their personal relationships. A few described going through their entire lives feeling somewhat numb.

For a long time afterward, I was really emotionally closed down. I definitely got a life going, but it took me a long time to do it. I really didn't want to be too involved with anybody. For one thing, it just leaves you too vulnerable and so in a kind of self-protective way I vowed that I would never get in that position again. I would never be that dependent on anybody again for my emotional happiness or for my direction.

I think it was a necessary position to take up and it certainly got me through. But, you know, it also becomes a little dysfunctional after a while. So eventually I did, you know, *need* people. That was hard, to sort of come back to the center again.

—Deborah

I think one way that it's been detrimental to me is that the things I should feel very excited about I can't really feel them. I know I'm excited but I'm not in touch with my feelings. I'm detached from a lot of things that I know I should be closer to. I just can't respond the way I'd like to because, I don't know . . . maybe I feel I was nullified, or just not considered a person. I wasn't considered a person worthy of receiving help to keep her child.

—Carole II

I got my bachelor's degree, I got married, I got a job, we moved, I got a master's degree. I kept going to school and I worked with emotionally disturbed children. It's like I had to work with the hardest kids, put in the most hours, and just keep doing and doing and doing, which is what I did for most of my life. I just kept doing, but something was missing.

There was a whole part of me, the emotional, compassionate part of me, that was just simply dead. I lacked a real, deep ability to feel and have compassion for people. I just couldn't. I had closed it off entirely. It was easy to be compassionate with strangers. It doesn't require the ongoing, deep intimacy. Especially if it's a stranger you do something for once and walk away. But an ongoing kind of compassion and intimacy, that's the kind I would close out, because it could hurt. There was nothing I could do except blame myself for not being a good enough person. Something was wrong with me. And that's how it went for thirty years.

—Glory

Many women became very successful in their careers but in retrospect felt that their drive to overachieve was an attempt to keep themselves too busy to think deeply. Others felt they needed to excel in order to prove to their family, or to themselves, that they were not the failures they had been made to feel they were.

> I did go on, but I kind of went on by myself. There's always this kind of depression, this sadness, but I never addressed it. I never paid much attention to it. I was always able to just be pretty functional, in fact, overly functional. I would be overly busy and I would juggle. I didn't just want to go to school, I wanted to go to Cal Poly. I didn't just want to get a degree, I wanted to get an engineering degree. I started running, I had to run marathons. It was, like, "Look at me. I'm really good. I'm spectacular. I can do this. I can do this. I can do this. There's nothing wrong with me." I was just out to prove that constantly, over and over and over again and I still do that.
>
> *—Suzanne*

Some women thought they had coped fairly well, but they developed recurring dreams or physical ailments that could not be suppressed. In some cases, they did not connect their symptoms to their surrender experience until they were reunited with their child years later and the symptoms disappeared.

> I developed a nightmare that stayed with me until I found her. The dream is: I'm at the hospital on the freight elevator. I'm trying to find her. I'm going up and down the floors. I get off but there's nothing there—no people, no nothing—so I get back on. Over and over, I'm trying to find her. Up and down and never any relief, just searching and frantic, always frantic. That dream went on for years. I found her when she was twenty-two, and we met when she was twenty-five. The dream started subsiding somewhere in that time period.
>
> *—Barbara*

> About a year and a half ago, I started having this dream about a baby in a grave, and I don't dream, or if I do I don't remember. I could see this coffin. It was just this little white box and I'm standing looking

down and I just got this haunting feeling. And at that point I didn't think about the child that I had so many years ago. But I knew something was bothering me. I decided to go into therapy, which kind of surprised me. But I just didn't understand why I'd been having this dream, and this sense of just missing something.

—*Sheila*

I gave my baby up when I was seventeen. When I was eighteen, I had my first migraine headache. I had them steadily until reunion. I ended up in the hospital on IVs because I had had a migraine for three months straight that would not go away. I've been in reunion for three and a half years now, and I cannot remember the last time I had a migraine. I think it was from holding everything in, you know, it all has to go somewhere.

—*Connie III*

Some of the women I interviewed turned to therapists for help with their relationship problems or intimacy issues, or for answers to unexplained physical ailments. Unfortunately, they did not always receive the help they needed. Many professionals were unaware that these symptoms were characteristic of women who had surrendered a child for adoption. Indeed, since many of the women did not attribute their problems to the loss of their child they did not always reveal their secret to the therapist, nor did the therapist ask.

Despite the fact that numerous small studies in the fields of clinical social work, nursing, family studies, psychology, and psychiatry carried out in the United States[9] and much larger studies completed in Australia[10] concur that "relinquishing mothers are at risk for long-term physical, psychological, and social repercussions,"[11] and even though millions of women have surrendered, there is still no widely accepted therapeutic model for counseling mothers who have lost their children to adoption.[12] Many women are still not able to find adequate therapy. In one study, 50 percent of the mothers participating reported ongoing pain and suffering as a result of their loss.[13] If this percentage holds true for the entire population of relinquishing mothers, millions of women today may be experiencing long-term problems resulting from their relinquishment, a great many undiagnosed and untreated.[14]

Some women spent years self-medicating with alcohol, drugs, or food, or years medicated by psychiatrists, before they found a knowledgeable therapist or learned through a support group that their symptoms were consistent with those of other women who had surrendered. Relinquishing mothers are not the only members of the adoption triad—comprised of the surrendering parents, adoptees, and adoptive parents—who seek counseling for adoption-related issues. Yet in one survey only 27 percent of practicing clinical psychologists felt either "well prepared" or "very well prepared" to work with adoption issues, even though 8 percent of their patients were triad members.[15] About half of these professionals had no graduate coursework that included adoption content. A similar absence of adoption research and study has been found in the fields of sociology and anthropology,[16] and in studies of marriage and the family.[17]

> I've been in therapy twice a week for six years. It took about three years to figure it out. He was trying to treat the symptoms: depression, trouble with relationships, a little bit of perfectionism, over-achiever, wrapped up in my kids' lives, and then this isolation. I said, "Don't you get it? It's not about not being able to have relationships or friends." I said, "It's about being a mother and giving birth and falling in love and then they take your baby away. And it's supposed to be okay. It's supposed to be a good thing. I lost my firstborn. But she didn't die and I didn't get to grieve."
>
> He said, "But you did the best thing for her." I said, "I abandoned my child! How could I be happy? I abandoned my child! Who wouldn't be depressed? Inability to have relationships? Well, who the hell am I going to trust?" So, yeah, we figured it out, and we work on it.
>
> *—Suzanne*

> I've tried therapy off and on for years. One time I was on so many different medications for picking me up, for relaxing me, that it was just unbelievable. That was prior to my finding my son and prior to the cancer. When I was diagnosed with cancer the first time, I told a nurse practitioner about my relinquishment and she

made a referral to a couple of therapists. I saw one but I remember not bonding with him well enough to talk about the adoption. His thing was just to medicate me. The nurse told me I needed to talk about it and she encouraged me to get in touch with the person I felt closest to and just talk to them about it. I thought I'd call my grandmother and talk to her, but I just couldn't do it. So I never really dealt with it.

—Carole II

My voice problem started when I entered the maternity home. I started getting a slight hitch, and it progressively got worse over the years. When I went to school at UCLA a year later, I finally went to a neurologist. I've been to many doctors over the years but this doctor pretty much hit it right on the head. It's been a waste thereafter. He said, "You've got a nervous tic and it happens to show up in your voice." He said, "When did this start?" And I could not get the words out. It took about five minutes. I'd open up my mouth to say . . . it's happening right now, I can't get the words out of my mouth. . . . I cannot say . . . "I had a child out of wedlock. I am an unwed mother."

Over the years, I went to voice specialists, ear, nose, and throat doctors. I also went to this famous speech therapist—two hundred dollars an hour—and he said, "When did your speech problems start?" I couldn't get the words out, just like earlier. Finally, I said, "At the home for unwed mothers." And he looked at me and said, "Do you think you're the only person who gave up a baby for adoption? Why are you taking it so hard?"

Then I went to a psychiatrist and he didn't know how to help me, either. He listened to the story and he comes up with the idea that I should pretend the baby was born dead and put it behind me that way. I said, "I don't think so, Doctor. I don't think so." I went on antidepressants at that point.

You know, years later when I was teaching school a little girl came up to me and said, "Mrs.—, when you talk it sounds like you're crying." And I think that's it. I've been crying all these years through my voice, because I didn't cry and deal with it then.

—Sheryl

In the 1970s, support groups for mothers and for adoptees began to proliferate. The first groups were sponsored by adoptees' rights organizations, such as the Adoptees' Liberty Movement Association (ALMA),[18] which was founded by adoptee Florence Fisher in 1971. Soon after, in 1976, Concerned United Birthparents (CUB)[19] was founded by surrendering mother Lee Cambell. Both ALMA and CUB continue to thrive and link members through either in-person support groups or the Internet. Many of the mothers I interviewed felt alienated and alone until they were able to communicate with other mothers through ALMA, CUB, or one of the many other support groups such as SunflowerFirstMoms,[20] OriginsUSA,[21] and Empty Arms—an online support group for mothers who surrendered and had no other children[22]—or one of the hundreds of other groups available. The Internet has become one of the best conduits for communication among mothers, because it has allowed women to share their grief anonymously and to gradually come out of the "birth mother closet."

I'll never forget the day I saw this flyer that said "Birth Mothers' Group." I was shocked. People talk about this in public? My God in heaven. This was in the mid- or early eighties. There was a phone number. I called the number about three times and hung up because I thought, "I can't utter this horrible word. How can I say this is what I am?" I couldn't get it out. I would have to hang up. Finally, I called and I stuttered and stammered it out, and the woman very nonchalantly said, "Yeah, they meet every month upstairs."

I remember going and peering into the room. I thought, "What are these women going to look like?" I looked at them. They were all sitting in a circle with their eyes closed and I left. But the next time I came and I sat. It was a beautiful group of women. We would just talk about day-to-day things. Diane would talk about how she couldn't be in a room with a baby. Marie would talk about how she was always so afraid to let her daughter go to school. We talked about the physical things, the emotional things, just everything. That was the real, true beginning of my healing process.

When my son was twenty-seven, my birth mothers' group celebrated his birthday because I had never done that. We had a cake and we weren't supposed to have alcohol in the Women's Center but I smuggled in champagne. We had this great celebration and when I came home I had this enormous bleeding, like a period, but I wasn't due. It was like this afterbirth coming out. I had to go to bed. It was the strangest experience.

—Diane IV

In April of 1983, I saw a notice in our local paper: "Adoptees and Birth Parents in Search." They were having a meeting at the library. So I called and made arrangements to go to this meeting. When I walked in, it was like I had come home. They had told us, "You'll forget, you'll get over this, you'll go on with your life." And for years when it would resurface I would think, "There's something wrong with me, they said I would forget." When I went to this meeting it was like . . . these were people who *knew*. They had been where I had been, they felt what I had felt.

—Pollie

The relinquishing mothers I interviewed who attended these group meetings or met other mothers through chat rooms on the Internet learned that the grief they felt over the loss of their child was not abnormal but was consistent with the grief felt by many others. Their realization was bittersweet. On the one hand, they learned that they were not alone and that they were not crazy because they could not "get over" the loss of their child. But on the other hand they realized that, despite the enormous number of people affected, few outside of this community knew of their experiences. It appeared that no one, other than those who had experienced relinquishment, cared.

Giving up my son was a seminal moment in my life. People will say, "Get over it." I can't tell you how many people say, "Aren't you ever going to get over it?" Never. You never get over this. Men often go to the military and fight in wars and they never really get over what they see. This is like one of those huge tragedies in your life. That's how I look at it, as a tragedy. It's a tragedy because it didn't have to happen.

They said, "You can't raise the baby alone." But no one expects a widow to give up her baby because her husband dies, do they? No. It's punitive. That's it in a nutshell. You don't deserve the baby. I think that parents whose children get into trouble should be the village for their family. It's as simple as that. When you've experienced this, you realize that every social problem is like this. People don't see themselves in the other person. I think this experience does make you much more aware. It comes from having other people not empathize with you. You understand what it is to be marginalized.

—Maggie

SUSAN III

I thought I might be pregnant. My period was late. So I called the doctor and made an appointment. I was very nervous. I was appalled when the nurse told me I had to get naked. I said, "Doesn't he only need to examine my bottom half?"

I figured I had plenty of time to tell my mother, that my boyfriend and I would have time to make a plan. I had been going out with my boyfriend for a couple of years. We met when we were freshmen in high school. On my sixteenth birthday, he gave me a beautiful pearl ring and asked me if I would marry him after we graduated. I was crazy mad in love with him. I knew he loved me, so I wasn't too worried.

The next morning when he picked me up for school, I told him I was pregnant and he said, "Now what are we gonna do?" I said, "We'll get married." He didn't say much. We never talked about it a whole lot. Later he said, "Where are we gonna live?" And I said, "Well, we'll figure that all out. I'm sure our parents will help us." His parents were wonderful people. My parents were wonderful people. I couldn't see that they wouldn't wanna help us.

A few weeks later, my mother was sitting on the chair by the telephone and she said to me, "Come sit on my lap," which wasn't uncommon for us. I sat on her lap, I put my arms around her neck, and she said, "Are you pregnant?" I said, "No, of course I'm not pregnant!" She said, "Susan, I checked your napkin; it wasn't soiled." I had been pretending to have my period and I would wrap up a pad and put it in the wastepaper basket in the bathroom. But the gig was up. I said, "I'm so sorry. I really hoped that we would have all this figured out by the time we told you and Daddy."

So that night Daddy came home and he said, "Don't worry, honey, this happens to a lot of people." He said, "You two will be married and you'll live here with us." The next morning when my boyfriend picked me up for school I told him that my father knew and that he understood. He was not angry with us, and that we can be married and live with them.

That following weekend, my mother invited his mom to come to our house to have a little powwow. He just kept looking down; he couldn't look me in the face. Finally he said, "Susan, I love you, but I'm not gonna marry you. I can't do this. I cannot live with your father. He's a cop. I couldn't live with his rules." Later, my parents made me tell him I had miscarried. I think my father's biggest fear at that point was that he'd change his mind and come looking for me.

Mom started making me new clothes to hide my weight gain. There was a new fashion called a tent dress, which was very convenient for me at the time, and that's what I wore to school. I don't know how many kids fell for the miscarriage. I worried that everyone knew I was pregnant and hiding it. I joined in nothing after school, none of the activities. I went to school and home. I couldn't wait for school to end. It was such a stressful thing, especially during the months I had morning sickness. Mom used to pack me saltines so that if I started to feel nauseous I could sneak one during class. I stayed at home until July 8. Then I was sent to St. Mary's home for unwed mothers.

I woke up in labor on September 16. Sister walked me over to St. Margaret's Hospital and placed me in the care of a nurse and I never saw her again. She didn't touch me—there was no compassion, no feeling. And, boy, did I need some compassion at that point. I was so afraid. As much as they gave us medical care, they didn't give us much emotional support, or even knowledge as to what labor and delivery was gonna be like.

The nurse who took care of me for the first few hours was an older woman and she was very distant. When they came to prep me, I had no idea that they were gonna shave me. I was, like, "You're gonna shave me where?" I was appalled. I was so embarrassed. As I lay in the room by myself, I began to cry and I don't know why I cried. I probably cried for more reasons than I could even absorb at the time. I was afraid of what was happening to my body and I was afraid that this was the end of my pregnancy and that I wasn't gonna be with my baby anymore.

After my daughter was born and they wrapped her up a bit, they kinda held her close enough that I'd get a good look at her, but not close enough that I could have reached out. She was so beautiful. The next thing I needed after seeing my daughter was to hear the sound of my mother's voice. I asked the nurse if I could call home. She wheeled me out in the hall and dialed the number. When my mother answered, I could tell I'd woken her up. It was two o'clock in the morning. All I could say to her was "I can come home now." She started to cry and, of course, I cried along with her and I told her a little bit about my delivery and my baby. And she promised she'd come up and see me in the morning.

I don't even remember my mother coming that first morning. I have no recollection of her being there. All I remember is when the nurse brought Madeline to me. I put her in my lap and I undressed her and checked her from head to toe. She was so soft! I was amazed by the sight of her. Once the nurse left, I pushed aside my nightgown and I laid Madeline against me and I covered us over with a sheet. I just wanted to make the most of every minute I had. I just remember how soft and smooth her skin was and her hair was tickling my chin. When the nurse came back, she brought cotton balls and warm water and we bathed her. I remember laughing. It was the happiest day I'd had in the twelve weeks I was away, that morning I spent with the nurse learning to care for Madeline.

We did that every day for eight days. On the last day, I fed her and rocked her and bathed her, and I made a promise to her that I would find her when she turned twenty-one. My father always said that I was very determined and I guess I proved it to myself then, because I knew I would find her. I knew that someday we would meet again.

When we left St. Mary's that day, I knew my life had been changed forever. I wasn't the same fun girl I had been. Going back to high school was very hard. I was very distracted. My grades suffered. I couldn't concentrate on the things my friends were saying or the things going on around me. Most of the talk seemed so trivial to me. I thought about Madeline constantly. I was trying to be so brave for my parents and I was trying to keep up the façade. Everyone told me I should feel fine and that I should go back to school and be a teenager and go to football games and parties and it just hit me that I'd never be the same. I would never be like the other girls.

Two days after I returned home, I went back to see the priest to sign the final relinquishment papers. My aunt went with me. We went to the priest's office and he was very nonchalant, very cavalier about the whole thing. You know, "Oh, how are you doing? How's school?" I said, "Well, I haven't returned yet, you know." "Oh, feeling good? You look wonderful, you'll be back with your friends, things will be good." "Yes, Father. Yes, Father."

He hands me a sheet of paper. None of the blank lines were filled in with my name, or with Madeline Jean's name, or the date of birth, nothing. It was completely blank. He pointed to a line and said, "Sign here." My aunt signed as a witness. I mean, I was only seventeen and I knew that was wrong. I knew those lines should have been filled in. I said, "Shouldn't this be filled in?" It was just a standard form with "said child . . . said child . . ." I remember feeling so hurt. My baby has a name. My daughter has a name. Her name is Madeline Jean.

But my feelings weren't any of their concern. Their business was to get my signature on that line. And that's how I signed my baby away, on a blank sheet of paper. The social worker sent me those papers after I found Madeline. She photostated everything and that paper was there. It was exactly as I had remembered it—my name on a blank sheet of paper, not the least bit legal.

I made up my mind that I would find a boy that my father and mother approved of and I would marry him and have his babies. That was my new mission. By Thanksgiving, I had found that boy. I knew exactly who I was going after. There was this boy that I had become friends with as a sophomore. He and I could talk about anything. He was on the football team; he was a starting player. He was tall, dark, and very handsome—the greatest guy ever. And I was gonna marry him. We spent the rest of our senior year together. He was wonderful to me. He treated me like the lady I pretended to be. I always felt bad that I didn't tell him what I had just been through. I let him believe that I was your normal, average teenager, that I was a good girl.

We went to the senior prom together. I loved being with him. He made me feel the way I thought I should feel. I didn't love him, not even in the slightest. I still loved the father of my baby. After we graduated from high school, my new boyfriend asked me to marry him and I said yes, even though I knew I didn't love him. I didn't know if I could ever grow to love him, but I hoped I could.

My reasoning was: Now that we're engaged, I'll fall in love with him.

Well, that never happened. Our wedding was planned. We were married the following September, in 1970. And as the wedding date neared I thought, "I'll fall in love with him once we are married." I wasn't gonna turn back. I was gonna be married because he was gonna give me the babies I wanted so much. I figured once I had his baby I will love him. I will fall in love with him then. We had two children. We had our first girl in 1973 and our second in 1976. I still didn't fall in love with him.

I refused to go to work. There was no way, not any chance, I would ever leave my children in day care or with anyone else. In 1978, when my second daughter was two, the indifference that I felt toward my husband was wearing on me. It's very difficult to have to get into bed with a man you don't love. I felt I wasn't being fair to myself and, more importantly, to him. I felt that he needed a wife who could love him and give him all the wonderful things he gave me that I couldn't give back. I had reached a point in my life where I didn't like myself for pretending. It seemed my whole life I pretended. I pretended I didn't have a child. I pretended I loved this man. My daughters were the only true happiness in my life.

I finally told my husband in October of 1978 how I felt. I came clean. He was crushed. All he kept saying to me was "This whole thing has been a lie?" And I couldn't even help him by saying it wasn't, because it was. The day that he moved out, I went upstairs to tell my parents; we owned a two-family home with them. At that point in my life, I had become such a good actress that even my parents, who lived in the same house as us, didn't know I was unhappy. I was able to hide any emotion I felt to suit my purpose.

My husband left right after New Year's. The relief I felt was beyond words. I felt happy that I didn't have to pretend to this man or pretend to anyone else that I was in love with him. I still loved Madeline's father. I thought about him every day. I thought about Madeline and I thought about her every single day. No matter where I was with the girls, I was looking for Madeline, always searching for a little face that looked like me or my daughters. There were times I'd be caught staring at little girls, like at swimming lessons or Brownies or dancing school and I would notice that their mothers were watching me watching their children. I'd feel so pathetic.

Even though the sister told me that Madeline had been given to a Boston physician and his wife, I never believed her. I always felt in my heart that she had been given to a family in Fall River, which is about fifteen miles from here. I would go to the Fall River Knitting Mills. It was always full of kids and parents shopping for school sweaters. Once I got married, I made that my Christmas pilgrimage. Santa Claus would be there giving out balloons and candy canes. I would go all by myself and sit on those benches and watch the children, looking for a little girl.

Once my husband left, I was broke. I wouldn't accept any money from him. I went on welfare. It helped, but it was still hardly enough. So I got a job working in a nightclub as a cocktail waitress. I would work eight to two on Tuesdays, Thursdays, and Saturdays. And my mother, because she lived upstairs, would watch the girls. There was this disc jockey there that I was very attracted to. I had probably gone out with him for two months when I knew how strongly I felt, how much I loved him. It had been fourteen or fifteen years and I finally wasn't thinking of Madeline's father. I thought, "Before I get any more involved with this guy, he has to know about my daughter." So I told him the story of Madeline. And he looked at me and said, "Well, if she's your daughter why wouldn't I love her, too?" We were married in 1982. My daughters were my bridesmaids. They were six and eight. I still hadn't told the girls about Madeline and I knew I had to.

Every time I thought about it, it made me sick. I've been quite ill for most of my life from the time of my relinquishment: pneumonia, urinary-tract infections, migraines, nightmares, depression, anxiety. But it was never so bad as it was after I had my fourth daughter in 1984. I was thirty-three and the pain and longing for Madeline just came rushing back at me after having that last child. I got sick with pneumonia shortly after her birth. I thought my depression might be due to my feeling so lousy all the time. My pneumonia lasted for about sixteen weeks. I was in and out of the hospital. They didn't know what was wrong with me because I didn't have a temperature. I had lung biopsies. My pulmonologist was absolutely baffled. He even wrote up my case for a medical-association meeting. He sent me to Boston and the doctors there couldn't find anything wrong with me, either. Years later, I received a post from one of my birth-mother groups that explained post-traumatic stress. I had all the classic symptoms.

Madeline's twenty-first birthday was coming up and my first daughter from my marriage was gonna be sixteen. I knew that when she turned sixteen

I would tell her about Madeline. She was very mature and wise for her age. I knew she'd have some good advice as to how I should tell her younger sisters, who were fourteen and five, about their sister. I couldn't wait for the day to come. Two weeks before her sixteenth birthday, she was diagnosed with leukemia. She died five months later.

My grief was so great. I felt God had punished me for giving my first baby away. I didn't know what to do. The night she died, we drove home and I didn't know how I was gonna get up the next morning. I had lost two daughters. I had two more and I wondered how long it would be before I lost them. I didn't know how I was gonna face the girls and my parents when I got home. I had nothing to say to them. I was totally empty. We pulled into the driveway and it was loaded with cars. My brothers were there. My godparents were there. My cousins were there. And I didn't want to get out of the car because I couldn't face them. When I opened the door and my daughters came running to me, I knew exactly why I was gonna get up in the morning: I was gonna get up for those two girls. I never felt so loved. The contrast between losing this daughter and losing Madeline was so different. Why could my parents and family see that I needed comforting after my daughter's death but not see that I needed it after the relinquishment of Madeline?

My search was put on an indefinite hold. I was emotionally unstable. Again, I received no counseling. I figured I was strong enough. My illnesses became worse: the pneumonia, the urinary-tract infections, the nightmares. The nightmares were the worst part; I call it my running nightmare. I was always running, running—sometimes in the street of the neighborhood where I grew up and sometimes on a beach. Always running after a little girl in a diaper. And I could never catch her because there was a man running after me and he would always catch me before I could catch the little girl. And I would try so hard to hit him and shove him away, but my arms were weighted down and I couldn't raise them. I would try to shout to the child to stop, but when I opened my mouth no sound would come out. This had been happening for twenty-eight years. I had to do something. I had to find this child. It was killing me, emotionally and physically.

At some point, I called Catholic Charities and told the woman there that I needed to contact Madeline because her sister had died of leukemia and I wanted her to know that if she or any of her children ever got sick they would have an entire family of bone-marrow donors available to them. And the reply I got from the social worker was "Do Madeline and your other daughter share the same father?" I said, "No." She said, "Is leukemia hereditary on your side of the family?" And I said, "No." "Then the chances of Madeline's having leukemia are slim." I was very angry. Who made her master of all medical likelihood? What gave her the right to decide that?

I searched the Internet for one year in secret. I searched every day, every adoption list. I registered in every site I could find. I joined the International Soundex Reunion Registry. Then after one year of searching, I knew I had to come out of this birth mother closet and start making some noise or I'd never find my child. First I told my husband and then the girls that I was searching. They were very happy for me. I told my brothers, told my parents, and I didn't receive one negative response. Everyone was happy for me. My parents couldn't believe it because I had always told them I'd never look for her. I didn't want them to think that everything they went through was in vain—all the secrets, sending me away, just for me to find her in the end. I always tried to protect my parents, but they didn't blink an eye. They encouraged me every step of the way. It was such a wonderful feeling to be able to tell people I gave up a child and I am looking for her. I am a birth mother.

I haven't had a migraine since I found her. I did, however, finally seek the counseling that I needed, not only for my relinquishment of her but for my daughter's death. My husband found a very awesome lady to help me. She said before you can grieve your daughter's death properly, you have to grieve the loss of Madeline. I finally feel peace.

My mother and I had never spoken about my relinquishment, even when I was searching and after I found Madeline. It had been a taboo subject. It wasn't until after my dad's death, a couple of years ago, that my mother was able to talk to me about her decision. At first, she tried to tell me she never felt guilty because it was "in my best interest." And all I could say to her was "If you never felt guilty, I'm disappointed in you." Because I could never understand how a kind and caring mother, like my mother, could give away a grandchild and not feel guilty. I think those words made her realize that she wasn't being honest with herself.

Through counseling, I finally realized that my feelings count, because I never thought they did. When you give up a baby, you don't feel you deserve much of anything, let alone happiness. After those conversations with my mother, it was the first time she told me she was sorry she gave my baby away. And she hugged me and told me she loved me. I know she was being honest. I know she really meant it. And the healing that took place within me, with just those two words: "I'm sorry."

Having to give my daughter away made me realize how precious life is and that it can be taken from you and that you're powerless to stop it. I was powerless because I was seventeen and unmarried. Society and my church and my parents felt that was the right decision for me. I had no voice.

I made sure that I spent every day with my girls. When my daughter died, I was so happy that I had spent every day of her sixteen years with her. I cherish those memories. And now that I have Madeline back we are making memories. I can't get back the thirty years I lost with her; they're gone forever. I can either choose to sit and dwell on that or I can just accept that they're gone and enjoy what I have now. And I have a lot.

I've been asked the question What is worse, adoption or death? Before I found Madeline, I thought adoption was worse, because I knew where my second daughter was—she was in heaven—but I still worried about Madeline and where she was. After I found Madeline, I now know death is worse because I'll never see my second daughter again.

The lack of counseling at the home for unwed mothers was a mistake. Many of us have had bad marriages. Many of us married men for the same reason I married mine—just to have a baby we could keep. That's not fair to anyone. It's not fair to the husband. It's not fair to the children. My girls were separated from their father because of me. The consequences are far-reaching. What I did was wrong, but I did it to survive. The only way I knew I could get up again was if I had more children. Little did I know back then that none of them, none of the children I had after, would ever replace Madeline.

MADELINE

I t was 1960 and I had just finished my freshman year of college. I'd gone to the University of Colorado. When I was applying to school my parents gave me the option of either going to William & Mary—which was my grandmother's college, and I could live with her and go to school—or to the University of Colorado, where all the other airline pilots' daughters were going.

Now, you have to understand, I was an extremely naïve young woman. I'd been out on maybe three or four dates. I knew nothing at all about the facts of life. My parents shipped me off to the University of Colorado, which was an unbelievable party school. And suddenly I was very popular.

In June of 1960, I was back on Long Island at my parents' house. I had done all sorts of terrible things, like taken out a charge account and charged five hundred dollars' worth of stuff at a department store. My parents were just furious with me. I was raised very strictly. We said, "Yes, ma'am" and "Yes, sir." We just did everything our parents said. I had never done anything wrong in my life and suddenly I had done all these terrible things.

So I came home and my parents insisted that I take two jobs so that I could pay off this debt that I had run up. I got a job as a waitress and a job as a salesgirl in a department-store type place called J.J. Newberry's. The other thing was, I wasn't getting my period.

I had had sex. Well, I guess you could call it sex. I had gone out on a date with someone I really liked and he was one of the few young men whom I really trusted. He was sort of like one of my brothers. We were necking at his apartment and I guess we had sex. I mean, he sort of pinned me to the floor and I didn't really know what was going on; I really had no idea what was happening. He pinned me down and pretty much raped me. We had necked a few times, then this thing happened. Then the next morning, he told my girlfriend that I was nothing but a slut and I was a bad fuck. I was a bad lay because all I did was lie there. So I guess you're really wonderful until they can stick it in you and then you're just this piece of shit.

I got on the plane and I went home to New York. I didn't really understand about sex and how babies happened and all that business. I was eighteen. I didn't know. My mother never told me the facts of life. My parents were very affectionate. They hugged, they kissed, but she never told us the facts of life. So I had no idea that that's what they did with the penis—that they put it in you and you got pregnant. I didn't know. I mean, it's so embarrassing.

There I was at home. I had these two jobs and I wasn't getting my period. I mean, I was just in this sort of state where I was not paying attention to reality. Then I started to get morning sickness. I would be in this place selling men's underwear and curtains in J.J. Newberry's department store and I would be throwing up. So in the corner of my mind I knew something was very wrong. Then I started reading books about what happened to girls who got in trouble. And I remember being in my parents' house and standing at the top of the cellar stairs. I had pillows wrapped around my legs and arms, because I thought if I threw myself down the stairs I would somehow be able to dislodge this baby. So part of me was accepting the fact that I was pregnant and another part was in total denial.

I went back to school. I was four months pregnant, but I wasn't showing. My roommate noticed that I never used any of my Kotex. So there was this rumor around that I might be in trouble, but I wasn't admitting it. Then lots of rumors started flying around campus about me. Somehow, I was becoming a slut because of these rumors. I was accused of doing things that, even now, I couldn't imagine doing.

I stayed with my parents the last two months that I was pregnant. I stayed in my grandmother's room because my grandmother didn't live there anymore. I just stayed in bed the whole time. Occasionally, my mother would sneak me out in this plaid coat that went almost to the ground and take me for walks at Jones Beach. My father was just enraged. I mean, you have to imagine, my father was like John Wayne. He was an air force colonel, and at that time he was an airline pilot. He's a wonderful man but everything with him was black and white; there was no gray. If you wore curlers in your hair and you go out in the street, you're a whore. So I'm there at home. None of my siblings know. Nobody could know that I'm pregnant.

My mom found this Park Avenue gynecologist where all the nice, Waspy unwed girls go to be taken care of and give their babies away. So I go to see him every couple of weeks. There's no question that as soon as I deliver this baby, this baby is gone. I mean, there's no question about whether I can keep this baby. No way. I mean it's not even considered. It's just, "You have done the worst thing possible and you'd better be quiet." My mom said, "This is the closest your father and I have ever come to having problems; you're killing your father. He's got to requalify on the jets now and he can't handle it because of you." It was horrible. It was really horrible.

Of course, nobody tells me a damn thing about what to expect or what giving birth is like. Nothing, there's no preparation whatsoever. And the night that I went into labor we had the worst snowstorm that had ever happened in the history of New York. My mother has to call 911 and an ambulance comes and of course all the neighbors are looking out their windows. It's her worst nightmare. They carry me out on a stretcher. My mother is making up something about my liver or my kidney or some kind of organ failure or something like that. I was supposed to deliver in New York at this fancy hospital. But instead I'm taken to Mineola Hospital. There's no power. They're on generators and they're very short-staffed. I can't describe it. I mean, still when I think about what it was like . . . they were so cruel to me. I can't tell you how they treated me, those nurses. It was so terrible. They tied me to a bed. They abused me verbally. After I delivered my baby, they left me lying in this bed with bloodstained sheets for a day and a half. I mean still, even talking about it . . . I can't understand how somebody who was supposed to be in a profession where you have compassion, and care about suffering, could do that. It was like I was fair game for them.

So I had my daughter. I remember very clearly the doctor in the delivery room holding her up and saying, "This is the most beautiful baby I've ever seen. She's not going to want to give this baby up," and the nurse just grabbing the baby and wrapping her up so I couldn't see her. I kept asking to see her, and they wouldn't let me until it was time for my mother and father to come and take the baby to the agency. They let me come into the room where they were dressing her. It was the same nurses. They wouldn't let me hold her and they wouldn't let me touch her. I was across one of those metal tables from them and they said, "I bet you'd like to hold this baby, wouldn't

you? This baby doesn't belong to you. This baby is going to a good home."
It was just horrible. It was like a terrible, terrible nightmare.

The only time I got to hold her was when they let me take her out to the
car. I carried her down these steps, concrete steps, with this kind of chrome
railing, down to my parents' car. Then my mother took her and I got into
the backseat. They dropped me off at the house and they took the baby into
the city. I remember the only one I could talk to, and cry to, was our dog.

My mom and dad came back and they never spoke about it. My mom
destroyed the papers from the adoption agency right away, all the papers
having to do with my daughter. She burned everything, supposedly to protect me. It was never spoken about again. I really wanted to talk about it, but
my mom treated it like it was her personal tragedy. I would try to broach the
subject and she would say, "You'll just never know what your father and I
went through. You'll never know. We came very close to separating at that
time. Your father could have had a heart attack so easily." It was always her
tragedy.

My daughter was born on February 4, and I spent that spring studying so
I could go back to take my exams at the University of Colorado. I took my
exams and then I came back and I went to school at Hofstra University,
which was within driving distance. My parents weren't going to let me go
anywhere again.

What I did after that . . . I mean, I'm amazed I'm still alive. It was in the
middle of the whole folk period. Bob Dylan made his first album. The
whole hippie thing was starting. I was supposed to be a poet and an English
teacher; that's what the women in my family did. You taught English for security and you wrote poetry. I was a really good writer but I took this art
class and that was it. I had to lie to my parents. I couldn't tell them I
changed my major to art.

I was going into the city all the time with my art friends, wandering
around the Lower East Side. If anybody wanted to sleep with me, I would
sleep with them. I had no boundaries—no sexual boundaries, no personal
boundaries, nothing. I would just put myself in these incredibly dangerous
situations and it was almost like I wanted to be destroyed. I just wanted it to
be over. I was filled with the most incredible rage that lasted until I was reunited with my daughter. I was fueled by rage all those years. That was a time

when you could channel it into political protests and the women's movement and so many other things. But it was really just this unbelievable rage at what had happened and this feeling of being totally powerless.

I met this guy at school and we wound up married to each other for a year. He was a poet. He got me to see someone who could help me. And it's a good thing he did, because I was really losing it. I mean, I really was very, very disturbed. My parents had no idea that anything was wrong. When my mother found out I was in therapy she was furious at me because I was telling my business to these people.

I think that on a core level I felt so worthless for giving my baby away. I was so beyond redemption that I just deserved nothing. Though I appeared to be very successful, I lived a life of complete lack inside. I couldn't have what regular people had. I could not have a home, for instance. I could not have something like a washing machine, anything that would make my life easier. That wasn't for me. I could not have anything, because I really didn't deserve anything. I never had other children.

When I got married for that one year, everyone started asking me when I was going to have a baby. If I had had a machine gun, I would have just gone out and killed an entire city block full of people. I was so enraged, because that's when it hit me that it was just a social convention. It had nothing to do with anything. Then later, when people like Madonna were having babies and keeping them and it was trendy, it made me so angry because it was just a matter of years. Now it's okay. *Then* it was the worst thing imaginable. I have been very angry for a long, long time. I didn't start out that way as a child. I feel like I lost my soul, in a funny kind of way.

My mom got Alzheimer's toward the end of her life and she died in 1998. Five days after she died, my daughter called me on the phone. I had been looking for her for years. I contacted the agency in New York and they said all of the paperwork from that era had burned. The records were all destroyed in a fire. I had no information, except I knew her birth date, where she had been born, and the name that had been put on her birth certificate. Then I saw something on television about adoption reunions and the Soundex Registry, so I registered.

As it turns out, my daughter had also seen that program on the Soundex Registry and she sent for the paperwork. But she hadn't sent the papers in because she thought she didn't have enough information. She just held on to them and held on to them. Then she said she woke up one morning and said, "I've got to go fill those papers out." She put all the information that she had on the papers and mailed them. I think they called her the day my mom died.

So five days later I was teaching and I came home and I was really, really tired. I came in the door and my husband said, "Sit down. I have some news for you." And I said, "Oh, for Christ's sake, can't you just let me get in the door? I'm so tired." He said, "No. You're really going to want to hear this." And I said, "Look, just give me a chance to take my coat off at least." He said, "Your daughter called." And I felt like I was going to throw up.

I just had all these mixed emotions. I had thought about it for so long, but then when it happened I was just terrified and excited. These two parts of me were coming into collision. The part of me that felt like this horrible slug underneath a rock that didn't deserve to peek up into the sunlight, and the part of me that was just, "Oh boy!" were kind of coming up against each other. He said, "You should call her back." And I said, "I can't. I can't. I just can't call her back." And he said, "You should call her." And I said, "I don't think I can. I don't think I can. Tell me everything she said."

He said she had called and had asked for me and he had said, "She's not home right now. She's teaching a class." And my daughter had said, "What is she teaching?" And my husband said, "She's teaching painting." And he said she got so excited because she had been raised by two scientists. She was this very creative child in a family of scientists. So she was very excited to find out her mother was an artist. Later, she told me she had never heard anybody speak about somebody with as much love as my husband did about me, which was really sweet.

The first time I drove over to meet her, it was really a shock to see how close she had been all those years. We found out that we both used to jog at the same reservoir. And we both took classes at the same college at the same time. I mean, it's just so strange.

I think that there's a thread running through my life that I probably came into this life with, which is the issue of betrayal. That's something that I feel is a big issue for me. I feel like my parents betrayed me, and then I betrayed my daughter by not being strong enough to keep her. So many of the decisions I made in my life involved not betraying her again. I would never have other children because that would be a betrayal of my daughter. Because I betrayed her, I really did not deserve to have too much. I should work very, very hard. I should do a lot of things for other people. I should be this force of compassion and protection, especially for other women. For many years I taught courses for women in creativity, in writing, in meditation, and in visual art. I would nurture other women, especially women who didn't have a voice. I felt a real sense of responsibility to nurture at my own expense, at my own creative expense. I let people take things from me.

I always felt like there was a huge scale and that I could never balance it. I held myself responsible. I had so many mixed feelings. I wanted to keep this baby. I felt powerless to keep this baby. I wanted it to be over. I wanted to go back to being a normal person. I wanted the baby out of my life. I wanted the baby. I didn't want the baby. I think it's that ambivalence that is so hard for people to look at and admit. Most people will say, "Oh, I wanted my baby with all my heart, and they took the baby from me." And they turn themselves into a victim. Anytime you get yourself into a situation like this, you have to see where you are partially responsible for it. It's a two-way thing. I've been in a lot of situations like that. I've been in situations where it seems as though I'm the victim but in reality I'm a part of the equation.

I think a lot of it started with that terrible betrayal that I felt by not wanting my daughter so much that I would have done *anything* to keep her—like run away, run out of the hospital, take the baby. It's like I *let* them take her. I let those nurses take her. I let my parents drive away with her. I let them do it, because part of me wanted them to take responsibility for making a decision that I couldn't make myself. I think that's where the horrible guilt comes from. It's not so much the act of surrendering, it's the passivity. It's allowing somebody else to take control. And when they take control they are also taking responsibility. You can slide so easily into the victim role and just say, "This terrible thing was done to me."

But the fact is that there is a complicity there that you have to look at. And that's been another theme that runs through my life. It's been really hard for me to face that. That's the hardest thing for me. And, you know, it's a really rough lesson to learn. It's really hard to be very, very honest with yourself and look at yourself and see things that are not so nice. I think that's something that is really important.

I don't see people talking about that. I don't think people want to look at that. I think it's so much easier to just say, "I thought the best thing for my child would be to do this." You know, I'm sorry. I have to say, I respect people who say that, but I find it hard to believe that anybody in that circumstance is so mature that they are thinking of what is best for their child. I think most people are surviving, and that's the thing they're so ashamed of. They're so ashamed that they're thinking of their own survival. The rock-bottom reality is you were thinking of your own survival more than your child's.

Once you realize that, it does something to you. It's like you've been put to a kind of test and you failed. You failed. So you punish yourself for a long time until you can get to a place where you can't go any lower. And there's something very liberating about that, because then you start coming back up out of it. You begin to see who and what you are. And you begin to see the importance of dogma and the importance of acting according to your principles and the importance of doing what you know is right.

I know in my heart I would never betray a trust again. Never. If someone said to me, "Your life will end right this minute and your daughter will be well, she'll be over her myasthenia," I wouldn't even hesitate for a minute. It's not because I'm some great soul or some highly advanced being; it's just that I know what's important now. And I will never compromise again.

In some ways, I wonder what kind of person I would have been if I had never lost my daughter. I would not have been the person I am now. I don't like to see people with power abusing other people. I don't like to see cruelty toward people or animals. I really hate cynicism and academic nastiness and all those little cruelties that people perpetrate on each other. I just have no tolerance for it.

I think this whole experience has made me incredibly strong. But if I had not been reunited with my daughter, I don't think it would have made me strong. I think I would have continued to be very, very, very angry until I died of a heart attack.

After my daughter and I were reunited, she and her husband came to our loft. I showed her pictures of my Abyssinian cat, Gatey, who had died. This cat was so beautiful. And she said, "Oh, I just love these cats. You should get another." And I said, "I'm saving up because I want to get two and they're expensive." So she and my husband, from November through Christmas, were doing all this stuff to locate breeders to get me Abyssinian cats. It comes time for my birthday and she calls and says she's got this present for me, and it's in Newton, a woman there is making it. It's something hand-made and I should go and pick it up. I hung up and I'm thinking, "*Newton, and it's handmade.*" What if she got me something like a Kitchen Witch or something like that, something really horrible. What am I going to do if it's really ugly?

We drive into this development of split-level houses and I'm thinking, "Oh my God, what kind of thing is this woman making?" We come up to the house and I see these two little heads sticking up, and it's cats. And I said to my husband, "Oh my God, look, she's got cats! Look, they're Abyssini-ans. This is so exciting!" So we go in and she says, "I'm finishing your pres-ent upstairs." And I said, "You just take your time. I'll play with your cats." There are all these Abyssinian cats and I'm so excited I'm playing with them, and my husband looks at me, like, "What's wrong with you?" And I'm just so happy hoping she's going to take her time making her Kitchen Witch up-stairs and I can play with her cats.

Then the phone rings and it's my daughter calling from L.A. and she says, "How do you like your present?" And I said, "Well, she's upstairs fin-ishing it right now, so I haven't seen it yet." She says, "Don't you *see* your present?" And I said, "Well, it's handmade, isn't it?" She said, "Yes. It's made by God." And then I got it. She said, "It's cats, two cats." She couldn't be-lieve that I would go there and be sitting there with these cats all over me and not think that she had gotten them for me.

She asked me about it later. She said, "How could you not know that they were for you?" And I said, "Listen, you know, I've gotten to the point in my life that when I see something that I really long for, I know it's not for me." That's when I realized what losing her had done. My expectation was . . . that what I wanted was going to be held up in front of me and I was going to look at it but I could never have it. Just like the nurses holding her up. That's what it does.

9

Search and Reunion

When I found my daughter and we started our relationship, I finally forgave that seventeen-year-old girl. It was a mending. I finally started doing things the way I had done them before. I regained the peacefulness that I used to have. I hadn't been able to stop the turmoil in me or outside of me. Then all of a sudden it was like . . . "It's okay, you don't deserve to be punished. You're not a screw-up." It was an amazing moment for me to feel like I got put back together. And that has helped my relationship with my children and with everybody from that point on. My husband and I have an amazing relationship now. I accept things. I make decisions. I have comfort with things. I'm my own person again.

—*Barbara*

OF THE WOMEN I INTERVIEWED, more than half have had contact with the child they surrendered for adoption. This percentage is no doubt higher than for the general population of relinquishing mothers because in many cases it was the reunion that brought women out of the closet. Mothers who are out are naturally more willing to tell their stories than those who are still keeping their secret. Of the mothers represented here who have been reunited, most all expressed great relief at knowing their child. They felt the reunion was the beginning of their healing process. However, a reunion is an emotionally complex process that is often fraught with anxieties for the many parties involved: the surrendering mother and father; their parents;

their subsequent spouses and children; the adoptee, his or her spouse and subsequent children; and their adoptive parents.

Many of the mothers I interviewed had not searched for but, rather, were found by their surrendered child. If an adoptee is able to obtain a copy of the original birth certificate the search can be relatively simple, but access to this document varies widely from state to state. In the 1930s, states began issuing revised birth certificates when adoptions were finalized. These amended birth certificates list the adoptive parents as the mother and father who gave birth to the child. The original birth certificate, with the name of the surrendering mother, is kept on file with the state, and before World War II these original birth certificates were generally available to adoptees and often to both sets of parents. But during the postwar adoption boom, most states sealed the un-amended birth certificates, making them inaccessible to all parties, in part to prevent possible interference from the natural parents.[1] In the process, most states closed the records to adoptees as well. The debate about reopening these sealed records is ongoing and emotionally charged, but the trend is slowly moving toward opening them.

Currently, there are only a few states that allow adoptees born in that state unconditional access to their birth certificate when they reach a partic-ular age, usually eighteen or twenty-one. These states are Alabama, Alaska, Kansas, Oregon, and, as of January 2005, New Hampshire. Eighteen other states allow access under certain conditions, such as adoptions that took place before or after a specific date, or access with permission of the surren-dering parent. The specific conditions vary considerably. In Pennsylvania, for example, records are open to adult adoptees if there is a waiver from the surrendering parent. In Ohio, records are open to adult adoptees if they were born prior to 1964, but not to adoptees born after that date. In Ten-nessee, adult adoptees may obtain a copy of their unamended birth certifi-cate except in the case of rape or incest, where additional conditions apply. The remaining states, about half, require a court order.

Adoptees, mothers, and many adoptive parents have been campaigning to change the laws state by state, as have national organizations. American Adoption Congress (AAC) was formed in 1978 from many smaller organiza-tions and is "committed to achieving changes in attitudes, policies, and legis-lation that will guarantee access to identifying information for all adoptees and their birth and adoptive families."[2] Bastard Nation, an adoptees' rights organization, "advocates for the civil and human rights of adult citizens who were adopted as children." Bastard Nation's Web site has a full list of state disclosure laws and provides updates on pending legislation.[3]

Most states will now provide adoptees with nonidentifying information. Such information may include the age, physical description, race, ethnicity, religion, medical history, and level of education of the surrendering parent or parents. About a third of the states will give surrendering mothers non-identifying information about their child, and some states will even help facilitate a reunion. The laws, services, and location of this information vary considerably, but the National Adoption Clearinghouse provides an online state-by-state listing with details about who may access information, what is available, and which agency or department to contact.[4]

Those who decide to search are generally categorized as either active or passive searchers. Active searchers work at locating the other person, whereas passive searchers generally limit their efforts to trying to make themselves findable. Hundreds of homegrown Internet Web sites have emerged to provide assistance, or space to post information. A quick Google search with the keywords "adoption reunion registry" will result in about 350 hits. It can be difficult to navigate through all of the information. Often those interested in a reunion join a support organization, where they can communicate with others who have conducted successful searches and who may be able to offer advice. Some mothers and adoptees try their hand at searching for a period of time and then turn to professional searchers, who can sometimes locate the missing person in as little as twenty-four hours. In some cases mothers, fathers, siblings, and adoptees pay private detectives or professional searchers considerable fees to locate a missing family member and in other cases "search angels," or volunteer searchers, help for free.[5]

With the trend toward more openness in adoptions, some adoption agencies will now facilitate a reunion between the parties they originally separated. But the willingness of agencies to cooperate in this endeavor varies. Some have systems in place and will, for a fee, conduct a search and serve as intermediaries between the parties involved. Other agencies will accept letters only from mothers, keeping them on file in the event that the adult child contacts the agency seeking information. It is a long-standing practice for agencies to allow mothers to leave a letter in their child's file and for several of the women I interviewed this later proved to be instrumental in their reunions. But this strategy has unfortunately left some mothers with a false sense of security, as in the case below.

> In 1974, I wrote a letter to the agency and I said, "I want this letter put in my son's file so when he's twenty-one, or whatever the age is, if he wants to find me . . . here's where I am." Here's my name, my Social Security number, and I gave them the name and address of relatives that I knew would never move. He went to the agency when he was twenty-one and the letter was not there. They never put it in there, or they chose not to give it to him. If they had given him that letter, I would have known him ten years before.
>
> —*Cathy II*

Those who conduct passive searches signal an interest in being found by signing up with one of the voluntary mutual-consent registries, in addition to leaving contact information with the agency that facilitated the adoption if it still exists. Mutual-consent registries allow mothers, fathers, adoptees, and in some cases siblings, to register. Often all that is needed is the sex of the child, the birth date, place of birth, and the name of the city where the adoption took place. If all known statistics match, the parties looking for each other are contacted to determine whether a match has been made. There are independent voluntary mutual-consent registries and state-sponsored registries. A 1998 survey indicated that twenty-one states operated voluntary mutual-consent registries, though some had made very few matches, perhaps because many adoptees and parents who are interested in reunions still don't know that the registries exist.[6]

Perhaps the most well-known and successful mutual-consent registries thus far have been independent registries started by those with a vested interest. Jean Paton, an adoptee and a social worker, is credited with originating the first registry and beginning the adoptees' rights movement in 1949. Her adoptee search organization, Orphan Voyage, and her 1954 book *The Adopted Break Silence* were firsts of their kind.[7] But it was not until the early 1970s that the registry movement in the United States took a firm hold, when Florence Fisher founded the ALMA registry. Today, the ALMA Society has a nationwide network of support groups and continues to facilitate reunions through its registry database.[8] The other widely used registry is the International Soundex Reunion Registry, more commonly called Soundex. It is a free registry that was founded in 1975 by Emma May Vilardi, the daughter of an adoptee. The current director, Marri Rillera, who is both an adoptee and a surrendering mother, estimates that the registry has between 200,000 and 250,000 active registrants at any given time. Approximately 60 percent of those who have registered are adoptees, adoptive parents, or otherwise related by adoption; 40 percent are members of surrendering families, including mothers or fathers, half- or full-blooded siblings, aunts, uncles, or grandparents.[9]

Although registries are an important part of the search process, mutual-consent registries depend on both parties knowing that the registry exists, taking the step to register, updating contact information, and being in possession of enough information to make a match possible. Both parties seeking contact must also, of course, be aware of the adoption—which many siblings, fathers, and even some adoptees are not—and, equally evident, both must be living.

Mothers embarking on a search generally have the same fear that searching adoptees have—the fear that the person they are in search of may not want to be found. The majority of the women I interviewed who had not actively searched said that they desired contact but felt they did not have the right to interfere in their son's or daughter's life. Many of these women had, nevertheless, registered and were trying to make themselves findable should their adult child decide to look for them.

> I don't think it's my role to look for her. I mean, I feel like I had my play and I played it and now it's her turn to make a decision that she can live with, if you know what I mean. It's not my privilege to say, "You need to know about me."
>
> I am waiting and hoping she will come and find me. I've tried to make myself findable. This unwed mothers' home has turned into yet another form of social-service agency and I keep updating

my file and saying, "Here's my cell number, here's my fax," and asking, "Has anybody come around, do you know anything?" "No, no. No activity on your file." So that's depressing. I really, really want to know that she's okay.

—Deborah

Women also worried that bringing a surrendered child back into their life might adversely affect their relationship with their husband or their subsequent children. Among the women I interviewed, only a few families had experienced difficulties with subsequent children who were not pleased with the news. The vast majority of the women had families that were accepting and children who were often eager to meet their newly discovered sibling. Some of the women recounted the healing effect of being able to introduce their surrendered child to their own mothers, who had pushed for relinquishment all those years earlier.

> From the time she was eighteen, my daughter had been looking for me. By the time she found me, my mother was very sick. She had lucid days, but most of the time she was in la-la land. My daughter and I went to see my mother in the hospital, because I wanted to tell her my daughter was back and she was going to be a part of my life. I wanted her to be a part of my mother's life, too. This particular day, my mother was lucid. She took a look at my daughter and started to cry. I said, "You know who this is, right?" And she said, "Yea. Yea. Oh, Bonnie, I'm so sorry." And I think when she told me she was sorry I let go of all the resentment I had felt for so many years. I was so glad that my daughter got to meet her before she passed.
>
> *—Bonnie*

First-person accounts of mothers who do not desire contact with the child they relinquished are much harder to gather, since these women are more reluctant to tell their story. But the mothers I interviewed who said they would not have searched–but were found by their child and who were initially very fearful of a reunion–described as the primary reason their reluctance to reveal their secret to family members and friends. They feared they might be judged harshly for their past behavior or for not being honest in the years since.

One thing that came through quite clearly in the interviews was that coming clean to family members can be extremely difficult, sometimes traumatic. It is best to have someone to lean on for emotional support, whether it's a close friend, a partner, or a support group made up of people who are familiar with the emotional ups and downs of reunions.

I came home from work one day and there was a slip in the mailbox that said I had certified mail at the post office. I knew that it was something from Catholic Charities about my daughter. I just knew it, because there would be no other reason to have certified mail coming here. The next day I went to the post office, and it was a letter from the social worker. She told me that my daughter wanted to meet me.

I was scared to death after all these years. My husband knew, but it was just never spoken about. First I tell Catholic Charities, "I can't have you open the records. I just can't do it after all these years." How can I all of a sudden have a twenty-five-year-old daughter? None of my aunts and uncles or friends or neighbors know. I'm scared to death because this has been a big secret all these years. In that era it was a shameful, dirty, nasty thing, and nobody talked about it.

I asked the social worker if I could write my daughter a letter through them, because I didn't want to give my address. So we did that for a while. I would send a letter to Catholic Charities and they would forward it to my daughter.

Even though my husband is a wonderful person and my best friend, I'm afraid to say anything to him about this. My daughter and I write back and forth; I send her a picture and she sends me a picture. She's a grown woman with children of her own, but in my mind I see the baby in the pink blanket.

For one year, I didn't say anything to my husband about the letter that came. Then one Saturday I went to church and I just lost it. I started crying and I cried all the way home. By the time I opened the door to the house, I was shaking like a leaf, tears were streaming down, and my face was all red. I couldn't stop the tears. I said to my husband, "I have to tell you something." After a year, I just couldn't keep this secret anymore. I mean, a thirty-year secret was enough. Now I have a one-year secret, too.

I told my husband that my daughter had found me and she wants to meet me. After I got that out, it was like the Hoover Dam burst. I was hysterical. I couldn't stop crying or shaking. I told him that he has no idea how hard it's been, because once I saw her in the hospital I didn't want to give her up.

By now he's dealing with a complete lunatic. I'm crying, sobbing hysterically, shaking. He didn't know what to do with me. I think he thought I was on the verge of a breakdown. I said, "I already told her that I can't all of a sudden have a grown daughter in my life. I just can't do that." He said, "You have to meet her and you have to let her be a part of your life if she wants to be. Why should you be without her now when you've already had to be without her for thirty years?" He said, "Things are different now. You're not a teenager who has to do what she's told. Don't worry about what anybody says. Who really cares?" He said, "Call whoever it is you have to call, your aunts, everybody, and tell them that you had a baby that you gave up for adoption and you're going to be reunited. If they can't deal with that, it's their problem."

I was so afraid, I probably wouldn't have done it if it wasn't for my husband. I still had in my head that it was very shameful, that I would be disrespecting my parents by telling my big secret thirty years later. So I wrote my daughter a letter. I wrote, "I have told my husband, we talked about it, and I want to meet you. I want you to meet my family, your aunt and uncle, your cousins, and I can't wait to see my grandchildren."

We knew we couldn't meet at a restaurant or any place where there would be people, because we would both be hysterical and crying. So we met in a parking lot. We hugged, we cried, we blew our noses, we held hands and then we cried some more. When I was able to drive the car without wrapping us both around a pole, we came to my house, sat on the couch, held hands, and cried some more. From the first day that we got together, it was like she belonged in this house. I never felt awkward or uncomfortable with her.

After I came home from the hospital, I said a prayer every night. And at the end, I would ask God to take care of my baby. God answered my prayers, because she wound up with the most wonderful parents. Her father was not a doctor, like Catholic Charities told me. It was better. He was a music teacher. All of the children played instruments. They sang in the church choir, there is a piano in the house, violins, everything was music. She has the best family I could have ever hoped for. There was so much love in that house; there was enough love for five children and enough for me and my husband when we walked in the door.

—Karen II

I have three sons and I couldn't see telling them, "You've got a sister *somewhere*." I wanted to wait until I found her. I had shared with my husband, but not with my sons. So I called the three boys in. They were five, fifteen, and eighteen. I was terrified: "What are my boys going to think about me? They're going to think I'm a slut and a whore and everything." I'd been called that. I was just weeping openly; it was all I could do to tell them. After I told them, my oldest grabbed the youngest and he was just jumping up and down and he said, "We've got a sister! We've got a sister!" And the youngest said, "What's a sister?" And the middle one said, "It's like a brother, only it's a girl."

—Pollie

Often mothers not only had to tell immediate family members or subsequent children about the baby who had been relinquished but, at the request of their child, they also had to locate and inform the father. In some cases, they had not had contact for more than thirty years and in a few instances the man never knew of the child's existence.

After the reunion, my daughter wanted information about her father and I had none to give her. I had a yearbook picture of him, which I gave her. This was the most horrific thing I'd had to go through in the reunion. I mean, it was easier to find her than to have to find him. I sat down at my computer and I tried to compose this letter to her father. I said to my husband, "Imagine this is you and you're getting this letter, what do you want to hear?" He said, "I want to hear that you don't expect anything from me, because I don't know if I can give you anything. I certainly don't want to hear anything about financial issues, and I don't want to hear that you need anything from me." So that's the kind of letter I wrote.

I wrote, "You may not remember that much about me but I can tell you that you were the only person that I had sex with for a period of several months and you are the father of my child." I tried to fill him in a little bit about who I was and that she was interested in her family history and did not expect or want anything from him other than information, if he felt that he could give it. I gave him her name and phone number and he contacted her within a few weeks. He's actually been lovely about the whole thing.

He called me one time and said, "I can't begin to tell you how awful I feel that you went through all of that alone." I was just blown away. I said, "Well, it's over and done with and it was my choice. I didn't give you the option to participate at all." You know, at twenty he seemed kind of callous. He was big, good-looking, a good student—he had everything going for him, so he was kind of arrogant. But I think he probably was a much better person than I knew. Either that or his wife, who sounds pretty wonderful, has had a really good influence on him.

—Nancy III

For mothers, the reunion is obviously complicated by the memories surrounding their pregnancy and the treatment they received. They have been living with the fact that they have a child somewhere out in the world. They have wondered what kind of life their child has had and have worried that it did not have the "better life" that was promised. They also fear that their child may hate them for what they did or, worse, that their child is dead. For the women who searched, their need to know what had become of their child ultimately outweighed their fears of bad news or rejection. A few of the mothers I interviewed did, in fact, find very bad news waiting for them at the end of their search.

> The agency located his family and I wrote a letter to them, which was sent through the agency, and I got a letter back with some pictures. He looked just like his father. He even had the same glasses that his father used to wear. I mean, those pictures were like a treasure.
>
> Then within probably a year or so, I got a call from the agency telling me that my son had Duchenne muscular dystrophy. It is a fatal disease—you generally don't live beyond your early twenties. So then there was another whole grief process. He was probably sixteen at this point in time and he was in a wheelchair and on oxygen, but he was still in school. They said that they had approached him to let him know that I was interested in having some contact and that my son had decided he wasn't ready to do that.
>
> Within a year, I got a phone call from the woman that I had been working with at Catholic Charities and she said, "I wanted you to know that your son died." She said it had happened earlier in the week.
>
> *—Susan I*

We finally found the names of my son's parents. I couldn't make the phone call. From searching, we knew he didn't have credit, he didn't have a phone, there was nothing in his name and he was in his mid-twenties, so there was something wrong. I had my best friend make the phone call to his adoptive father. He told her that my son was in the state prison.

It just about broke my heart, especially when his father said, "Ever since he was six years old he wanted his real mother, he'd been asking how to find his real mother." He said he started doing drugs when he was in high school. Well, his birth father had committed suicide when he was twenty-seven because he could not get off drugs. His mother will not speak to me. She thinks I gave him the bad seed.

He's in prison because he committed murder. He and his roommate were up in the mountains with guns and doing some kind of drugs and he shot him. He will be in the state prison until I'm sixty-seven, I think. I got to go visit him five years ago, and he was so apologetic. He said, "I just can't believe you're having to see me in this situation. I am so sorry. I'm so sorry." I said, "We all make mistakes, but the mistake you made was one that I don't know how you're ever going to be forgiven for."

I communicate with him by letters and occasional phone calls. I'm a mother. Mothers just have that bond with their children. I don't know how to describe it. You just can't break that bond, I don't care what your kids do. I guess that's how I was raised.

—Nancy II

There are mothers who do not want to search or be found, but their numbers would seem to be far fewer than those who welcome contact. Some evidence of this can be found in data compiled by states that have recently passed bills granting adoptees access to their original birth certificates. The state of Oregon began giving adoptees access to unamended birth certificates in 2000. The Oregon system allows both mothers and fathers to send in a nonbinding Contact Preference Form indicating whether they would like to be contacted directly, contacted through an intermediary, or not contacted at all by their adult child. A Birth Parent Updated Medical History Form must be filled out by any parent who does not want to be contacted. As of August of 2005, 8,615 birth certificates had been requested by adoptees and 503 parents sent in Contact Preference Forms, 391 indicated that they wanted direct contact, 29 wanted to be contacted through an intermediary, and 83 indicated that they preferred not to be contacted.[10] The New Hampshire system, which was modeled on the one in Oregon, began issuing unamended birth certificates to adoptees in January 2005. Eight months after inception, 717 adoptees had requested their original birth certificates, 51 parents had sent in Contact Preference Forms, with 12 requesting that they not be contacted.[11]

As with mothers, not all adoptees want to search or to be found. Some search because they have a powerful desire to know where they came from or why they were relinquished. They describe a feeling of emptiness and longing that they believe can be filled only by finding their mother, or both parents. Others simply have a natural curiosity about their family of origin—their genealogy and nationality—and a desire to parse out how they have been shaped by nurture and nature. Some are simply in search of medical information.

Often mothers have attempted to pass on updated medical information but, as with most aspects of adoption, there has been no clear or uniform process to facilitate the transfer of this important information. It has been known for some time that many of the most common and deadly diseases, such as heart disease, cancer, and diabetes, are genetic. In 2004, the Surgeon General and the Department of Health and Human Services launched a Family History Initiative to encourage everyone to chart a family-health history. Regrettably, this is not possible for millions of adoptees.[12]

I contacted the woman who is at the agency now. I told her I wanted to pass medical information. She said, "Oh, we have medical information." I said, "You do?" She said, "Yes, we have that your mother and brother wore glasses for reading and your dad wore glasses all the time." I said, "Well, that was true when I was sixteen. Twenty-two years have passed since that time. My mother has developed high blood pressure, heart disease, she had thyroid problems, she was also diabetic." I mean, she had a number of problems. I said, "I cannot leave this world until I let my daughter know the truth. I have to know that she's okay and I have to pass this medical information to her." She said, "We just can't do that. We can't pass medical information. We *have* medical information."

—*Pollie*

I don't think a day went by that I didn't at least think, "I wonder if she's okay? I wonder how she is. I wonder if they take good care of her." When her father was seventeen or eighteen, he was diagnosed with Hodgkin's disease and at that point I worried that there could potentially be something hereditary there. Plus, his father was a brittle diabetic. I knew I had answered a lot of questions, and given them as much information as I had, as far as medical records and stuff like that. But, I mean, you're asking a sixteen-year-old. What does a sixteen-year-old know about medical history?

—Wendy

Adoptees quite often begin searching as they reach a milestone in their life, such as marriage, the birth of a child, or the death of an adoptive parent. As they age, their heritage and genetic history may become more important to them. Often when contact is made there is an initial euphoria, which is sometimes referred to as the "honeymoon phase" of the reunion. One of the most powerful aspects of a reunion for adoptees is the experience of meeting, for the first time in their lives, someone who looks like them or laughs like them or has the same voice or gestures.

I had signed up with Soundex International Reunion Registry and then kind of put it in the back of my head; I didn't even think to change my address with them. One day I came home and there was a message from a lady with Soundex: "I've been trying to track you down for two weeks. I think I've got some news you've been waiting a long time to hear."

I am going berserk. I knew what news they had for me; it had to be. It's the only thing they could be calling me for. I don't know what I'm going to do. With the time difference I can't call until noon tomorrow; I'm going out of my mind. I hardly slept all night. I get into work and I am just watching the clock. At the stroke of noon I closed my door, picked up the phone, and called Soundex. They told me just a few things about her. She was living in Kansas.

I dialed her number and she answered, and the next four minutes was nothing more than "Oh my God, I don't believe it, oh my God, oh my God, I can't believe this is happening." Tears, the works. Unbelievable. We asked serious questions, we asked silly questions. I said, "Okay, tell me, how big are your boobs?" Because I was always totally flat as a kid. She starts laughing hysterically and she said, "I told my fiancé that was the first thing I was going to ask you." I mean, she was just so happy to finally know who she was. She said she would just sit and stare in the mirror and go, "Who am I?"

—Serena

The day we met, I primped as if I was going on a first date. I wanted to look my very best for her but my legs were like jelly. I was staying across the street from where we were meeting and I could not walk over there. My sister-in-law had to drive me across the street and turn the car around so that I could get out on the passenger side next to the sidewalk. Of course, my daughter was sitting there scanning everyone. We knew each other instantly, because we look amazingly alike.

I got a sense of the loss that adoption can bring when she held my face in her hands and I realized that she was looking at someone who looked like her for the first time in her life. I've always been surrounded by people who, if they don't look like me, they walk like me, they have my quirks, the same sense of humor, and we all have this same voice. For the first time in her life, at the age of twenty-eight, she was looking at someone who looked like her and it was overwhelming.

—Mary III

It is not uncommon for adoptees so lose interest after they have found the information they were seeking. Some of the women I interviewed described joyful reunions followed by a lot of contact, but said that after a while their child's interest gradually waned. Some mothers saw this as a natural course of events. In other cases, mothers experienced considerable pain and turmoil because their child did not want to establish a relationship. These women felt like they had lost their child a second time.

I got a phone call on a Saturday evening. I was having a little dinner party for my nephew, his college roommate, my sister, and my husband, and the phone rang. I picked up the phone in the kitchen and this young man said to me, "Is this Carolyn?" Well, most people call me Carol, so I thought it was somebody trying to sell me something. I said, "This is she." He said, "Is this a good time to talk?" I said, "About what, sir?" He said, "About December 14, 1965." I said, "Could I put you on hold for just a minute?"

I went into the guest room and told my husband just to hang up the phone in the kitchen. I was in there for one and a half hours. My husband came in a few times and I gave him a hand motion that everything was fine. I have a brother who's a Vietnam vet, need I say more, so my husband thought it was something to do with that.

It was my son-in-law on the phone. When I hung up and came out, all my company had gone except for my sister and my husband. I told them who it was and my husband started crying, my sister started crying, and I was hysterical. I was just . . . you couldn't even console me, I was so upset. It was just fear of the unknown. My daughter has always known she was adopted, but maybe five people in my life knew she existed. My father did not know, my *own* father. So it was very, very difficult.

I called my son, who was at his girlfriend's house, and I said, "I need to talk to you about something." He was here in ten minutes. Now, you have to realize that my son, his whole life, wanted a brother or sister. When I was twenty-eight years old I had to have a hysterectomy for cervical cancer, so I never could get pregnant again.

I told him. I was so hysterical. Telling him was the hardest thing. Telling my grandmother and my dad wasn't as difficult, as emotional, as telling my son. But he was so good with it. I'm so proud of him. He was so accepting and understanding.

The next day, I called my daughter and spent two hours on the phone talking. We planned on meeting that next Friday. Oh, God, I lost nine pounds. I couldn't eat, I couldn't sleep, all I did was cry. It was just so emotional.

When my daughter came to the door and I looked at her I said, "Oh, my God, you look just like my sister." And my son said,

"Mom, she looks just like *you*." And she does. She looks just like me. We had a wonderful reunion. By the end of the evening, there were probably twenty-five people here. I called my friends. She called her brother, who's also adopted. I mean, we had this wonderful, wonderful reunion.

We were talking every day, then it went to maybe a couple of times a week, and then it sort of peters off, you know. But she got to meet my father. I'm so happy, because he has since passed away. And she met my grandmother, who has since passed away. So she got to meet all the really important people in my life.

—Carolyn I

He found me in 1999, when he was thirty-one years old. He found me, I think, for medical information and curiosity. I thought that if he wanted to find me he would want to know me, but that wasn't true. It's been heartbreaking. I did not have other children. I never had someone who looked like me and he looks like me. To see that is so overwhelming. It's just . . . I can't describe it . . . it just kind of blows your whole world.

I wanted so much to just hold him and he didn't understand that at all. That isn't why he found me; he had a mother. He wasn't going to upset her. We've had some tough, tough times. I've had to do a lot of grieving. I've had to grieve all the initial garbage, and I've had to grieve all my dreams and hopes of wanting to be a mom. I guess I never realized how much I wanted all of that. I still grieve. It's easier now, but it's such a loss and it doesn't heal. It's never going to heal, ever.

My husband is so tired of seeing me hurt. He and my mother just want to say to me, "For crying out loud, why don't you just walk away from it, just forget about it. Quit trying. Quit making gifts for him. Quit. Walk away." They're baffled that I can't do that; they're just baffled. They don't understand. Most people don't.

People don't get the depth of our connection with the child. They can't believe it. When I first met my son as a man, I was so overwhelmed and just shocked at how much I loved him, the first sight of him. I can't put a name on it but boy, *it's there.* You know that baby's yours. You know he's *from* you. There's some connection there that does not break. I don't know what to call it, but it's there.

My marriage has been affected. Since reunion, my husband's gotten much more distant. At first he was real empathetic and close, but it goes on and on and on and takes so much of my emotional energy. He feels shafted and helpless. There's nothing he can say or do. So it's had a huge effect. I guess the question would be, Is there any part of my life where it hasn't affected me? I doubt there is.

—Glory

A common reason for adoptees' not wanting a reunion, or backing away, is anxiety over conflicting loyalties to their adoptive parents. Perhaps the saddest reason that adoptees cite for not wanting a reunion is the belief that their mother has already rejected them by her act of surrender. A few of the women I interviewed located their adult child only to find that the child did not want to meet them. But sometimes adoptees who do not initially desire contact change their minds with time.

I called the Crittenton League and the woman said, "I will contact his parents. I cannot give you the information, but I can tell him you're looking for him." A few days later, she called back. I was so excited. But she said, "He doesn't want to meet you." I was devastated. I was completely devastated and my daughter, who very much wanted to meet her half brother, was very disappointed, too.

Then about two and a half years ago, my daughter called me and she was crying. I thought she had a fight with her boyfriend. She said, "Mom, guess what? My brother wants to meet me." I guess this communication had been going on for about a month. She said he sounded really nice and they had a lot of similar interests. They're both artsy, music-y type people. Then she said, "Mom, he wants to meet you. He and I are going to arrange everything."

My son said he had a great life but his personality was so different from his adoptive family's. Once he started to meet all of us, I think it made him understand where he came from. He's very outgoing; he's a singer. It has just been wonderful. I never in my wildest dreams thought I would see him again.

—Charlenea

I didn't give myself permission to search for my daughter until after my dad died. He died twenty years ago and one of the first things that came to my mind is it might be safe now to look for my daughter. It still took me a while to get up the courage. I was really afraid. Maybe I was afraid of the rejection. I don't know what it is that scares you.

I called Catholic Welfare. I wrote a letter and they sent that letter to her. She sent one back to me, through them, telling me about her life and included a few pictures. The letter concluded with her saying that she wanted to thank me for giving her life and for giving her to the family she had, and that she had never made room for me in that life and she hoped that I could accept that. In other words, this would be our last correspondence.

I could accept that. I knew now that she was happy and I knew that things had worked out. As much as I would have loved to have been able to meet her, at least I could see a picture of her and I knew that everything was okay.

Close to a year later, my friend who had been prompting me to do this all along said, "You know, so many times kids will change their minds. Why don't you just call Catholic Welfare and ask that social worker to contact her again and ask her if she's considered changing her mind?"

So I called Catholic Welfare one morning and the gal came back on the phone and said, "I'm sorry, but I can't find a file with your name on it." I was angry. I thought, "What do you mean you can't find a file?" Good grief, you know, it was only a year ago. She said she would leave a message for the gal I had worked with. Well, she called me at my office about three hours later and she said, "I have to tell you. I am shaken up by this whole situation." She said, "The reason we couldn't find your file, it was because your daughter called here about an hour before you did this morning and someone put your file on my desk and that's why the other person couldn't find it."

Yeah. We just kind of both knew that it was meant to be at that point in time. We exchanged a few more letters and finally decided that it was safe to give each other a phone number.

Her family was given so many misconceptions when she was adopted. Her husband is just a super, super guy, quite a character, very Irish. Her family is all Irish, so the agency told them that they had an Irish baby for them. I mean, my dad wore a shamrock on St. Patrick's Day, but that's about it. My mother is a full-blooded Swede and my daughter's father's parents are both full Swedes. So she's 75 percent Swedish and the rest is kind of a mixture. The weekend that we finally met, her husband said, "You know, first of all I was told I had an Irish wife. Now I find out she's a Swede. Secondly, I get two mothers-in-law."

—Mary I

Whether a search is initiated by the mother or the adult adoptee, the person who searches generally spends quite a bit of time contemplating the process and possible outcomes. They have had time to prepare emotionally for the reunion. The person who is found most likely receives a call or a letter out of the blue. The emotional intensity of that first, unexpected letter or phone call can be powerful indeed.

It was the day Dale Earnhardt died; it was that Sunday. We were watching the race and I remember seeing it happen. About nine-thirty that night, the phone rang and I said, "Hello?" And a man's voice said, "Um, yes, I'm trying to reach a Cathy that used to live in . . ." Now, my high-school reunion is coming up next year, thirty-five years, and I figured that's what it was. I've been married for twenty-six years and no one knows me by my maiden name. Then he said, "Does the date April 29, 1970, mean anything to you?"

I literally fell on my knees. I was standing right there. My knees gave right out on me, 'cause I knew right away who it was. Then he started saying, "I weighed..." and I would say, "Yeah, you weighed..." And he said, "I was born at..." and I would say, "Yeah, you were born at..." And then he said, "You remember all that?" I said, "You don't forget that. Don't you know I thought about you every single solitary day of my life?"

When I got married and I was walking down the aisle, I talked to him. When his sisters were born, I talked to him. I would say, "You have a sister now. You have another sister now." I can honestly say that when my parents died I stood at the coffin and I said some really nasty things to each of them. I'm sad that they died, but my relationship with my parents was never the same after that. Never the same. I hated them for what they made me do.

None of my family knew. I never, ever, ever talked about it until he found me. My children didn't know about him. I had to tell my husband; he didn't know, either.

My husband was sitting right here, and I said, "I gotta tell you something that's going on in my life that you need to know about." Well, he thought I was sick. I could see the look on his face—he had that scared-to-death look. I said, "I had a baby in 1970 and I had to give it away for adoption." He just looked at me and he went, "I hope it's not another girl." That's exactly what he said. My husband is the only guy in this house. We have two daughters and the hormones fly. I said, "No, it's a son." Next question: "Does he play baseball?" That's all he wanted to know. He's a baseball coach, so he wanted to know, "Is he an athlete?" "No, he's not. He's an electrician, he's not an athlete."

He said, "I need to deal with this in my own way." We kinda kept away from each other for a couple of days. I gave him his space and he was fine with it.

—Cathy II

I'm looking through the mail and I saw a little card that looked like my girlfriend Lorraine's handwriting. I opened it up and it began, "Dear Kathleen, it was twenty-one years this past December since we last saw each other. I hope you will remember me..."

The letter went on and she gave me her address, her phone number. I had to read it a second time. I couldn't believe it.

I immediately tried calling her. She came out to see me that night, that very night. I think we stayed up most of the night talking. She had so many questions. I can't tell you what it felt like to be looking at her. I was waiting for it not to be real. She wanted to hear the story and I told her the story the best that I could.

She was graduating from college that May and she asked me to go to her college graduation. She was going to tell her adopted parents and I have adopted children, so I was sitting on both sides of this. I asked her if she would just please not tell them until after graduation, because they had brought her to this point in her life, in their life, and it was very important that they had that day. But I said I would go.

I sat at her graduation all by myself over in a corner, sobbing. The people around me were probably thinking, "Oh, that poor woman, she must have been scrubbing floors to put her child through college." If they only knew. I just sat there thinking, "My God, when I left that infant in a nursery I never thought I would be sitting here at her college graduation."

—Kathi

Many mothers describe their reunion as an emotional roller-coaster ride. When talking about their relationship with their adult child, they often sound like someone recounting their first experience of falling in love. These newly formed relationships are filled with intense emotion that, as in many romantic relationships, is not always equally or simultaneously felt. The emotions described by mothers I interviewed included extreme highs, being obsessed with their adult children, wanting to know everything about them, wanting to be with them every minute, wanting to hold and touch them. It's not uncommon for women who reunite with a son who looks exactly like their boyfriend of so many years earlier to find themselves momentarily attracted to him. The lows included revisiting the feelings of loss, betrayal, and shame that occurred around the surrender; reverting to the age they were at the time of their loss; experiencing rejection, anger, or ambivalence from their child; or feeling a new sense of profound loss that comes with realizing that the baby they have thought about all these years is a grown person, and that the lost years can never be regained.

Only two of the mothers I interviewed said they questioned whether they would have a reunion, given the opportunity to do it over again. For the overwhelming majority, it was the beginning of the healing process. For mothers who had internalized their grief for thirty or forty years, the reunion was an important awakening, though sometimes an incredibly painful process. Whether set off by seeing baby pictures of their adult child for the first time or by a simple act of kindness and acceptance, the result for some was an eruption of grief and anger that had been bottled up or denied for years.

About 1989 I started thinking more about my daughter. I never allowed myself to go too deep. I was just wondering . . . is she okay? Sometimes I would pick up the phone and call the agency in Illinois and hang up. I didn't even know what to ask. I had read nothing on adoption. I didn't know about nonidentifying information. I didn't even know what questions to ask. Then, I think it was 1991, I sent a letter to the agency and I put my address and phone number, so if she ever contacted them . . . this is how they could get hold of me.

When she called me the first time I cried, but it was stilted; I still wasn't letting it out. I sent her pictures right away, but I had a hard time getting pictures from her. Finally, I came home from work and in the mail is this big envelope. Oh, I just couldn't wait to look at the pictures. I was by myself in the house. I was standing in the kitchen, and there was an eight by ten of her as a baby. I can't describe the sound that came out of me. It was a wail. It was not crying, it was an animal sound. It was like a wounded animal. It scared me. I was so glad nobody was home.

I hadn't cried all through the years, but looking at the pictures— that's what burst the dam. That's what did it. She was about three months old. That made it so real. The reunion unlocked it, but those pictures really burst it wide open. I cried a lot more after that.

One day when we were together I said, "I wish I could put you back in here and start all over again." And she said, "But I'm too big now." And that's the loss. You can't get it back.

—Christine

While I was pregnant, I wouldn't look in the mirror at myself other than from the waist up. I had this whole denial system. I thought I was being sensible. If you're not gonna have a baby, then you can't have it in your head, either. I didn't want to see her when she was born. I heard her cry and she was taken away. I stayed in the hospital for a week and I would walk up and down the hall, but I would never go as far as the nursery. Three weeks after I gave birth, I was living in New York. I started summer school at Columbia. I got a job. And it was as if it hadn't happened.

So what this story becomes is how I don't feel anything about it after that. But there was this problem about not being able to hear infants cry. I couldn't *stand* to hear infants cry. I couldn't stand it.

I gave birth in '64 and in March of 1988 I somehow found the wherewithal to sign up for this registry in the state of New York for people who had given up children. I registered and nearly nine years later I came home and there was a slip saying I had a registered letter from the State of New York. I knew what it was. It was like I was in another world.

I know I must have slept some, but I felt like there was somebody sort of outside of me, watching me. I felt like I was losing my mind. But I was at the post office the next morning at nine o'clock.

There had been a match. "If I was still interested in having contact I was to sign and notarize. . . ." I walked out of the post office and over to the bank. I swear it was not me walking, doing this. I got the letter notarized. I turned around and I walked back to the post office and I put it in the mail. The rest of the day I felt like I was high. There was this amazing sort of feeling. The numbness certainly was still there, but I was so excited.

A couple weeks after that she called me and that's when I knew something was really, really wrong with me because I was so numb. I couldn't feel anything. Physically, I felt this incredible pit in my stomach and my heart was racing, but I just didn't feel anything emotionally. The shame now is that I could just cut myself off like that. I mean, I know I had a lot of help in doing that, but it feels like I was inhuman and that's horrible to live with. That's what I struggle with now, trying to not feel like such a robot. I had to make myself into that in order to do what I did.

After I met my daughter, I was getting major dental work done. My dentist is an American-born Chinese woman who is also an adoptive mother. One day I was holding a magazine that had an article on adoption, and I said, "Oh, another thing on adoption." And she said, "Are you adopted?" And for the first time in my life, in this kind of situation, I said, "No. But I'm a birth mother." And we both started crying. She said, "How old is your daughter?" I said, "She's thirty-seven." She gave me a hug when I left.

I had to go back a few days later and, having told her, it felt scary. When people have asked me if I have children, I've always said no. At the end of our session, she gave me this wrapped present. I went out to the car and I opened it up and it was a book about birth mothers. At first, it was like it wasn't real that I was getting this from her. And then all of a sudden I started to feel her kindness and I started to really cry. I cried for the next three days. I went to work. I functioned. I saw my patients. But I was a wreck.

All of a sudden it really hit. What did I do? I had been this robot and I gave up this child. I just fell apart. I started getting flashbacks of being with my parents and then being in the hospital and not walking down the hall to the nursery. All this came back in wave after wave after wave. I was out of my mind. I just hurt. I hurt about who I was and what I had done. You just don't take somebody out of your body and deposit them someplace where you won't see them or know them. You just don't do that. I just felt I was so inhuman that I had participated in this. I was just frantic and nobody got it. Nobody understood the hell that I was in, including my therapist. I was having nightmares, one after another and they were always back then, thirty-five years ago. I told my therapist, "I think I have post-traumatic stress disorder." The next time I saw him, he said, "You're right. That's what you're describing."

I began to see how my whole life had developed around this. It had a hell of a lot to do with why I had no children, and why I was so lonely, and why there was no man in my life. There've been men, but really inappropriate men who didn't mean anything to me. There was a certain kind of depression that I'd lived with for years and years. I did everything I could to not feel that attachment. With that wall breaking down, I started to feel just what I had done and what had happened to me, in a way and at a level that I had never felt before. I was no longer numb.

—Judith III

SUSAN II

The guy that I had been dating had problems scholastically, and his parents decided to send him to private school. So he came to say good-bye. My parents had a very, very big yard and he parked his car under the trees and we were out there necking and petting and doing the things that boys and girls do. He had been after me for some time to begin a sexual relationship and I had not done it. We hadn't even really explored. I mean, beyond petting there wasn't any exploration. And to this day I really have no clue what possessed me to do this, but I decided that this was definitely the night that I needed to give myself to my boyfriend and give up my virginity. And that was the night I got pregnant.

My boyfriend came to see me during winter break. I remember him in the living room of my grandparents saying to me, "Sue, I'll marry you. I will marry you." And I said, "What, are you out of your mind? You're eighteen." I wasn't even seventeen, I was sixteen. I said, "We can't get married." And it was then that he told me that the year before he moved to our town he had gotten another girl pregnant and he didn't want to lose another child.

The agreement was for me to go to Florence Crittenton Home in March. From January to March, I went to day school there. My mother drove me every day. My grandmother was enlisted to take care of the two little kids while my mother took me in so that I could keep up my schoolwork. I mean, I graduated from high school at Florence Crittenton, and it's really thanks to my mother, who insisted I was going to finish school.

In March, I went to live at the Crittenton home and I stayed there until my baby was born in June. When Karen was born the doctor, who was the only female on staff, came out to the waiting room and she said to my mother, "Would you like to come in and see your granddaughter?" Think about that. It's 1965. That is not what happened for most women. That is not the treatment women were given. But my mother went in and actually held Karen before I did. My mother was there when they cut her cord. So she saw her first grandchild, and held her even before I did.

At that time, the rule at this Florence Crittenton home was if you chose not to see your baby, then you never saw your baby. But if you chose to see your child, then you lived in for the next seven days. You fed the baby several times a day, changed diapers; they brought the baby to you constantly. And I wanted to be with my baby. So Karen and I spent the next seven days together bonding. I mean, I remember every day, I remember every moment, I remember every feeding—I remember it all.

And I also remember, and this is really hard to say, but I also remember wanting to get home. I wanted it over with. And that's hard. Because the memory I would much rather have had was that I didn't want to let her go. But I was so conditioned by that point—so many people telling me that I couldn't do this, there weren't any options, it was a fait accompli. So I just wanted it over. And I didn't realize how precious those days would be later on.

When I look back, the social worker who had worked with me was wonderful. There was never any question this baby was going to be given up for adoption, so there was never any discussion about keeping her. Never. But I think it was either on day two or day three I decided I wanted to go home. I was done. And I called over to Florence Crittenton and I left a message for this social worker and I told her, "I want to go home. Please take the baby, I want to go home." And she wrote me a letter and had it delivered and said, "No. You'll want these days later. You have to do this. You have to go through this experience, Susan. You wanted to be with your baby and, believe me, in the years to come you'll be glad that you did this." And she was right. I needed to spend those days with my baby.

My parents and my boyfriend's parents had spent a lot of money on my incarceration, so my future was very different than all of my other friends'. Going to college was out of the question. I went to work and I went to night school. But one thing I can say unequivocally: my daughter drove me all my life. I never ever wanted her to find me and to find somebody less than the most successful woman on this earth. Karen was my beacon; Karen was my beacon all through those years. I was driven to be the very best that I could be for her. I knew the day I kissed her goodbye that we would see each other again. I never doubted that she would be back in my life ever. Ever.

And knowing that she'd be back in my life, I wanted her to be proud of me. I wanted her to find a woman that she could really be proud to call mother. Whenever my life went crazy, and it did, I was very self-destructive for the first five years after her birth. Every time I would start to self-destruct, I would remember that little girl. So Karen was my beacon.

The first year after Karen was born, my mother sent me a Mother's Day card, and she sent me a Mother's Day card every year. My mother always was very empathetic to me on her birthday. She so, *so* deeply regretted her decision and it haunted her for years before it haunted me. My mother never forgot that baby, ever.

Interestingly, when Karen turned thirteen, my mother went bananas. I don't know how to describe it any other way than that. My mother was absolutely convinced that Karen was living in the neighborhood. In truth, Karen had moved from Georgia to New Hampshire, to a town just up the road from where my mother lived. She was working as a lifeguard. She was a swimmer, like I had been, and was a lifeguard at a place where my older brother taught diving and where her two cousins were in the pool as often as she was. That's how close we were to her as a teenager. My mother has always been a woman who has had a sense. She's got that gift.

When Karen was twenty-five, my next-door neighbor at that time, unbeknownst to me, was the child psychologist at the agency where I surrendered her. And she and I were planting tulips that spring on either side of our borders. She was well into her seventies then. I asked her, I said, "You go off somewhere a couple of days a week. You can't still be working. Where do you go?" And she told me who she was and where she worked. I looked up and she looked at me and she said, "Let me think, you don't have kids so you must be one of our birth mothers." We talked about it, and she said, "So why aren't you searching?" And I said, "I don't really have a right to search." And she said, "Oh, yes, you do. Start the search now." So I have her to thank. She was an incredible woman. Everybody at the agency loved her. She died that December. Before the search could even happen, she was dead.

Karen was found in six weeks, on the day that her first child was born. And she and I were reunited a month later. There are no coincidences in life. Years back, my husband and I would have dinner on about a quarterly basis with two of the other executives in the company we worked for. One of them had a daughter Karen's age. Every time we would have dinner with them, I would leave the house and I would sob. *Sob.* And my husband would say, "Okay, princess, what's the problem?" And I would say, "I'm absolutely convinced that their daughter is my Karen." He would say, "Cut it out, she looks just like them." I would say, "But I don't care, it's a feeling I have. Honest to God, that's my kid." She didn't look a bit like me, didn't act like me, but I was convinced she was my kid.

When Karen and I reunited, I asked her where she grew up. Well, in her thirteenth year she came to live in New Hampshire. That was the year that my mother went mental. She lived right next door to the house where my husband and I had dinners. My daughter and their daughter went to school together and were best friends. And it was very likely that my daughter was in the house the nights they had dinner parties. My daughter was right there under my nose. It just wasn't for us to see at that time.

So we make plans to meet at the agency. I really didn't know how it was all going to work out. I gathered up family photos and put together an album. I found all the poetry I had written in the years that we were separated. My attitude was if this was our only meeting I wanted her to walk away with something genetically connected to her. If she chose not to have a relationship, it was okay. I just wanted her to have that information.

The Wednesday we were scheduled to meet, I was training a group of about three hundred salespeople, one of whom was my niece, and she could not believe that I could work and then get in my car and go for my meeting with my daughter. I just shut it off.

I got to the agency and they put me in this little room, an interview room, and the social worker said, "It will probably be about ten minutes and then I'll come to the door and I'll knock and I'll let her in." So I sat there waiting. And I was totally shut down. I mean, devoid of any worry, of any fear, of anything. And I remember thinking to myself, "You know what, this is it. *This is it.* You get one shot at feeling this feeling. You can put it away, you can shut it down, but you know what, this moment will never come again and if you stay shut down you're not going to show your daughter who you really are and what you're really all about." It was a physical thing I had to do. I mean, I physically had to get in the moment. And I did. I mean, when the knock on the door came my daughter got to see who I really am. Not a fake, not a phony, but somebody who really was in that moment for her. The social worker opened the door and she said, "I want you to meet your mom. This is Sue. Sue, this is your daughter." And this beautiful young woman walked through the door.

We looked at each other. I mean, we were both stunned, because she looks just like me. We were totally stunned. We hugged each other, that wonderful sustaining hug, and then we leaned back and the tears were streaming and we started to laugh. I mean, how could you not laugh? It was like looking at yourself.

I tell people about that moment and I tell them that the rest was this blur; it was like my life in fast forward. We could not get enough. It was as though she had gone away to college and she was back and she had to tell me all about what had happened. We were there for three hours by ourselves. All of a sudden I looked down and she had started to leak. She had been nursing her daughter and she said, "Oh, the baby." I said, "Where's the baby?" It was six at night. Her stepmom had been sitting out in the lobby with the baby for three hours.

So we asked her to come in and here was this baby. Here was this *baby*. I shut down. I saw that baby and I shut down. She nursed the baby. She sat there and nursed this child and I totally shut down. I mean, I held my granddaughter, but I can honestly tell you I don't remember it. There are pictures of it, but I didn't feel that baby. I could not. It was too close.

You know, it's twelve years now that we're reunited and twelve years we've been back in each other's lives. It's not been easy for either one of us. In the early years she would say to me, "You know, you can't ever be my mother." And I'd say, "I understand that but you will always be my daughter and that's the way it will be for life." I think about three to four years into the reunion I started receiving birthday cards, Mother's Day cards. She doesn't call me mom. That's okay. I'm Grammy Sue to the girls. I've been totally integrated into both of my grandchildren's lives. The years that I missed with her I've been able to make up with her two daughters. I'm very blessed.

But I never knew until after the reunion how angry I was. It's hard to even describe it, but it interlaced my being. I was angry at everybody. The world. I was cheated. I was screwed. I mean, I was *had*. I was had by society, by people who were bigger than me, who were more educated than me. Certainly some of them were well meaning. I mean, some of them were very well intentioned. But I should have had the right to parent my child. I didn't realize how the anger permeated my life until we were reunited and until I was able to finally articulate who I really was, until I was able to come out of the closet of shame. It really was a closet of shame that we were all put in. We were all locked into it. And they did it so beautifully that if you ever revealed what happened to you, *you* would pay the price.

Birth mothers do not forget. I know a lot of birth mothers have drilled it down, but they don't ever forget. My shame came afterward, because I couldn't talk about the experience. I had an incredible fear that if I revealed who I was I'd lose everything. For a woman, I attained incredible stature in my career in the business community. And for all but the last twelve years of it nobody ever knew who I really was.

When I came home from meeting my daughter at the agency, I brought home all of these Polaroid pictures of her and in the morning my husband picked out a couple of the pictures. I said, "What are you doing with those pictures?" And he said, "I'm a father, I'm a grandfather, I can't wait to show everybody at work." And I said, "You can't *show anybody*. Oh, my God." He said, "What do you mean, I can't show anybody? Sue, there's nothing to be ashamed of."

I was still trying to preserve the status quo of this persona that I had created for myself. I was terrified that it would destroy my career. Thank God, he said, "Pfft, get out of here. This is a joyous moment, this is the best thing that's ever happened." I often wonder if he hadn't been here what would have happened. It was my husband who absolutely blew my cover. And by revealing who I was, I was destroying the person I had created.

I hope that my story helps other women heal. I do feel healed. That closet of shame is huge. There are a lot of us in it. I had my moments of sadness but, truly, when I lay my head down at night now, I'm thankful. I know where my baby is. She's all grown up. She's a beautiful woman. I'm blessed and I feel healed. It kills me to think that there are women who are not out. I hope talking about this allows women who have not been out of the closet to get out and, hopefully, change their lives—by getting them on the Internet, getting them to join the groups, and letting them hear their own voices for the first time.

As you requested.

your sheets have not been changed. Should you choose to have your sheets changed tomorrow, please place the Sleep Sweetly card on the bed.

Your choice makes a difference.

Thank you.

JENNIFER

I grew up in a small town on the east coast of Florida. My father was an attorney and we were big churchgoers. At thirteen, fourteen, people started dating. At fifteen, it got a little more serious. Some of the boys were driving. That's when I started dating my first real boyfriend. I'd had a puppy love before, but this was what I considered to be my first real love.

He was a lifeguard at the country club and he was just this gorgeous man, strong, and a few years older than me. I was pretty astonished when he asked me to go out. We started dating and I had decided that virginity was a burden. It had lost its glamour. I wanted to get past it. I wanted to be a woman and I just wanted to get in the game and I wanted to get it over with. So we started having sex on a regular basis. I just felt completely protected and insulated from anything bad. I grew up in a very nice home with nice friends, nice family.

He had used condoms a few times and fumbled with them and I just did not have a good experience with them, either. I just still didn't get that I could get pregnant. I thought, "Well, if I have sex when I'm close to my period, or right after my period, then I won't get pregnant." Then that next cycle didn't come and didn't come and didn't come. We were both terrified. Three weeks later, I got my period: "Phew, we're fine." So, feeling invincible, I went ahead and continued to have unprotected sex. Then the next month my cycle didn't come and didn't come and didn't come. I thought, "Well, it's happened before. This is no big deal. I couldn't be pregnant."

Then the signs became very evident. I was rushing around the house before school, and I ran back upstairs to brush my teeth and all of a sudden I just threw up. I thought, "Wow, that's weird." Then probably about two weeks later at church we stood up to sing the last hymn and I felt really woozy, like I was going to pass out. I looked down at the pew and I can remember the musty smell of the hymnal, and the organ going, and the

Reverend, and I'm in my Easter clothes, with my shoes, and I all of a sudden I just went down.

From that day on, my boyfriend and I knew I was pregnant. I can't get in touch with the person that I was then. I was in a dreamworld. We were not doing anything about it. We just sort of continued, biding our time, waiting for something to happen. I tried to imagine how I would tell my parents if it ever came to that, and I just couldn't even imagine.

Then one Sunday my boyfriend and I came home from the beach and we were in our family room having sex on the carpet. My parents were supposed to be out on the boat. Well, they had boat trouble and had docked near our house. My father and my uncle came in the back door with the little jalousie windows. I heard the door opening and there we were. I had been wearing a bikini and there's no way you can quickly put on a bikini. It was a nightmare; it was an absolute nightmare. I can't imagine how I looked. I know that my boyfriend looked as white as a sheet. He got behind the draperies and I threw him his bathing suit and picked up a towel. My father just looked at me and said, "Go upstairs. Go upstairs and get dressed." Poor Daddy. So I'm upstairs in my beautifully decorated room, trembling, with the towel still around me, and my father came in and said, "Let me see your stomach." He looked at my breasts. He looked at my stomach and he said, "You're pregnant." I thought, "How in the hell could he know?" Thinking back on it, of course, he had four children with my mother. He knows what a pregnant woman looks like. Later that evening before dinner, I heard my father crying. I heard him sob in his room and I'd never heard that before. It was just gut wrenching and I figured, "Whatever they want to do, I'm going to do."

That same night they went down to my boyfriend's house and spoke with his parents. I was still holding out hope that we would get married. I really wanted the baby. It just felt like love to me. They came back and my father called me into his den and we had a conversation without my mother, which was kind of unusual. He told me that my boyfriend's parents felt that the best thing would be for me to have the baby and give it up for adoption. I must have looked horrified at that suggestion, because he said, "It's hard for me, too. It's my flesh and blood, too." We were both crying and he was comforting me and he said, "You know, Jenny, you've got your whole life ahead of you. If you can just get through this, you're going to have a wonderful life. It will all be like a bad dream. You'll get through it, and you'll have fun again, and you'll have a full life. You're still Daddy's little angel." It just broke my heart. It totally broke my heart. It didn't occur to me to protest. The main feeling I had was just to not make any more problems, do whatever they wanted me to do, just basically be invisible.

I was whisked off to Texas to live with my sister. My mother went to my high school and cleared out my locker. She told me that I shouldn't talk to anybody, that she was going to tell everybody that I had rheumatic fever. I didn't even know what rheumatic fever was—it sounded like "romantic" fever to me. All I knew was it was some sort of disease. I got set up in the extra bedroom in my sister's house. I never looked more beautiful. My hair was glossy. My skin was clear and beautiful. I had roses in my cheeks. My breasts were full. I would just look at myself in the mirror and wish so much that my boyfriend could see me and we could share this.

I didn't have a sense of shame, ever, during the time that I was pregnant, even when they found out. Maybe when my father walked in on us having sex I felt embarrassed or ashamed, but shame was never part of my pregnancy. It was either sadness or love and wonderment, nothing in between. I would go to bed early and my baby would start kicking. I would talk to him. I would tell him how perfect he was, and that I would always love him. It was our time, and our space, and nobody else got into that bubble. I felt like I was feeding him little bits of love, and nurturing and taking care of him, just like if I was holding him in my arms.

I was, allegedly, meeting with this caseworker throughout my pregnancy and discussing my adoption plan. I met with a woman once. She jotted down all my vital information and asked me to please obtain baby pictures of myself and my boyfriend. She basically just gave me assignments to gather information, like list any special talents that ran in my family or in his family. There was never any discussion about how I felt about giving my child up for adoption. I never thought there was supposed to be. It was never explained that it was an option. I was basically just going through the motions. I was being told what to do, and I did it. They asked me if I wanted to see my baby when I delivered and my mother piped up and said, "Oh no, that would be too difficult. You should say no." So of course I said, "Well, no. I don't want to make things difficult." I couldn't imagine seeing, or not seeing, my baby. I couldn't imagine delivering. It still wasn't me that this was happening to.

One Saturday I did my exercises and went to bed and later that night I couldn't get comfortable. They walked me over to the hospital and I was already dilated. This was it. I sort of felt this shade being drawn down on my life, like one of those old window shades. It just came down. I'm thinking, "Oh no, oh no, I'm not ready for this. This is good-bye." I just couldn't bear it. They gave me something to knock me out and I was in la-la land. I don't remember much of anything, just some stainless steel and some tile and some voices. It seemed like about a minute later a nurse was saying, "Well, you did just fine. You did just fine."

I have very few memories of being in recovery. The rule was that you had to stay there for eight days. They said it was eight days to fully recover, but later I put it together that it's eight days before you can sign the adoption papers. Every time the door would open into the room, I'd hear the nursery. I picked out my baby's cry. I said, "Do they just let them cry?" And the nurse said, "Oh no, there are nurses in there. They're holding the babies and talking to them. They're cared for." But they were crying.

The caseworker presented me with papers. She said, "This will finalize the adoption." I asked if my baby had been placed in a home yet. She said, "I think we've found a wonderful home for him." I said, "When will he be placed?" And she said, "After you sign the papers he will be placed." I read through this paper, legally cutting off any connection to him, took a deep breath, and signed my name on the bottom. I put the pen down and I started to get up and go and she said, "You have to sign these, too." There were about twelve papers to sign. It was the first time I showed anger. I yelled, "Can't you use carbon or something? Why do I have to sign each one?" I said, "You've got my signature. You've got my soul. You've got my baby, and now I have to sit here and sign twelve pieces of paper for you?"

Before we went home we were at my sister's house and she and my mother were in the kitchen making dinner and there was some happy chatter going on and I guess I was supposed to be helping them. The house had a screen door leading off the kitchen and I can remember opening it, hearing that screen-door noise, and looking out at the huge Texas sky that I hadn't taken in the whole time I was there. I looked up at that big sky and something just lifted out of me. It was like a part of me was flying off, separating, and leaving the other part of me there. Later, when people would ask me what it felt like to give my baby up for adoption, the only words I could find to describe it was it felt like an amputation—like half of my body had been removed. I can still feel that very powerfully.

I went through horrible depression. I didn't want to kill myself, but I didn't want to have the burden of living, either. It was just too painful. I was feeling so much grief. Ten years later I realized, "This is not going away." If anything, it was getting worse. So I started therapy. Then I found a little classified ad for a triad support group, which I had never heard of before. So I went to the meeting. Most of the people there had been adopted. I told the woman that I really wanted to find out where my son was. She asked me why and I said, "I just have to know. I don't know if he got hit by a car when he was on his tricycle or if he broke his leg or has brothers or sisters or if he died. I just want to know how he is." She gave me the name of a searcher and within twenty-four hours I had his name, his parents' names, their address, phone number, and a brief description of them. I thought, "Ah . . . he's fine, that's fantastic. I can get on with my life now."

Another ten years passed. During that time there was lots of therapy, lots of healing, lots of trying to peel back the layers and begin to express what I couldn't when I was sixteen years old. Then I wrote his parents. I wish now that I hadn't. I wish I'd just written directly to him, but I wrote about three or four pages explaining who I was. I tried to be completely gracious: "You are his parents, you are his family, you are his history, you are his world, but I'm his birth mother and I will always love him and I want to reach out and make myself available to him should he ever want me for any reason. If he ever wants to talk to me, or see what I look like, anything." I said I wasn't trying to intrude or bring problems.

His mother wrote me back: "We showed him the letter and he isn't interested in contacting you at this point, but he asked us to hold on to the letter should he change his mind in the future." She said that he was nineteen and he had just moved out of the house. She described him as being healthy, happy, very much his own person, handsome, fun, strong. It was all good. I was relieved that she wrote me. She asked that I let the next contact come from him. She thanked me for writing. I think I had closed my letter with something like "I was hoping that they could keep their minds and their hearts open . . . that all that I had, and all I was sending, was love." She responded to that and said everybody could use more love in their life so she would hold on to the letter for him, and, sure enough, she did.

Another ten years went by. I was getting anxious again and felt like I shouldn't have written to his parents. I'm thinking, "It should have been between the two of us. He's not a kid any longer. I'm going to call him. I'm pretty sure I'm going to call him." Then one night I went to see a movie with a girlfriend of mine. We went to see *Good Will Hunting* and I just lost it during the scene where Matt Damon is backed into a corner by Robin Williams. Williams is trying to get Damon to confront being an abused child and he's shouting at him, "It's not your fault! It's not your fault! It's not your fault!" And I felt like my son might think that there was something wrong with him, that it was his fault that he was given up for adoption, and I wanted to say to him, "It's not your fault. It's not your fault. It's not your fault. I'm so sorry that I couldn't take care of you. It's not your fault." After the movie, I was driving home by myself and it was pouring down rain and I was just sobbing out loud by myself. And I thought, "God damnit, I'm calling him. I'm not going to wait. I'm not going to be a chicken. I'm just going to call him."

I came home and I walked in the door and there was my husband with a glass of water, a glass of wine, and the portable phone. I don't know how he had all three in his hands at the same time, but he did. I looked at him and my eyes were all swollen and red and he looked at me and his eyes started tearing up and he said, "Your son called. He's waiting for you to call him back."

When I called and he answered, there was this voice that I just knew. I knew him. He has the sweetest, softest, most reassuring, most grounding voice of anyone I've ever known. He's just . . . he's pure perfect. He's perfect love to me.

I told him everything that I always wanted to tell him. It was the first time that I'd ever talked to anyone that way. It just all came out. Shortly after, my husband and I went out to visit him. We visited a few times and then I went out by myself. He was in a band in Austin that was very popular, and they were breaking up. So I went out for their final concert. I'm so glad that I did. The place was absolutely packed and when he started playing everybody started screaming and there was a mosh pit. I went down in a mosh pit for my son.

People were going nuts, throwing things, and then he stopped and said, "Okay, everybody settle down. Where's my mom? Is my mom okay?" He's just so sweet. I never expected or anticipated or would ever have allowed myself to think that he would call me mom. He's the one who reassures me.

I had a lot of anger toward my son's father. I called him when I first located our son. Then ten years later, when we were reunited, I wrote a letter to his mother. He contacted me and said, "You know, you need to get a life." I had to laugh at that. I have a life. I do other things, but I do this, too. This is my life.

When I came back from giving birth, my mother had told me to snap out of it. I said, "Fine, if you're taking my baby away and telling me I can't feel this way, then I'm just going to be a party girl. I just can't walk the straight and narrow and date a nice young man. I'd go out of my mind." I had to distract myself. I needed *big* distractions, so I was wild. I partied, I experimented with drugs, you know, I did a lot of stuff. I was a child of the seventies and I enjoyed it. I wasn't horrible. I wouldn't put myself in dangerous situations, but I was escaping, big time. I was trying to numb the pain. I was always looking for distractions. Bad relationships, anything.

I numbed it all out, but every once in a while it would just well up and I would just start sobbing from my core. All of a sudden I would just cry and would feel this intense grief, really intense grief. I remember one time I was watching the movie *My Life as a Dog*—I had one of the biggest cries of my life during that movie. My husband had some friends over playing cards and he came back into the room and said, "Do you want me to turn this off?" I said, "Leave it on. Let me go ahead with the process. I'm giving birth here."

I think in many, many, many ways I am stuck as a sixteen-year-old. I dress like a sixteen-year-old. I like the music. I can make mature decisions, I have a husband, a son, and a house. I have a job. I've been functioning as a seemingly mature adult, but I do feel like there's a part of me that's in arrested development. I will probably never get past that. I don't know if that's the trauma of having something like that happen, the splitting off, or maybe it's wanting to be back there again, pregnant.

10

⟁

Talking and Listening

What can people do? What can any of us do to help another human being? How do you find the right words or amount of support? I don't know. That's very, very difficult. Sometimes just listening, just letting a person talk it out, and work through it, is probably the best . . . not being judgmental or having all the answers, just accepting.

—Jill

ALTHOUGH ALL OF THESE women share the experience of surrendering their baby for adoption, they are not of one mind when it comes to many related issues. As individuals they hold a range of opinions about women's reproductive rights as well as about current adoption practices. Despite economic, generational, religious, racial, and geographic differences, they are in complete agreement on one point: most people do not understand their loss. Corroboration and validation from like-minded people is extremely helpful, but these mothers still exist in a world that knows little about their experiences. The simplistic and stereotypical characterization that these women are mothers who simply did not want their babies has damaged not only the mothers but also many adoptees. It has also allowed the pain to spread to partners, husbands, subsequent children, and siblings.

I have not yet formally interviewed extended family members or the men who fathered these babies, but I received hundreds of e-mails from adoptees and adoptive parents, as well as from sisters, sons, daughters, and later children who either attended one of my exhibitions or read about the project in the newspaper. It is clear from their responses that surrendering a child affects not only the mother and the child but also generations of family members related by blood and adoption.

> *Dear Ms. Fessler:*
>
> *My mother gave up a son (my half-brother), I believe it was in 1970 and it has bothered her tremendously ever since. She tried to find him later to no avail. I used to think it was the "weak" thing for her to do, that maybe she should have tried to raise him. After reading the article, I feel like I have had no idea how it was back in that era for single unwed mothers (I am 24) and I feel sorry that I ever thought of my own mother negatively because she gave up a child for adoption.*[1]
>
> *Jennifer*

> *Ann,*
>
> *I have recently begun a search for a half sister my mother gave up almost forty years ago, a baby she had when she was twenty. I am finding that knowing she had this experience explains to me so much about who my mother was and how she felt about herself and her family.*
>
> *She never spoke to me about the baby and she died ten years ago when I was seventeen. I found out "accidentally" when asking my uncle questions about her childhood. My mother never told any details to my father or her close friends. I find the people who were close to her at the time of her pregnancy are unable to remember much or are dismissive to my inquiries. They have told me it is not my business and that if the baby wanted to be found she would have found me. I'm shocked that STILL, after forty years people are so ashamed. This is very much a secret for my family, one that my mother, her parents, her siblings, and her friends were told to put away for good.*
>
> *I think back to all the times my mother insisted to my brother and me that she was the black sheep of her family and I understand a little better where that feeling came from.*[2]
>
> *Eloise*

Hi Ann,

I'm age 52, my mother is now 74. She gave birth to my older brother in 1949. She had become pregnant and my grandmother sent her to a home for "Wayward Girls" in Boston. When she was giving birth, in pain and in need of medication, she was required by the medical staff to sign her child away and then, and only then, would she receive medication. She never signed any papers and she never received any medication and she never saw him until he was 26.

I had known since my early teens that there might have been someone missing from the family and was finally told at age 15. (I was quite wild and my mother was in dread of losing another son, I'm sure it would've killed her.) Now I knew why we (myself, sister, father & mother) had often taken trips to a particular area of Massachusetts for no apparent reason. My mother had somehow found out the location of his adoptive parents and always wanted to catch a glimpse of him, which never happened.

My sister and I convinced our mother that I should go to his parents' door and see if they would put him in touch with me. When I was around 25 his mother arranged a meeting between him, my mother, sister and me. The meeting was hell on my mother. She was a total wreck. She had waited 26+ years for this moment.

It went remarkably well and we arranged to meet his family (wife, first daughter & son) at his house. That meeting also went very well–from hell to heaven for my mother.

I don't know if she ever forgave her parents for shipping her off. She did make her peace with them, though the reasons I'm not sure of. Still after 53+ years, if asked about it, she remembers it like yesterday and it's obvious to me that it's still a very deep wound and it'll never close up and heal. Though since finding him she's been able to find a peaceful place for it all.[3]

Barry

Unlike the women whose stories are chronicled in this book, there are many mothers who feel they cannot come forward, like the anonymous woman who left the following message in an exhibition comment book.

Ann,

No one knows. Not my friends. Not my sons. When I became preg-nant my boyfriend left town and I was left very, very, very alone–just turned 16. It was the 1st time I stood up for myself, refusing to get an abor-tion believing that eventually I'd be able to keep my baby. I wanted him more than my own life. I wanted him. I talked to him and sang to him and prayed he knew how much he was loved. But when he was born, he was taken from me. I had to promise I'd never ask about him and I kept my promise. That was 1971. Now, I see that I can at least register and maybe if he does too, I will have the incredible blessing of a reunion. I married and had 2 sons that do not know. I am sad inside and believe there is no rea-son to make my sons suffer with the inner sorrow of a phantom brother they may never meet. Many unanswered questions. That's why they don't know, but I want to tell them. I want to open this wound and let it heal once and for all. It took guts for me to come to this exhibition. This may seem strange, but it is true. I took off work, drove here and told no one. This is my way of living. Living with this secret.[4]

The burden of shame that was thrust upon unwed mothers in the post-war period has made it difficult for them to share their secret. The shame and secrecy that are still attached to adoptions that took place during this time period have caused tremendous misunderstanding on the part of the public and adoptees. The lack of information about the conditions and complex forces that contribute to relinquishment has left adoptees specu-lating about the scenario that led to their adoption. As a result, many have misplaced anger or have been haunted by the fact that they were "given away" by their own mother.

Over the years, whenever I met an adopted person I would pick their brains. I would ask them, "What do you think about your mother? Do you want to meet her?" I would hear things like, "F—— that bitch. She gave me away. Why would I ever want to meet her?" I'll never forget that one. That was the husband of one of the girls who worked for me. That's what he said. I tried to explain to him why his mom gave him away, but he just didn't want to hear it.

And then I had a delightful girl who's still one of my dearest friends, who came to work for me when she was fifteen on a student program. She was adopted and she wanted very much to meet her mother. She was just the opposite and had made her mom a fairy princess goddess.

—Joyce II

An adopted girl had posted to one of the Internet lists and she was just expressing such bitterness and anger about being given away and being discarded like trash. I felt so touched I was compelled to write her a private e-mail. She was talking about the shame that she felt about being discarded. From what she said, her mother and I were about the same age, so I shared some of my experience with her. It's really sad. It's sad all the way around.

—Joyce I

Dear Ms. Fessler,

My adoptive mother just gave me this article to read over Christmas, she knows I have struggled with "abandonment issues" due to my adoption. I have done some research on my birth mother and received quite a bit of information. I also contacted an organization that told me they could find her in two weeks after I pay my fee for the search. I decided not to for many different reasons. First out of fear, what if I contact her and she doesn't want anything to do with me? I know intellectually she is not rejecting me, she doesn't know me, so how can I take it personally, but my heart tells another story. The other reason is—do I have the right to invade her privacy? Hopefully, she has gone on to have a family and live a happy full life, maybe her family doesn't know her history. Will I cause her pain? It's so hard because I cannot answer these questions.

Christmas night some friends and I were playing a game called "If" and the question was, "If next New Years day you could be anywhere, with anyone, what would you choose?" My answer was, "On the beach anywhere with my biological mother, spending time talking, getting to know who she is, and to thank her for giving me the gift of life." The tears poured out, there is so much emotion I just haven't dealt with. I think about what she looks like, is she happy, do I have half brothers and sisters? I would love to send her pictures of my three beautiful daughters, her Grandchildren!!! I understand in 1961 things were not easy for unwed mothers, your article gave me more to think about when it comes down to the pain she has been through. Being a mother, I can't imagine what it must have been like for her. My parents love me and did the best they could, it hasn't been an easy life. I wouldn't change a thing, my life is full, and everything I have been through has made me the strong independent woman I am today.

There are mothers and children alike with so much grief and so many unanswered questions.[5]

Nancy

Dear Ms. Fessler,

I recently read an article about you in The Boston Globe *and was brought to tears. I am an adoptee who has never had any interest in finding her birth mother until recently. A close friend of mine came down with a rare form of breast cancer. I went with her to all her medical appointments and chemotherapy sessions. Her cancer was found to be genetic and they spoke a lot about how she should prepare her children for their high risk of breast cancer.*

Then I thought about my own children and how I had no medical background to share with them. That's when I decided to search for my birth mother. I found her just about a year ago and we have been exchanging e-mails about once a week. I have never met her, or heard her voice, but am enjoying getting to know her slowly. Her story is very similar to those in your article—the unaccepting parents, inhumane unwed mothers home, etc. She actually had a nervous breakdown and subsequent long-term therapy after she gave me up. She was so glad to hear that nothing awful happened to me after I was adopted. She had reoccurring nightmares of my abuse and mistreatment. We are taking our relationship very slow. My parents have been supportive but hesitant. My dad is the one who actually cut out your article and gave it to me. I couldn't have asked for more wonderful parents. It has given my birth mother such relief to know that.

I'm not sure why I just wrote all of those details. I think these women have suffered in guilty silence for so long.[6]
    Debbi

Simple acknowledgment on the part of the public, professionals, family, and friends that these women have, in fact, suffered a loss and that grief is a normal reaction to their loss would be an enormous step forward, not just for those women who have shared their secret but for all who have been unable to come forward because of fear of further recrimination. Perhaps the example set by Australian social workers and the Tasmanian Parliament could serve as a model. The social stigma of single pregnancy and the treatment of unwed mothers in Australia in the 1950s and 1960s were virtually identical to the situation in the United States. In 1998, urged on by organizations composed of triad members—Adoption Jigsaw and Origins—the Parliament of Tasmania held hearings to determine whether the practices of the 1950s–1980s were "unethical and/or unlawful, or practices that denied birth parents access to non-adoption alternatives for their child."[7] It stated, "The main purpose of this inquiry was to provide those birth mothers that believe they were not treated fairly or appropriately in adoption practices between 1950 and 1988 with an opportunity to put their case forward."[8] The committee listened to the testimony of mothers and professionals and concluded that due to the lack of records, the death of some potential witnesses, conflicting or insufficient evidence, it could not make definitive findings regarding unethical or unlawful practices, but it stated:

> In hindsight, it is believed that if knowledge of the emotional effects on people was available during the period concerned, then parents may not have pushed for adoption to take place and birthmothers may not have, willingly or unwillingly, relinquished their children. Witnesses and respondents, who include some adopted children, would not therefore be experiencing the pain and suffering, which continues to influence their lives.[9]

The report also cited the statement below, with the comment, "Perhaps the statement by the Australian Association of Social Workers Ltd on 12 June 1997 has already made the wisest conclusion to this report." The statement reads:

The Australian Association of Social Workers Ltd (AASW) expresses its extreme regret at the lifelong pain experienced by many
women who have relinquished their children for adoption. In doing this, we recognize that decisions taken in the past, although
based on the best knowledge of the time, and made with the best
of intentions, may nevertheless have been fundamentally flawed.
Many individuals and professionals, social workers included, were
in the past involved in the process that led mothers to give up
their children for adoption. With the wisdom of hindsight, and
with an awareness of the knowledge, resource, and support now
available, we believe that in the same situations today, the same
individuals and professionals would give very different advice.
This in no way diminishes the pain felt by the mothers and children who were separated at birth.[10]

Acknowledgments by professionals that they, too, were the products of
the social forces of the time, such as the one above, can go a long way
toward facilitating conversations within families about the pressures that
parents felt. But within most families there has been silence. They were unable to talk about it at the time, and perhaps time has only made it more difficult to broach the subject. It is clear from the interviews that women who
have finally been able to have an honest and frank conversation with their
own mothers have experienced a tremendous sense of healing. Although
these women cannot retrieve what they have lost, some were finally able to
mend the relationship with their families. The exchange was cathartic and
healing but, unfortunately, often took place thirty or more years after it
should have.

My mom got struck down by cancer. We were told it was terminal,
so my husband and I took her into our home and, with Hospice,
we saw her through her last two months. Hospice told us that
we're supposed to go to the dying person and tell them how much
we loved them and thank them for raising us and apologize to
them for things we have done wrong. So, of course, what did I
apologize for? I apologized for being such a problem when I was

a kid. She said, "What do you mean?" And I said, "You know, the baby." She had only three weeks to live then. She grabbed my hand and looked at me and she said, "Are you kidding?" She said, "Joyce, I am sorry."

After she died, we were going through her things and she has a scrapbook that started out with her oldest child—that was me. We each had a page, then there was an empty page. Then the page after that started with my sister's children, all in order of their births down to the last baby born. Everybody had their page and there was an empty page where my son would have gone. I opened that book and I started crying. I said, "Thank you, Mom."

—Joyce II

If readers scratch beneath the surface of their own family history, they may find a story of unwed pregnancy. Many stories, of course, have been lost to history because mothers carried their secrets to the grave. In some cases, women have not been able to talk about their experience until their own death is imminent and the fear of earthly judgment no longer matters. Deathbed confessions about long-lost nieces, nephews, brothers, sisters, or grandchildren are not uncommon. Two of my oldest and dearest friends each had family members who were unable to talk about their secret until they thought it was their last opportunity. One friend's seventy-nine-year-old mother confessed to her daughter—as the mother lay on a gurney about to be wheeled into surgery—that the person the daughter knew as her uncle was really her half brother. The mother had a baby just before she married, and the baby was raised by her parents as their own. My friend's father would not allow his wife to bring "that bastard" into their home. The mother had been asked to choose between her child and her future husband.

In the other instance, a girlfriend's sister had become pregnant by her high-school sweetheart. They later married, but the baby had already been relinquished. The sister would not talk about the surrender until the week leading up to her death from cancer at age fifty-one. In both cases, the effects of the ongoing secrecy and silence strained relationships between family members, who could not speak of the elephant in the room that had affected all of them.

In all my training in social work and family therapy, the phrase is,
"Secrets keep families sick." You never keep secrets in families, because even if the child doesn't know what the secret is, they will always know there is a secret.

—Leslie

Certainly, a recurring theme in the interviews is just how damaging secrets
and withholding information can be, and not just to families. If parents—and
society in general—had been more realistic about the likelihood of young
people engaging in sexual relations before marriage and had provided them
with adequate information about pregnancy prevention and access to birth
control, perhaps fewer unplanned pregnancies would have occurred in the
first place. Obviously, no one would want to advocate early sexual activity
among teenagers, but leaving young people uninformed only postpones and
complicates the problem—a problem that ultimately becomes one of unplanned pregnancy. With each stage, the problem becomes more complex
and the solutions more difficult and life altering.

In spite of the long-term negative consequences of surrender for those I
interviewed, there are many examples of mothers using their painful experiences to a positive end. One example is the importance that many of these
women placed on sex education for their own children.

I really am very thankful that I had that experience, because I
would *never* want my girls to go through that. *Never!* Nobody
should look down on *anybody* who's using birth control. In these
times there isn't a high-school girl who should not have birth control available to her, and *good* birth control.

Knowledge about birth control to young girls is the most important knowledge you can give them, because if they don't have that
knowledge and they get pregnant, it's going to be a struggle from
that day on. If they go for an abortion, it's still a struggle because
80 percent of abortions are never followed up with counseling.

Women are the future of this country. If they're not screwed
up in some way, they'll get an education and they'll be good
teachers to the next generation. If they're going to do away with

Roe v. Wade, I'm afraid I'm going to have to get on a train. I'll be in Washington to protest, because I can't even imagine the injustice of it for every girl who follows behind me. It's such a knife in the heart of the women of this country. And that comes from a Catholic!

—Maureen II

Part of telling my boys about my pregnancy was also to say, "When you love somebody, no matter what your age, you have a responsibility to that female to not put her in the position I was in." I was very honest with my boys. I didn't want them to put another woman through that loss, because it is a loss. You feel like a part of your soul has been taken away from you. I told them, "I'm not telling you this because *your* life would be destroyed. I'm telling you because it impacts that *mother,* it impacts that *baby.*" Men don't suffer this the same way a woman does. I don't care what anybody tries to tell me. I understand that it's painful, but it's not the same. They didn't carry that baby for nine months.

—Pam

Another positive outcome was that many women chose to work in fields where they could help others because their experience underscored the importance of empowerment, communication, and tolerance. And though it is not uncommon for women to enter the "helping fields," quite a few women arrived at their chosen profession as a result of the lack of communication they experienced in their own family or the powerlessness they felt at the time of their surrender. They understood the importance of advocacy and of open and honest communication. Many felt that a positive outcome of their experience was that it made them less judgmental than they might otherwise have been.

I was a Women's Day speaker at a church one time and I had all these little index cards written out with what I was going to say. I put the cards up there, but I was just led to go ahead and talk from the heart. I had worked in excess of ten years in the court system.

I worked several years in administration and probation/parole before I worked in protective services. And I talked about how when
I sit across the table from a person in the courtroom I try and deal
with that person the way I would want my loved ones to be dealt
with. For all I know, I could have been thinking subconsciously
about the fact that I had a son out there and I didn't know who
was dealing with him, and in what manner. I want everyone to be
treated with dignity. That's how I've tried to give back.

—*Carole II*

People in my family didn't talk about things. I think that's probably part of the reason why I've been drawn to working with people
and talking about the hardest things, because we never did that in
my family. So I've always found myself working with people and
talking about the things nobody else wants to talk about.

When I returned to college after going through the pregnancy,
I chose sociology. Later I went back to get my master's in marriage
and family therapy, because I wanted more knowledge and training about families and how families work, how families cope with
things and negotiate things.

I think part of the reason why I do the work that I do with sexual abuse is when I work with families who have experienced sexual abuse, there's a victim and there's an offender. And I've always
felt like both. I could relate to the offender, because I was the bad
guy. But then on the other hand, I can really feel like the victim because of the times, because there were no alternatives, and because
nobody ever explained to me what I would experience when I went
through an adoption. That was never explained. I don't know that
I would have been able to do anything different, but I wouldn't
have felt so much like a victim if I had been given more information about what that experience was really going to be like.

With this experience, there's a lot of shame. Birth mothers are
kind of the shame receptacle. They quietly carry it around and nobody really knows about it. And nobody wants to hear it. I mean,
nobody . . . because that's too scary. It's too uncomfortable. Peo-

ple don't really know how to listen. When you really listen, you have to take in all those feelings, and some people have a hard time tolerating the pain, the hurt, the shame, or the sadness. Those are the hard feelings.

One of the things that I've often said to people is that one of the greatest gifts, really, that you can give to somebody else is to just listen to who they are, and what they have to say, what their experience is. Just to be able to talk and feel like somebody is really hearing what you have to say. Sometimes that's all you need. If you think that somebody else really hears you, and understands you, that can be very healing. That's a wonderful gift that people can give.

—Sandy I

The public's lack of understanding of these women's experiences—and the notion that they did not suffer a loss—is a result of the women's lack of voice, not their lack of feelings.

Ann,

I am writing to you in response to the article I read in The Boston Globe *about adoption. I would like to share my experience with you because, like your article, it gave me a different perspective regarding the birth mother. However this experience took place in 2003 and not 1966.*

I always felt adoption was a win, win, win situation. I often thought of the birth mother as unfit, or really not wanting her baby for whatever reason. What could be better for a child than to go from an unwanted situation into a loving situation?

Then, really good friends of mine had one child and wanted a second. After so many unsuccessful attempts, they decided to pursue adoption. After extensive research on their part, they put ads in several newspapers in the Midwest. Mostly they were contacted by young unwed women who were pregnant. They finally connected with one, who was as interested in them as they were in her.

No one knew the woman was pregnant, and wanting to keep it that way, she moved closer to them. They brought her to the East Coast and even provided her with a therapist to help her cope with her decision to give up her child.

The birth mother was young, not college educated, and did not come from an affluent family. The father of the baby did not want the child. My friends are a good family. He is successful and she is a stay-at-home mom.

After the baby was born, the birth mother had a hard time signing the papers. My friends were traumatized at the reality of not being able to keep the baby. In speaking with them, they felt betrayed; after all they did for her along with the relationship they developed. She finally signed the papers after several weeks. My friends were of course delighted. The baby is now part of a wonderful family.

I was saddened by this story, and to my surprise, I felt for the birth mother. I didn't see this woman as unfit, or not really wanting her baby. I saw her as someone who could not give her child the same life that my friends could. It seemed to be a "timing" issue and because of her mistake, my friends will raise her baby as their own. I also couldn't help wondering what if she had support financially and emotionally?

So when I read your article, I wasn't sure how far we have come regarding adoption or what the truth about adoption is. Too bad we can't adopt mothers.[11]

Patricia

The voices of surrendering mothers need to be included in ongoing debates regarding adoption policy and law, women's reproductive rights, and sex education. The double standard is still very much a part of our cultural psyche. It is still tolerated within institutions and families and ultimately damages generations of men and women alike. These women were made to carry the full emotional weight of circumstances that were the inevitable consequence of a society that denied teenage sexuality, failed to hold young men equally responsible, withheld sex education and birth control from unmarried women, allowed few options if pregnancy occurred, and considered unmarried women unfit to be mothers. Asking the women to keep their secret and deny their child may have worked out well for others, but not for many of the mothers. Their experience and their motherhood have been silenced and denied for too long.

I feel lucky. I feel lucky because I know my daughter is out there and she's fine, and healthy, and productive, and beautiful. I feel lucky that she says she loves me. I feel lucky that my children love me and understand what happened. I feel lucky that I survived cancer. And I feel lucky that I now have a voice. I didn't for so long, but you're not going to shut me up now. Keeping things inside kills you. You rot from the inside out. I did a great job of punishing myself for thirty-two years. But you just have to set yourself free, and that's what talking about it does.

−Ruth

LYDIA

I was sixteen and lived in Southern California with my parents. I did things that girls in Southern California do: I went to the beach and had a good time. I liked school. I met a very nice young man, a musician, and we started hanging out together. He went to the other school in our valley and he would come up to see me. We became very, very close and very devoted to one another. I had never been intimate with anyone before because I was pretty young. At one point we did find out that we were pregnant and we were both shocked . . . I mean, I don't know why we were shocked, but we were.

My parents got together with my son's father's parents, to make the so-called problem go away, disappear. They decided the best thing for me and for everybody, I guess, would be to send me to a facility—they called it a home, but I called it a facility—to sort of warehouse me in Los Angeles for the duration of my pregnancy.

I just felt like I had done this horrific thing and I was not in any position to protest or say what I wanted. Certainly I wasn't in any position to say, "Is there any way that my baby wouldn't have to be taken?" You know, "You have done quite enough, young lady." In those times, and certainly in my family, I would not come up against my father or my mother and say, "I'm gonna do this or I'm gonna do that." If they put their foot down, that was pretty much the way it was going to be. So the decision was made that I would be sent away and that our baby would be put up for adoption and that was just how it was.

When the time came, my parents loaded me up and took me down to this place and I just remember never being as fearful and distressed. I mean, looking back, I can't imagine sending my child away in that condition. I just don't know how they could do it, but they did. We went to this place and it was institutional looking; it was just cold. I remember there was this aquarium in the sitting area, with all these little fish in there, and I was just mesmerized. I just wanted to be in there with the fish, just take me away from this place and from these people. I didn't want to be deposited there. They left and I was in such shock, I just clammed up and I think I just went inside myself.

I was taken to this long, long room with a bunch of beds. I don't know how many, there had to be twenty or thirty beds right next to one another, each with this little tiny two-drawer stand. After I was there for ten days or something, I told my parents that I was going to run away if they didn't come and get me. My dad finally came down and took me to dinner. I was very, very lonely and unhappy there.

There was just a constant sort of indoctrination with these meetings. They'd sit us all in a big group and tell us what a wonderful thing we were doing, and that whoever the families were that would get our babies they were these sort of idyllic sort of families, they were perfect. That sounded good to me. I was sixteen and I thought that's what my baby needs. It doesn't need me.

At some point my dad did come and take me home. I don't know which place was worse because they really did not want me to be there; that was really evident. They were very angry with me. I pretty much stayed in my room and at one point I put a lock on my door because my mother was especially unhappy with me and treated me badly. They called me terrible names that I would never call my daughter. First they tried to get rid of me and then they brought me home and called me terrible names. That stuck with me, too. To have your mother call you a slut or a whore. I mean, it sent a real message about being pregnant and having children. Those were my memories, that's my experience.

My boyfriend and I were very much in love, we saw a future together, whatever that would mean. The message I got as a young expectant mother was I wasn't good enough. I mean, basically that was the message. I wasn't good enough for my child. That stands out as a message that I carry to this day. That's probably why I never had any children after my son.

Ironically, my son's father didn't have any children of his own, either. I think that message really hit home with us at a point in our lives when we hadn't really developed the ego strength to withstand that kind of onslaught. I felt denigrated, marginalized. I couldn't put it into words then, but

I just thought, "I'm not good enough," and that never went away. I also didn't want to have children again because I really felt strongly that–how do I put this?–I didn't want to do that to my son. If I couldn't raise my son, why would I have another child to raise? That would dishonor my son. I honestly felt that all my life. So I never had children. But I was always striving to be better and better and prove that I was good enough or that I was mother material, that I could be respected in that way, and I never got there.

I wasn't looking forward to going to the hospital and giving birth because then I knew that was going to be it. I'd be separated from my baby. They let the father stay with me for quite a long time and so that was very comforting. I guess they finally told him that he would have to leave. It's very painful even now, thirty-five years later. I gave birth to a little boy and they let me see him, but they took him away pretty quickly. I remember he screamed really loudly and they said he had a really good set of lungs.

The first morning, a couple of people came from the county in suits. I was flat on my back with my head flat because I had had an epidural. I remember I had to sign the paper; it was only about nine hours after I gave birth. I had to do it, like, upside down. She said, "This is just so that we can give your son any medical attention. This is your permission, that's all this is." Well, come to find out that it wasn't just that; it was also for foster care. No one had ever said the words *foster care*. I had no idea. I signed it, and I guess a day or two went by and finally a nurse came in with my son all wrapped up and she gave him to me.

I was really surprised because they had told me that he couldn't get out of his incubator. They told me that he weighed three pounds three ounces, or something like that, and that he was so frail that he had to be in this incubator or he would get sick. And, of course, I believed the doctors. So, anyway, this nurse brought him and let me hold him for about an hour and that was just the best. I never forgot that time. It was the best thing that I can ever remember. I was so happy, I felt peaceful. I thought this is how it's supposed to be.

I'm fifty-two now. I had my son thirty-five years ago and to retell . . . to recount what happened during that time and to talk about this even after all these years, I'm trembling. I think a person could see that my body is trembling. It's just as intense as it was when they first took my son away.

We got to see our son one more time when we went to sign the papers at the social-services office. We got to sit with him and hold him and then we were brought into a little area where we were supposed to sign these papers. I just remember shutting down even more so, just going on automatic. They told me what to do and where to sign and that's what I did. The father was right there with me and he held my hand and I signed everything that they wanted me to sign. I distinctly remember walking out of that building and leaving my little boy in there.

I was never the same person after I came out of that building. I became much more introverted. Definitely not trusting, I didn't trust people after that, really. I had a pretty good self-image right up to that time. I think going through that, and being told by all kinds of people—parents, doctors, social workers—that I wasn't what I thought I was . . . I guess I thought they were right.

I became very depressed. I didn't know what was happening to me. I had never been depressed before. I had been a pretty happy young woman, pretty well adjusted, I loved life, I looked forward to things, I was pretty smart, I was resourceful, I was creative, I liked who I was. Not that all those things went away, but I think to have your baby taken—and I want to make the point that he *was* taken from me. I never gave him away. He was never meant to be a gift. If anything, the gift was that I thought I gave him the parents that he needed. *They* were the gift. *They* were the gift to *him*. My son was not a gift.

My boyfriend and I were still together. He graduated and we actually got a little home together. A beautiful home up at the top of a hill and we were very happy for a long time. I think as time went by, though, I had changed so much, I really became a different person. So eventually we went our separate ways. I decided that I would go ahead and get into college; I was a good student. I really enjoyed creative writing. My professors encouraged me to send my work off and I got published in some very good journals. That sort of lifted me up and I thought, "Well, there is something that I'm good at." I think I had to prove something to myself. I had to find something that I felt like I could do, that I was good at.

I think at that point, emotionally, I was trying to cover up and just, as they say, dance as fast as I could to not think about what had happened. Then one day I just couldn't get out of bed. I was at school and I was in the midst of all these midterms and I couldn't move. I really didn't see it coming. I simply broke down. My parents had to come and get me. Even then, they didn't recognize that I was having a very serious problem coping with this loss. I can't imagine that they didn't know what this stemmed from, but they didn't acknowledge it. We never talked about my son ever, ever, until he found me thirty years later. It was like a big dead horse on the dining-room table that we all danced around.

Eventually, I just got on with my life. When I thought of my son, I had to put a positive spin on it because what else could I do? He was gone. I just had to think that he was in a wonderful place. It was sort of a recording. I would say, "It was a wonderful thing I did for my little boy. He has a wonderful family. I'm sure he's having a great life." I started believing that, and still there was just something *so* missing. I mean, I was just bereft under all of that. I didn't *really* understand why it was supposed to be a good thing. I'm still sort of perplexed.

I still don't know what hit me. It was like an eighteen-wheeler came at me, or a train came at me, and here I am still standing. That's kind of how I feel. You just keep going, you know, the emotional wreckage aside, you just keep putting one foot in front of the other and you go through the motions and you look like you're a normal person among all these normal people. You just go on.

But that young woman in me was always there. There was just a little place set aside somewhere; she was locked away and not allowed to have her voice. People did not want to hear what she had to say. Believe me, she was very angry. I can say that with a second voice that I have. This young woman that they locked away had feelings, she had emotions, she wanted her son and nobody wanted to hear that. So the older woman just took over and that's how it had to be to survive.

I got married in my early thirties and after that I actually did some interesting advocacy work. I worked for about five or six years for the Romanian orphans who were discovered after Ceauşescu was deposed in 1989. In the early nineties I worked doing direct emergency relief for those children—airlifts with food and medicine and clothing. Looking back, I feel that I was

sort of compelled to work with children in some capacity. I felt I was helping rescue them or something, these little children. I'm sure that has some
sort of meaning, you know, because of what I had gone through in losing
my son.

After that, I became involved with a very large animal sanctuary in the
United States. I coordinated a volunteer corps for them and I helped put to-
gether a manual they've been disseminating to shelters around the country.
I would help put on very big animal-adoption festivals. I kept pretty busy.

Then, I guess it was in 1999, I had gone out to have lunch with my mom
and we were sitting in a little restaurant, and she told me that she had gotten a call from a very nice young man who had left his phone number and
wanted me to call him. She was still in the same home and had the same
number. He had not told her exactly what it was he wanted to speak to me
about, but she felt real strongly that it could be my son.

So as it turned out, yes, it was my son. I was just stunned. I had never
thought that this would ever come to pass. I went ahead and called his father, we hadn't talked in years and years and years. I just said, "Are you sitting down?" He says, "I can be," or something to that effect, and I let him
know that our son had found us. He was as elated as I was. We were just so
shocked and happy. We both got to speak to our son that evening. When he
got on the phone, the voice was familiar because he sounds like his father. I
think one of the first things I said to him is "You sound just like your father."
I remember he said no one had ever told him anything like that before.

We had a long talk and just filled each other in, and it was very . . . it was
very emotional. It was happy, and a relief, and everything rolled into one. It
was just . . . I mean, I can't describe the feelings . . . to talk to my son for the
first time after all those years. We decided that we'd try to see each other as
soon as possible. His father wasn't going to wait. He got on a plane the next
morning. Then I flew in, and there he was. I definitely recognized him. I
mean, he *had* to be our son.

He's just very sweet and he's a very intelligent young man and he's ac-
complished all these things. We continued to talk on the phone after that
and see each other back and forth. He came down and visited me and met
his grandmothers and cousins and brought his wife and everything and
it was very, very happy. Through all this, you know, it's difficult . . . he's

known a family that he calls his own all his life. And, of course, that's his family and he has wonderful memories with them. It is difficult to sort of be added on. So over these last five years it's been difficult at times and happy at times and sad at times, for both of us, for all of us—trying to figure out where we all fit. We really want to be in each other's lives in some way and I guess we're just still working through all that. So at this stage we're just looking to the future and I'm hoping that we're going to have a good, productive, loving relationship from here on.

When my son found us, we were all extremely happy and just so relieved that he was with us. We wanted to see one another and talk with one another and that continued for many months. Then I'd say maybe nine or ten months into our reunion it hit me like a ton of bricks. It was as though a trigger had gone off and I started to experience all of the trauma that I wasn't allowed to experience, or didn't even know I should be experiencing, when I was much younger. I think I was coming out of denial.

I feel as though I was preyed upon by this system, by these people that I was surrounded by. Not some nebulous thing but real human beings, real people had a hand in taking my son away. I knew this, but to this day I really haven't been able to express this to my son in such a way that he accepts it or understands it completely. I was not able to ever mourn my loss of him or be able to express how sad I was. Nobody ever said, "Oh, I'm sorry. . . ."

All of that came to a head when I realized that this wasn't a good thing. It was in everyone else's best interests. It was the convenient, expedient thing to do at the time, but it wasn't really in our best interests. It was not a win-win situation. In my opinion, it was a loss for him, too. He didn't get to know his mother and father. We didn't get to know our son, and be with our son, which we should rightfully have been able to do. The winners were the adoptive parents and the social workers who got to do their job in the way that they thought they should do it. We lost and we lost big. I mean, we lost the most precious thing in our lives that ever was or ever will be—our baby. Nothing can ever make up for that.

After my son and I reunited, I experienced what was probably post-traumatic stress. I can only describe this as a sort of out-of-body experience, but at one point I felt like I was not human. I didn't feel the humanness in me and that was really scary. It was just like a big, ugly, dirty, dark hole. I realized that I had been used. I wasn't recognized as a human being. I was a mother. I was not a breeder or an incubator for somebody else. I was a young expectant mother and I was treated like I was this thing used to produce a child for somebody else.

At that point, my marriage started on a downward slope that never stopped and I eventually divorced after a twenty-year marriage. My family couldn't understand and it was making everyone very uncomfortable. I refused antidepressants. I really felt like I was silenced before and I was not going to cover it up or make everybody around me comfortable by taking a happy pill. I'm sorry, everyone needed to see what this had wrought.

I was very determined that I was going to make it through and it wasn't going to be on pills. I did reach out and go to some pretty good psychologists who understood adoption issues. Unfortunately, it's not recognized as a loss, so no one has worked up a nice psychological model to treat us and to get us healthy again. I knew that I needed to vent or at least talk about this, but I would not take pills. I wanted to be able to mourn and grieve the loss of my child, and I wanted to be coherent when I did that. I had a right to be sad and angry and I didn't want to be shut up again. That had already been done to me for thirty years and it was not going to happen again.

It makes everybody real uncomfortable to think that they took a mother's baby away, that she didn't give it up happily and voluntarily and as a gift. Nobody wants to face the fact that this is very traumatic. Even back in the sixties, it was a matter of finding a child for a family instead of finding a family for the child. It leaves a lot of emotional wreckage and it usually goes unaddressed because it's not even seen as a problem.

It always comes to mind whenever I see somebody on the news who, God forbid, has their child kidnapped. Or you see in a magazine that a child anywhere in the world has been killed, and the mother is just grieving inconsolably, hysterically. We have all the same feelings but the public doesn't know that. They don't want to acknowledge it because it is so unpleasant. It makes everybody so uncomfortable to think that in this civilized society anybody could actually take a baby away from a young woman and expect her to not cry or be sad, or not want that to happen. We have those same hysterical, out-of-control, inconsolable, never-goes-away grief, you know, "Please, where's my baby?" sort of feelings. It's just that no one recognizes it and they don't want to hear it. We have those feelings and they're all bottled up. I mean, talk about people raging inside. . . . When you have your child taken away and nobody cares and nobody wants to help you or even recognize that you might be sad, that's rage.

Before my son found me, if I would share that I had had a son and that he had been taken into adoption, people would not have sensed any kind of rage in me. They would have thought that I was very much at peace with what they thought was my decision. I actually had to think it was my decision because otherwise I would have been enraged for thirty years and I probably wouldn't be here now.

I came to really resent the language that was used to describe me and my experience. Everyone who would talk about adoption in general, or about adopted people or mothers who had lost their children, seemed to all use the same sort of jargon, what I would call "loaded language," that's emotionally charged. It's very judgmental and biased to one side of an issue. Calling young expectant mothers "birth mothers" or any kind of mother other than just simply *the mother* simply serves to put distance between that mother and her baby. That serves a real purpose. It makes everybody comfortable with the fact that she's not a "real" mother. You have terms such as "first mother," "life mother," "birth mother," "natural mother," "biological mother," like she was just this surrogate receptacle that carried this child to the real family. So there is a lot of language surrounding adoption which is very disentitling, disenfranchising, marginalizing to both the child and the mother, and in favor of the industry and the potential adoptive parents.

Every mother is inexperienced the first time she is pregnant. Somehow, whether they're married or unmarried, thirty or eighteen, they learn to be a mother. I can only speak from my experience, but as a seventeen-year-old woman I was educable, I was trainable, I was looking for guidance in every facet of my life. I was very resourceful. I was very loving and gentle. I would have made, I believe, an excellent mother. Unfortunately, that opportunity was taken away from me. If I'd had support and mentoring, I would have made a wonderful mother for my son.

I think there should be opportunities to mentor young expectant mothers in established homes, to see how parents act in a healthy home, to learn from that. A mentoring experience and classes in parenting–all of these things could help a young woman who is single at the time of giving birth. She may eventually get married and maybe have more children. But I think that these young women just need some guidance and education. They have all the natural inclinations to be the mother to their child and most want to be, and would be, if given the opportunity.

LINDA I

I grew up in Waco, Texas, and we were raised very strict Baptist. There was right and wrong and you didn't stray. That's more or less the way I'd lived my life. Then right after I graduated from high school, things were getting bad in Vietnam. We lived just outside of James Connolly Air Force Base. A lot of the boys in my high-school class were drafted. My cousin was drafted and my other cousin was killed there in 1968. I was a fairly good nursing assistant and I wanted to be a nurse but didn't have the money for school. So I joined the army. I thought this would be a way I could help the army and our country and also get a good education.

I went to Fort Sam Houston, Texas, where I was on the receiving end when they brought the wounded in. So many men were being killed. We were told to never tell how many men were brought in, because the U.S. didn't want to alarm the general public. We weren't to talk of the wounds or anything we saw. I worked with the men who were brought back with contagion due to their wounds, or jungle diseases that there was no cure for—things of that sort.

They trained us to be combat medics. We learned how to crawl on our tummies and pull the stretchers. We were sent out in the field with little plastic things to make tents out of. The Air Force tried to kill us. They would drop bombs on us. They were teaching us not to get shell-shocked. Only one person in my class had a nervous breakdown. They sent her back home, but all the rest of us went right on through that. We were trained and ready in case they needed us. As far as I understand, no woman ever went to the lines; they were at the field hospitals. A friend of mine went and she came back and committed suicide. She couldn't deal with what she saw.

I had lived, I guess, a fairly sheltered life. I didn't know it at the time. I thought I was typical of the sixties, but I guess I wasn't. I hadn't ever had sex or anything like that. Like I said, I grew up in Waco and the Baptist headquarters is there. But during the war everything was going fast. A day then was like a month now. It was terrible pressure, taking care of the wounded. Men died in my arms. I was their mother, I was their priest, I was their sister, whatever they needed. I would talk to them and I'd pray with them. I'd hold them in my arms and tell them that they were a hero and that I'd never forget them, and I haven't. I still dream of that. They say that's post-traumatic stress syndrome and I should go to the VA. No, what that is, is just caring for people.

There at Fort Sam Houston, I met a soldier who had been injured. They brought him back to recover and I fell in love with him instantly. He looked like Dean Martin. He said that he fell in love with me at first sight and he asked me to marry him. I thought it was the most wonderful thing in the world. Before we were supposed to marry, I became pregnant. I wasn't even worried. Of course, I knew my family would be counting the months.

I knew I could get pregnant, but I never even thought about it. Some way or another, falling in love with him just erased my mind. I had been putting him off for a good while, but I was in love with him and we were going to get married soon. So I went ahead. Two weeks later, I was pretty sure I was pregnant. So yes, I knew better, but reason left my mind.

When I told him I thought I was pregnant, he told me that he was married. It just broke my heart. Later I found out—and this makes me really furious—that there are many military men who propose marriage to women who are not very worldly. They will give you a ring and say they're going to marry you, with no intentions. I had a ring. I was already wearing it and I had made plans for the wedding.

Several times during my pregnancy I thought of suicide. I didn't see how I could go on. I knew I didn't dare confide in my family or close friends. I knew my days in the army were short. I was about to be kicked out. I heard a lot of sermons from my commanding officer about how I had dishonored the whole army. It wasn't bad enough to dishonor myself; I had gone after the whole U.S. government. I cried. I wasn't acting like a trained combat soldier, I can tell you that. I was sobbing and apologizing and saying how sorry I was. I had to write something on it and I wrote how sorry I was that I had dishonored the army.

They gave me an honorable discharge but they told me the reason they did was because of the child. If she were to see my records someday she would feel guilty because I had been kicked out of the service due to her. I didn't know it at the time, but the law said after she was born I could go back. They didn't tell me. Since they were talking about how dishonorable I had been, I didn't think they wanted me back. The father got a pension. He got a pension that he still draws to this day. So the whole thing was much harder on me than it was on him.

My mother let me stay at home for a few weeks, then she said, "You don't look pregnant now, but you will soon. I want you out of this house." She told me that if I kept my baby I could not come back. She also said, "You'll never be able to find a job with a baby. All you're going to find is more trouble like you've had. No decent man will want to marry you and if you keep your child people will call her a bastard and they'll be mean to her. Who do you love the most, you or your child?" She said, "You go to that maternity home and you give that baby up."

Being that I really didn't have any resources, that's what I did. At that time, people were talking about it being a sexual revolution—free love and Woodstock—but it didn't happen in Waco, Texas. There was no way that I could have had my daughter with me. I lived in the maternity home for six months and I gave birth at Fort Sam Houston. I heard helicopter after helicopter landing outside my window. I would crawl over and look out and cry because they were bringing in wounded soldiers. Fort Sam is the burn center of the world, and some of these young men were burned so badly. I thought, "I'm supposed to be down there helping these men into this hospital. I'm supposed to be saving lives."

I saw her after she was born. I couldn't believe she looked just like me. They let me hold her and I told her I don't want to do this but I have to. I swore to her that when she was eighteen years old I was going to find her. I said, "I love you and I don't want to do this." When I did find my daughter she told me, "I never worried, I knew you'd find me and I knew you loved me." So her soul remembered what I said.

I returned to the maternity home and stayed until I was considered healed. While I was there, I put together a baby book for my daughter. I didn't put in names or anything, just things about me and her father. I was hoping that she could use this to avoid the mistake I made. I also bought her a christening dress. I had changed my religion to Lutheran. I didn't have any use for those Baptists because they were rather condemning. They didn't give her the book. They just told her that I was in the army and that I was musical. I had sung backup on some of the sixties music. It was enough to make me sound a lot more interesting than I am.

I never let the people at the home see me cry. From then on, I put a face on for the public, but I grieved. It was like a child had died, and I have lost some babies since then, so I know exactly what I'm talking about. It was very difficult for me to sign those papers. One of the things that hurt me desperately was that where it said "Father" they put "unknown." I knew who my baby's father was and he knew she was his child. I thought, "If she ever gets this birth record, what is she going to think of me?"

Every July 3, I would remember. Usually I was sick. One time I had a heart attack on July the third. I had a whole list of illnesses. I had ovarian tumors that came out one time in July. If you go back and look at my medical records, I was always physically ill around that time. I spent a lot of those days in the hospital. I know it was nothing except the stress and the sadness. There's no way that I can describe the sadness that was in my heart. It was like she was born again on that day.

I went on to nursing school and halfway through I started seeing a friend who was a Green Beret. He had actually been in the same company at Fort Bragg as my cousin who was killed. We began corresponding and later we were married. I always liked him but I don't think I loved him. I didn't ever want to be in love with anybody in that way again. He was a POW for a short time and was wounded. He had scars, you know, and he became very mean. When my daughter was two we were divorced. Later, I met my husband that I'm married to now. It was love at first sight. We've been married, I think, thirty-five years; I have to add it up. So there *is* life after doing everything wrong.

I always wanted to know where my daughter was but I knew that it was against the law for me to even think about looking for her until she was of age. I kept counting down the years. Every birthday was one year closer to eighteen. I thought about it a lot, but I was afraid. I thought she might hate me, like the doctor had told me in the army. Every July 3, I would put a birthday greeting in the San Antonio *Light* for my daughter. I'd say, "Born

7/3/66, Happy Birthday, your mom loves you." When I located her, I sent a letter and she called the day she got it. She said, "I know you're my mother. I don't have to investigate. When you answered the phone, I thought I was talking to myself."

I found out later that she played violin. We both participated in musical programs. She has a beautiful voice and did many professional appearances. She was also in the army and was a trained combat medic for Desert Storm. Her military pictures look just like mine. We were both EKG technicians, we work with hearts.

And she's interested in history like I am. I was able to tell her about our ancestors, like the ancestor who was the youngest man killed at the Alamo. I belong to the Western Cherokee Nation of Arkansas, Missouri. My great-grandmother was Cherokee and she was born on the Missouri River. My father's grandmother was Chickasaw, so I have ancestry on both sides. My daughter's father is also Cherokee. I think he has more Cherokee blood than I do. She didn't know she was part Native American. She wasn't told. I don't think she was told anything about her heritage, just things like . . . I played the French horn. I think it meant more to her to know some of her background. She said knowing made her a whole person.

I'm a Texas Search Angel and every person that I have reunited I've done it in honor of my daughter, because it's made a difference in her life. She felt there was always something missing. She says it doesn't take away from her other family; she just has two families, and she loves them both.

Finding her and becoming close to her did not end the pain. I took a lot of psychological counseling and I don't think it helped. I just wasted my money. The only thing that helped was time and honesty. I had to become honest and say, "I gave my child up for adoption."

After the reunion, my mother told me that if I was going to have my daughter in my life, then I couldn't have her in my life. She said, "I will not be embarrassed by you having this illegitimate daughter. You're going to have to make a choice." And I did. I chose my daughter. My mother wrote letters and I put "Return to sender" on them. I told her, "I made the wrong decision in the first place. I should not have given up my child, I should have been able to find a way." Back then I chose my family, today I'm choosing my daughter.

My father became ill and I took care of him until he died. I did the same, more or less, with my mother. My father wanted my daughter in his life and would ask about her when my mother wasn't around. He would say, "I'm sorry, I'm sorry." It broke his heart. I blamed my mother for not helping me. I was angry and, to be honest, I never got over that completely. I took care of my mother and did everything I could for her, but it left resentment in my heart.

I am an activist for open records. Any adoptee who is eighteen years old should have their original records if they want them. Adopted people need to have their medical history, know their genealogy, their ancestry, that's their right. My daughter has inherited a genetic disease from her father. Someday she will be paralyzed. Without those records, she wouldn't have known and without early treatment she would have had serious problems. With the right medication, the disease is progressing slowly. So I'm one of the people that you see down in front of the capitol building with my signs. There's no reason for any state, any court of law, to withhold that information.

I had to do what I did because of the times. What you have to do is make that bad into something good. That's why I'm a Search Angel and that's why I'm always writing letters to the senators. I'm trying to keep others from suffering what I have suffered. I want everybody to have a chance to be reunited and to heal. Had I not been able to reunite with her, I think I'd probably be in an institution. I don't believe I could have dealt with it all these years. I just don't think I'm strong enough. I've had a lot of pain in my life, relatives and loved ones I was really close to who died. It hurt so bad, but there's nothing that comes close to this. Death is not the same, because death is final. You know that loved one is in heaven. But with adoption it's never final because that child is walking this earth somewhere, so it never ends.

I also talk to teenagers about pregnancy. I tell them my story. They need to know in order to avoid the pain I suffered. I say, "If you have unprotected sex, this is what could happen to you." So I put myself right out there on the firing line and, believe me, I've been fired at more than once. I've helped a lot of people and I wouldn't have done that if it hadn't been for my daughter. So I think that the Lord created my daughter to help others and to make this a better world. She's done a lot for me. She has shown me that I don't have to be a doormat. She says, "You don't have to smile and say okay.

That's why you have an ulcer, Mom. You've got to be honest and truthful and stand up for what's right."

Not only has my daughter done a lot for me, so has her family. We've all made changes. We've grown together. We might not be the all-American recognized family, but we're one family and at the center is our daughter.

11

⁂

Every Mother
but My Own

A S I MET WITH WOMEN across the country and asked them to reveal
the most intimate details of their lives, most asked me if I had met my
own mother. "No," I would always say, "but I know where she is." I suspected it was an unsatisfying answer for many of them. After the tape
recorder was turned off, the interviewees often took over the role of inter-
viewer and pressed further. Some asked politely why I had not made contact, but the underlying question was: "Why are you traveling around the
country collecting the life histories of all these surrendering mothers but not
your own?" It was a legitimate question.

Usually I would launch into the story that began, as this book begins,
with the chance meeting with the woman in the gallery and ended with my
journey through the farms and fields of the rural Midwest in search of my
mother's yearbook picture. I would tell the story in more or less detail, but
it didn't really answer their question. They were usually too polite to press
further, but they would often encourage me to contact my mother and some
would offer advice on how to go about it. Or they would simply give me a

knowing look, perhaps identifying with an earlier point in their own measured progress.

I have always approached important decisions slowly. I look at the options and potential outcomes from all sides. I circle around and around the central problem, seemingly covering the same territory while inching ever so slightly closer to a decision. Then one day I simply act. In fact, the conclusive action feels like a nonchalant move, impulsive even, as if I were acting on a whim.

Perhaps the visual work I began fifteen years ago on the subject of adoption was the first step of the slow, spiraling path to my mother. If so, as with earlier decisions, I am thankful I took my time. A more direct path would not have encompassed all the mothers I met along the way.

My rationale for waiting so long was my concern for my two mothers, but perhaps it was also my own fear of the unknown. My mother, Hazel, made it clear that she thought it was a bad idea for adoptees to seek out their mothers. She would always talk about it in the abstract, in response to a made-for-TV movie or talk show about adoption. Otherwise, it never came up. Her sweeping generalizations about all adoptees and her contention that "*they* should not look for their mothers because *they* never know what they might find" was a message clearly aimed at me. It was a warning meant to protect me, but I knew she was equally concerned about herself. She feared I might prefer my "real" mother to her; it is a common fear among adoptive parents. But for adoptees the adoptive family *is* their family. The bonds that develop over a lifetime together are not broken by the introduction of additional family members. Yet, knowing how my mother felt, I respected her wishes and waited. Hazel was seventeen years older than my natural mother, Eleanor. I calculated that there would be time enough.

My concern for Eleanor was the second reason I had not attempted contact. I assumed she had not told her subsequent children about her experience. I knew that her husband had passed away years before, as had her parents. Her secret, most likely, had been buried with them. Maybe she wanted it to stay that way.

Hazel passed away in 2003, almost a year to the day after I began interviewing. I waited for what I felt was a respectable length of time and then wrote Eleanor a letter. It was not the first letter I had composed, but it was the first I sent. As so many years had passed since I had gone on my journey to find a yearbook picture and was given her address by her unsuspecting brother, I decided to send the letter by certified mail. I could not be certain that she still lived in the same house, or even that she was still alive.

Dear Eleanor,

I hope that this letter does not come as too much of a shock to you but I am an adoptee and my search for information about my biological family has led me to you. I believe you may be my mother.

I sent for my original birth certificate quite a few years ago and have weighed the pros and cons of sending you a letter for a very long time. My hesitation was, for the most part, due to my concern about whether or not you would welcome contact. I worried that this letter would bring up painful memories that you may not want to revisit. I also worried about hurting my adoptive mother's feelings, but she passed away in June and thus the only thing holding me back since then has been my concern about invading your privacy. But I decided to take a chance and write.

First, I want to reassure you that I have never had any negative feelings about being surrendered for adoption. Having grown up in the fifties and sixties I am well aware of the social stigma and shame that single women had to endure as a result of getting pregnant. I always felt very empathetic towards you, knowing how difficult it must have been.

I also want you to know that I did have, and continue to have, a wonderful and fulfilling life. My adoptive parents, who have both passed away, were completely devoted to my brother and me. Like many couples who turn to adoption, they wanted children very badly but could not have their own. Three and a half years after I was adopted, my parents adopted my brother. We lived on the edge of town in a rural setting. My father had grown up on a big farm in Iowa and though he didn't make his living as a farmer he raised crops on our 5 acres to keep his hand in it.

I had a fairly idyllic childhood growing up in the country. I was, and still am, a huge animal lover and spent my days exploring the fields that surrounded our house with my dog by my side. My mother, who would have loved to put me in frilly dresses, was always somewhat dismayed that she could never get me out of my cowgirl boots and jeans. I always preferred

*building forts and growing things to playing with dolls. I loved art and at-
tended Saturday classes at Toledo Art Museum throughout my childhood.*

*Though I was pretty shy as a small child I became very outgoing and
social in junior high school. I used my sense of humor and interest in story-
telling to entertain my friends and make them laugh. I always received
good grades, but I must say that I was much more interested in socializing
and boyfriends than in my education when I was in high school.*

*I majored in art in college and later went on for two graduate degrees.
I have been teaching photography, video, and related art courses at the college level since the mid-1970s. Though I studied drawing, painting, and
other traditional mediums, I preferred using photography, film, video, and
writing to tell stories based in real experiences. There is much more to say
about the specifics of my artwork, but I don't want to overwhelm you with
information in the first letter. I'll save that for the next one if you want to
continue to communicate.*

*I've been living in Rhode Island for the last 10 years and have lived in
Baltimore, Philadelphia, Tucson, and St. Louis, since leaving Ohio. My
husband Peter works in New York so we have a small apartment there as
well. On the weekends we try to put our busy week behind us by working
in the garden or repairing one thing or another on our old house.*

*So now you know a little bit about me and I hope you will be willing
to write back and tell me about yourself. I have many interests and personality traits that are quite different than my parents' and I have always
wondered if they were genetic.*

*My mother was always very open about the information she was given
from the adoption agency, though I know that agencies are not always
honest about the information they pass on to adopting parents. My family
was told that you were from a big farm family and that my birth father
was a football player. My adoptive father had been a star athlete in high
school so I suspect that his farm background and his athletic ability both
contributed to me being matched with my adoptive parents.*

*I would, of course, also love to know about the circumstances that led
up to my birth. I'm hoping that you are willing to share the information
and will not hold back for fear I might pass judgment on you. Please believe me when I say that I do not judge you, anything you did, or any de-*

cisions you made. I have talked to many mothers who have surrendered
children for adoption and have heard every kind of story, so you don't
have to worry about hurting my feelings if the circumstances were anything
less than conventionally romantic. It's just that if I am ever to have any in-
formation whatsoever about my paternal lineage, it must come through
you. So after telling me about yourself I would really appreciate any infor-
mation you have about my biological father.

I have no particular expectations or ideas about where to go from here.
I will not contact you again unless you contact me first. Take all the time
you need. I fully understand if you do not want to take this any further, but
I do hope you will at least write once, so I will have the answers to the ques-
tions that only you can provide.

All my love,

Ann

I mailed the three-page letter and waited for the card confirming receipt.
But nothing. I envisioned her refusing the letter, or purposely allowing it to
languish in the post office until the ten days were up and the letter would
automatically be returned. The U.S. Postal Service Web site indicated that a
delivery attempt had been made, but not whether it would attempt another.
After a week I called the post office. Three days later the 3½" x 5½" green card
arrived in my mailbox with her signature neatly and beautifully written out
in uniform script above the line that reads "Recipient."

A year later, I still had not received a response to my letter. But I could
wait a while longer. After all, it had taken me fourteen years to write her and
I did tell her to take her time. I did not tell her that I already knew quite a
bit. I did not mention the conversation with her brother, my uncle, or the
dull gray copy of her senior picture that I had photocopied from her high-
school yearbook, which was now tucked away in a manila folder alongside
the obituaries of her parents, my grandparents.

I said that I would wait for her to contact me, and I believed that when I
sent the letter. But once that first big step had been taken it was hard not to
take the next. Since I had not heard from her in such a long time, I concluded that she didn't want anything to do with me. I was convinced that
she was either scared out of her wits or simply did not want this intrusion

into her life. Of these two possibilities, I hoped it was the latter. By now I had heard stories of women curling themselves into a fetal position after receiving a letter. I had visions of her in a heap on the floor. I had sent pictures. Maybe I shouldn't have.

At some point my focus shifted. Now it seemed clear to me that she didn't want to communicate, but I wanted to know why. I thought I knew. After more than a hundred interviews, I knew the most common reasons, but I wanted to know if the same was true in *her* case. I mulled it over. I had said I would let her make the next move. Could I really break the first promise I'd ever made to her? I decided to send a little card. The card said, "Still waiting to hear . . ." I didn't really expect her to respond. This time I was sending a signal. The card was the promise breaker.

My husband will tell you that what I said about circling and mulling things over is true. I've been talking about building a studio in the pasture behind our house for eight years. I draw up floor plans on the backs of used envelopes. I build scale models. I get estimates on the foundation, I speak to builders, I save money, but I don't build the studio. Instead, I think, "With that same money I could put a down payment on land in Arizona. It would be a start on a winter getaway for retirement." I look at property in Arizona. I research straw-bale houses. My husband is sick of hearing about the studio I'm going to build and the winters in Arizona.

Two months after sending the card, I called her. "Eleanor?" "Yes?" "This is Ann Fessler." I had given a lot of thought to how I might keep her on the phone when she tried to hang up. Perhaps I would not even have a chance to ask for a moment of her time. She might say nothing at all and simply return the receiver to the cradle.

She said, "Well, hello . . ." It was a drawn-out hello, the kind with a slight rise in tone that suggests a pleasant surprise. I said, "Are you willing to talk to me . . . a little?" "Sure . . ." I was so unprepared for this response that I forgot everything I wanted to ask her. I said, "Well, I wasn't sure because you hadn't responded. . . ." She said, "I actually bought you a birthday card this year, but . . . I didn't send it." I still couldn't remember my questions. I asked her if she had any questions for me, and that's how we began.

She asked me about being a photographer and I explained that I taught photography but that I had been making video installations and short films.

She asked more questions and I told her that I had been working autobiographically with the subject of adoption for years but that more recently I had been collecting the oral histories of mothers who had surrendered children, and the conversation continued from there. It was a steady stream of questions and answers in both directions that continued for two hours.

As I had always suspected, she got pregnant on New Year's Eve. I had already counted backward from my birthday and guessed as much. Her story was not the story of ill-fated love that my parents had been told by the social worker at the adoption agency. They were not a couple who wanted to get married but were prevented by his family, who did not want him to drop out of college. He was not in college. None of that was true. It had always sounded a little too much like a Hollywood script to me. He was not a football player, either. He played basketball. I don't even like basketball.

The truth, it seems, had been stretched in both directions. By now, I knew that agencies routinely fabricated information when describing the adoptive family to the mothers. But for some reason I had never contemplated what Eleanor might have been told about my parents. The story she was given was that my would-be adoptive mother was a nurse and that my father owned a factory. My mother was a practical nurse but my father certainly did not own a factory; he worked in one. The agency assured her I would go to my new family right away. She seemed a bit taken aback to learn that my parents were not able to take me home until I was three months old.

She, like many of the women I interviewed, had gone to a Crittenton home. Her story was familiar. She had stayed in her parents' home, hiding her pregnancy with a girdle and oversized blouses until a month or so before she was due. At the maternity home they had to do chores and they were told not to reveal their last names. She learned about the maternity home from the doctor who confirmed her pregnancy.

I asked her who in her family had known. She had told her father, but not her mother. I asked her if that was because she was closer to her father but she said no. She had been close to both of them but she just thought her father would be able to handle it better than her mother. She assumed her father had told her mother at some point but her mother never said a word to her. As far as she knows, none of her sisters or brothers know, nor do her subsequent children, my half siblings.

Her father visited her a few times during her short stay in the maternity home. It could not have been easy for him to leave his farm for a day and drive more than two hours there and two hours back. Her boyfriend also visited. In fact, her boyfriend and her father drove her to the home together the day she checked in. This boyfriend was not my father. Between the time she discovered she was pregnant and the time she went away, she had met the man she would marry. She didn't know she was pregnant when they began dating. They married a month and a half after I was born. He had left the decision about whether to bring me home to be raised by the two of them up to her. He did not want her to resent him later. She felt it would not have been fair to him.

I asked her if she could tell me who my father was, and she said she didn't know if she should. She had written him from the maternity home once, because she felt he had a right to know, but she did not hear back from him. She thought he was still alive and probably married. Maybe his wife did not know. She didn't want to cause any trouble.

We moved on to medical information: she has problems with her heart. Then we covered genealogy. After learning her identity, I had visited a family-history center and scrolled through lengths of microfilmed census records to chart the maternal side of my family tree. We compared what we had learned about our ancestors and then returned to the present.

We are both gardeners. We talked about the varieties of lilacs we have in common. We discussed the perennials and roses and shrubs we plant. She has a nice selection of trees, including a couple of catalpas. She said the pods make a mess but it's worth it when they bloom. She said, "They're real pretty when they bloom."

I asked if she would be willing to meet and she said she would, so I asked her to think about what she would like to do with our day together. In the meantime, I would look into reservations and send her pictures of my garden. Afterward, I felt baffled by what had just taken place, shocked even. It was not at all what I expected. I thought the conversation would be short or she would hang up. It was so hard to absorb the fact that the woman I'd just been speaking to, and whom I had just made plans to go visit, was my mother.

We decided on a town south of where she lives and a month later I returned to the farmland I had traversed fourteen years earlier in search of her picture. I checked into a hotel the night before and that is where we met. I was less anxious on this trip. The wondering and circling were done. The desk called my room at 10:00 A.M. and I walked down to the lobby, where my mother was sitting in a chair waiting for me. We had a quick, brief hug and then set out on our day together. We had made plans to visit a public garden. I drove and we talked the entire time. It was easy and comfortable and she was generous and open with information about everything except my father, whom she said I resemble. I studied her face and kept an eye out for mannerisms, but I recognized nothing. I could have known her all my life and never guessed.

As we meandered on back roads, we talked about the chronology of major events in our lives. She and her husband built two houses; I have renovated three. I must have gotten my fort-building and power-tool gene from her. She told me about family members and their interests and I confessed that I had already met her brother. He had never mentioned the stranger who stopped by and asked questions about her.

At the end of our drive we returned to my room to look at the pictures she brought of her garden. It is elaborate and impressive and I was awed by her ambitiousness. She arranged a group of snapshots end to end, so I could try to make sense of the layout and see how the flower beds connected. Still not understanding, I asked another question and she flipped over the envelope that had held some of the pictures and began to draw a schematic that looked precisely like my sketched plans for garden plots and studios and houses in Arizona. And though I said nothing to her, I think that was the moment that I knew she was my mother.

I'm still not sure whether she was eager to meet or merely felt she owed it to me. She said she was told at the time of the relinquishment that she was never to have any contact with me. And though she did not say it directly, I suspect that the agreement she made was at least a part of the reason she did not respond when she received my letter. She is from a generation of women—unlike my own—that generally did what they were told.

I cannot fathom this event from her perspective. At seventy-five years old, she has just sneaked off for the day to meet a woman who is a both a stranger and the newborn she surrendered almost fifty-six years ago. But like the women I interviewed who were near her age, she does not talk easily, or emotionally, about her experience. We talked about feelings and about adoption in the abstract, as Hazel and I had done earlier. But at one point she did ask, "So you *did* have a good life?" And I assured her I did. There were only two times that I detected a crack in her voice. The first was when I was talking about how some of the women I interviewed had suffered and she said, "Yes, when you walk down the street you look at every little face and wonder." And the second was when we were leaving my room to walk her to her car and she pulled a ring from her finger and gave it to me.

And so our reunion has begun, with neither of us terribly emotional—at least on the surface—and with no particular expectations and no specific plans. We will start with our common interest in gardens and sketchy plans on the backs of envelopes, and move forward. Not knowing whether that visit will be our last, I tried to write down the details before they escaped me. But my mind kept returning, again and again, to the image of a ring. Not the one she gave me when we parted but the one she mentioned in passing—an old high-school class ring that belonged to my father that she said is still in the bottom of her dresser drawer.

Though I cannot express it precisely, that ring seems emblematic to me of everything that has happened—of my endless circling and of returning to the place where it all began. It was a ring once given to my mother by my father as a symbol of his commitment. And in the years since, it has no doubt served as a reminder to her of that relationship and of me—the child born of it—a pregnancy for which society made my mother, and many women like her, pay dearly. Perhaps what I have been trying to do is to rectify that wrong. But I think my drive to record the stories of the girls who went away, and my belief that what they have to say is important, is linked to the endless circle—of love and family and mistakes and second chances—symbolized by that ring.

A Note on the Interviews

W HEN I TALKED about the stories I was recording for this oral-history project, the first question people asked was "How do you find these women?" But more often than not, after I responded they told me about a mother or sister or aunt or friend of theirs who went away. Simply talking to others about what I was doing led me to many of the women I interviewed.

I have also met women through the exhibitions, films, lectures, and the visual and audio installations I have produced on the subject of adoption. Descriptions of the oral-history project were sent to regional coordinators of American Adoption Congress and Concerned United Birthparents with the request that these organizations forward the information to potential respondents, who were then asked to contact me directly through e-mail if they were willing to be interviewed.

Public-radio interviews and newspaper articles about the oral histories generated the largest number of responses and volunteers. Feature articles in the *Boston Globe* and the *Providence Journal* precipitated hundreds of e-mails from mothers who had surrendered, as well as from their subsequent children and friends, adoptees and their half siblings, and adoptive parents. Newspaper articles led me directly or indirectly to women who had told very few people about their experience and had not been part of support groups. I still receive e-mails in response to articles published years ago that someone has just located through an Internet search or received in the mail from a friend.

My goal was to interview as many women as I could reach, but no fewer than one hundred, before publication of this book, while attempting to be mindful of age, geographic, and ethnic diversity. I did not ask the women about their relinquishment experience or their sentiments about adoption in advance of the interviews, nor did I prescreen potential interviewees based on their story. I indicated that I was interested in diverse stories and welcomed all perspectives. I asked potential interviewees to send only their name and current city and state of residence, in addition to the year and place of the surrender. I also asked that the women be willing to give me permission to record their stories and to later publish excerpts in written or audio form. This naturally eliminated women who did not want to reveal their story or were fearful that I would not respect their anonymity. I was contacted by more women than I could possibly interview, and I regret that I still have a long list of willing participants whom I was unable to reach in time for this book.

Notes

CHAPTER 2: BREAKING THE SILENCE

1. Sandra L. Hofferth, Joan R. Kahn, and Wendy Baldwin, "Premarital Sexual Activity Among U.S. Teenage Women Over the Past Three Decades," *Family Planning Perspectives* 19, no. 2, Alan Guttmacher Institute, New York and Washington, D.C. (March–April 1987), 46–53, table 3.

2. Kathy S. Stolley, "Statistics on Adoption in the United States," *The Future of Children* 3, no. 1, The Center for the Future of Children, The David and Lucile Packard Foundation (Spring 1993), 30, figure 2, citing P. Maza, "Adoption Trends: 1944–1975," *Child Welfare Research Notes* no. 9, Administration for Children, Youth, and Families, Washington, D.C. (1984).

CHAPTER 3: GOOD GIRLS V. BAD GIRLS

1. Sandra L. Hofferth, Joan R. Kahn, and Wendy Baldwin, "Premarital Sexual Activity Among U.S. Teenage Women Over the Past Three Decades," *Family Planning Perspectives* 19, no. 2, Alan Guttmacher Institute, New York and Washington,

D.C. (March–April 1987), 46–53, table 3. See also Lewis M. Terman, *Psychological Factors in Marital Happiness* (New York: McGraw Hill, 1938); Alfred Kinsey, *Sexual Behavior in the Human Female* (Philadelphia: W. B. Saunders, 1953); Alfred Kinsey, *Sexual Behavior in the Human Male* (Philadelphia: W. B. Saunders, 1948).

2. Martin O'Connell and Carolyn C. Rogers, "Out-of-Wedlock Births, Premarital Pregnancies and Their Effect on Family Formation and Dissolution," *Family Planning Perspectives* 16, no. 4, Alan Guttmacher Institute, New York and Washington, D.C. (July–August 1984), 157–62, figure 1.

3. Ibid.

4. Ellen K. Rothman, *Hands and Hearts: A History of Courtship in America* (Cambridge: Harvard University Press, 1987), 289. Paula Fass, *The Damned and the Beautiful: American Youth in the 1920s* (New York: Oxford University Press, 1977). For 1930s studies by Lewis Terman, see *Psychological Factors in Marital Happiness* (New York: McGraw Hill, 1938). See also John D'Emilio and Estelle B. Freedman, *Intimate Matters: A History of Sexuality in America* (New York: Harper & Row, 1988).

5. Robert S. Lynd and Helen Merrell Lynd, *Middletown: A Study in Modern American Culture* (New York: Harcourt Brace, 1957), 135–41.

6. Elaine Tyler May, *Homeward Bound: American Families in the Cold War Era,* rev. and exp. (New York: Basic Books, 1999), 68.

7. Beth Bailey, *Sex in the Heartland* (Cambridge: Harvard University Press, 1999), 45–46.

8. Rothman, *Hands and Hearts,* 301. For a sociologist's perspective on "going steady" in the 1950s, see Winston Ehrmann, "Dating Characteristics," in *Premarital Dating Behavior* (New York: Henry Holt and Company, 1959).

9. Hofferth, Kahn, and Baldwin, "Premarital Sexual Activity Among U.S. Teenage Women Over the Past Three Decades," 46–53.

10. Roger J. R. Levesque, *Adolescents, Sex, and the Law: Preparing Adolescents for Responsible Citizenship* (Washington, D.C.: American Psychological Association, 2000), 69, citing Edward O. Laumann, et al., *The Social Organization of Sexuality: Sexual Practices in the United States* (Chicago: University of Chicago Press, 1994).

11. Linda Gordon, *Woman's Body, Woman's Right: A Social History of Birth Control in America* (New York: Grossman Publishers, 1976), 26–46.

12. Ibid., 64–66.

13. Ibid., 26–46.

14. See Gordon, *Woman's Body, Woman's Right,* for a thorough history of birth control in America.

15. Beth Bailey, *Sex in the Heartland* (Cambridge: Harvard University Press, 1999), 106.

16. John D'Emilio and Estelle B. Freedman, *Intimate Matters: A History of Sexuality in America* (New York: Harper & Row, 1988), 246, citing Kinsey, *Sexual Behavior in the Human Female,* regarding use of the diaphragm.

17. *Griswold v. Connecticut,* 381 U.S. 479 (1965). Argued: March 29, 1965. Decided: June 7, 1965.

18. *Eisenstadt v. Baird,* 405 U.S. 438 (1972). Argued: November 17, 1971. Decided: March 22, 1972.

19. June Machover Reinisch with Ruth Beasley, *The Kinsey Institute New Report on Sex: What You Must Know to Be Sexually Literate* (New York: St. Martin's Press, 1990).

20. Phillips Cutright, "Illegitimacy: Myths, Causes and Cures: A Family Planning Perspectives Special Feature," *Family Planning Perspectives* 3, no. 1, Alan Guttmacher Institute, New York and Washington, D.C. (January 1971), 25–48, table 3.

21. Alan Guttmacher Institute, "Facts in Brief: Teen Sex and Pregnancy" (www.agi-usa.org), 1999, updated February 19, 2004.

CHAPTER 4: DISCOVERY AND SHAME

1. Martin O'Connell and Carolyn C. Rogers, "Out-of-Wedlock Births, Premarital Pregnancies and Their Effect on Family Formation and Dissolution," *Family Planning Perspectives* 16, no. 4, Alan Guttmacher Institute, New York and Washington, D.C. (July–August 1984), 157–62, table 2.

2. Elaine Tyler May, *Homeward Bound: American Families in the Cold War Era,* rev. and exp. (New York: Basic Books, 1999), xii, table 1.

3. The 1972 Title IX Educational Amendment Act forbids the expulsion of pregnant girls from federally funded schools. Title IX prohibits discrimination on the basis of gender. See also Roger J. R. Levesque, *Adolescents, Sex, and the Law: Preparing Adolescents for Responsible Citizenship* (Washington, D.C.: American Psychological Association, 2000), 216.

CHAPTER 5: THE FAMILY'S FEARS

1. Kathy S. Stolley, "Statistics on Adoption in the United States," *The Future of Children* 3, no. 1, The Center for the Future of Children, The David and Lucile Packard Foundation (Spring 1993), 32.

2. Ibid.

3. Stephanie Coontz, *The Way We Never Were: American Families and the Nostalgia Trap* (New York: Basic Books, 2000), 24–25. See also William H. Chafe, *The Unfinished Journey: America Since World War II*, 2nd ed. (New York: Oxford University Press, 1991), 112.

4. Chafe, *Unfinished Journey*, 112–13.

5. Elaine Tyler May, *Homeward Bound: American Families in the Cold War Era*, rev. and exp. (New York: Basic Books, 1999), 67.

6. Delores Hayden, *Building Suburbia: Green Fields and Urban Growth, 1820–2000* (New York: Pantheon Books, 2003), 131–32.

7. Ibid., 132–35. See also Chafe, *Unfinished Journey*, 117.

8. Hayden, *Building Suburbia*, 132.

9. May, *Homeward Bound*, 151.

10. Ibid.

11. Chafe, *Unfinished Journey*, 111, 117.

12. May, *Homeward Bound*, 148.

13. May, *Homeward Bound*, "Marital Status of the Population," 15, table 7.

14. Rose M. Kreider and Tavia Simmons, "Census 2000 Brief," U.S. Department of Commerce, Economics and Statistics Administration, U.S. Census Bureau, Marital Status 2000, issued October 2003.

15. May, *Homeward Bound*, "Median Age at First Marriage, Male and Female, 1890–1995," xii, table 1.

16. Chafe, *Unfinished Journey*, 123.

17. May, *Homeward Bound*, 121; Chafe, 137.

18. May, *Homeward Bound*, 207, and evidence from U.S. Census reports.

19. David Riesman, Reuel Denney, and Nathan Glazer, *The Lonely Crowd: A Study of the Changing American Character* (New Haven: Yale University Press, 1950).

20. William H. Whyte, *The Organization Man* (New York: Simon & Schuster, 1956).

21. May, *Homeward Bound*, 16.

22. Chafe, *Unfinished Journey*, 144.

23. Hayden, *Building Suburbia,* 135.

24. May, *Homeward Bound,* 20; Whyte, *The Organization Man.*

25. C. A. Bachrach, K. S. Stolley, and K. A. London, "Relinquishment of Premarital Births: Evidence from National Survey Data," in *Family Planning Perspectives* 24, no. 1 (January/February 1992): table 1 (Alan Guttmacher Institute, New York and Washington, D.C.)

26. Social Welfare History Archives, University of Minnesota, Florence Crittenton Collection, box 14, folder 2, *Florence Crittenton Bulletin,* March 1952, vol. 2, no. 1, page 7.

27. Ibid., 4.

28. Dawn Davenport, "Born in America, Adopted Abroad: African-American babies are going to parents overseas even as US couples adopt children from other countries," *Christian Science Monitor,* October 27, 2004.

29. For an excellent overview of race and surrender, see Rickie Solinger's *Wake Up Little Susie: Single Pregnancy and Race Before Roe v. Wade.*

30. B. C. Miller and D. D. Coyl, "Adolescent Pregnancy and Childbearing in Relation to Infant Adoption in the U.S.," *Adoption Quarterly* 4 (2000): 3–25.

31. May, *Homeward Bound,* 136.

32. Chafe, *Unfinished Journey,* 97–110.

33. May, *Homeward Bound,* 82–83. Quote from Republican Party national chairman Guy Gabrielson.

34. Ibid., 82.

35. Ibid., 59–60.

36. For a thorough account of the American family in this era, see Elaine Tyler May, *Homeward Bound: American Families in the Cold War Era,* and Stephanie Coontz, *The Way We Never Were: American Families and the Nostalgia Trap.*

37. May, *Homeward Bound,* 83.

38. Ibid., 69.

39. Chafe, *Unfinished Journey,* 126–27.

40. Ibid., 124.

41. May, *Homeward Bound,* 172.

42. May, *Homeward Bound,* 66.

43. Stolley, "Statistics on Adoption in the United States." See also Brent C. Miller and Kristen A. Moore, "Adolescent Sexual Behavior, Pregnancy, and Parenting:

Research through the 1980s," *Journal of Marriage and the Family* 52, no. 4, National Council on Family Relations (November 1990), 1025–44.

44. Roger J. R. Levesque, *Adolescent Sex and the Law: Preparing Adolescents for Responsible Citizenship*, 123, citing Michael Resnick et al., "Characteristics of Unwed Adolescent Mothers: Determinants of Child Rearing Versus Adoption," *American Journal of Orthopsychiatry* 60 (1990): 577–84.

CHAPTER 6: GOING AWAY

1. Regina Kunzel, *Fallen Women, Problem Girls: Unmarried Mothers and the Professionalization of Social Work, 1890–1945* (New Haven: Yale University Press, 1993), 17, 19, 29, 30.

2. Rickie Solinger, *Wake Up Little Susie: Single Pregnancy and Race Before Roe v. Wade* (New York: Routledge, 2000), 104, 114.

3. *Life*, February 19, 1951, 101. Fifty dollars in 1951 is the equivalent of $376 in 2005, according to the Inflation Calculator provided by the U.S. Department of Labor, Bureau of Labor Statistics, Consumer Price Indexes, http://www.bls.gov.

4. Solinger, *Wake Up Little Susie*, 115.

5. The conversion of 1964 dollars to 2005 dollars is based on the Inflation Calculator provided by the U.S. Department of Labor, Bureau of Labor Statistics, Consumer Price Indexes, http://www.bls.gov.

6. Solinger, *Wake Up Little Susie*, 26–27.

7. Kunzel, *Fallen Women, Problem Girls*, 26.

8. E. Wayne Carp, *Family Matters: Secrecy and Disclosure in the History of Adoption* (Cambridge: Harvard University Press, 1998), 16. Quote by child-welfare reformer Galen Merril at the National Conference of Charities and Corrections in 1900. See also Rickie Solinger, "Prewar Attitudes Toward Illegitimate Babies and Mothers," in *Wake Up Little Susie*, 149–52; Regina Kunzel, *Fallen Women, Problem Girls*, 32–33.

9. Kunzel, *Fallen Women, Problem Girls*, 32–33.

10. Solinger, *Wake Up Little Susie*, 150.

11. Kunzel, *Fallen Women, Problem Girls*, 38.

12. Ibid., 53–54.

13. Ibid., 54, citing Stuart Queen and Delbert Mann, *Social Pathology* (New York: Thomas Crowell, 1925), 163–64.

14. Kunzel, *Fallen Women, Problem Girls*, 52–54.

15. John D'Emillo and Estelle B. Freedman, *Intimate Matters: A History of Sexuality in America* (New York: Harper & Row, 1988), 189.

16. Social Welfare History Archives, University of Minnesota, Florence Crittenton Collection, box 13, folder 1, Application Form, "Rules Governing Scholarship, Rule #1, To be awarded to a girl who wishes to continue her education to enable her to care for her child," c. 1941.

17. Ibid., "Rule #4, Board of Home from which application is received to assume responsibility of board of child."

18. Ibid., letter from principal of school district in support of applicant, January 9, 1941, box 13, folder 1.

19. Ibid., letter from superintendent of Florence Crittenton Home in support of application, box 13, folder 1.

20. Ibid., handwritten thank-you letter, box 13, folder 1.

21. Ibid., box 12, folder 8.

22. Kunzel, *Fallen Women, Problem Girls,* 169.

23. Ibid., citing Rose Bernstein, "Are We Still Stereotyping the Unmarried Mother," *Social Work* 5, Boston University (1960): 24.

24. See Regina Kunzel's *Fallen Women, Problem Girls* for a thorough overview of the professionalization of social work and the shifting definitions of single pregnancy. Explanations, including the psychiatric diagnosis, are scattered throughout the book but a condensed explanation can be found on pages 144–56.

25. Social Welfare History Archives, University of Minnesota, Florence Crittenton Collection, box 14, folder 2.

26. Social Welfare History Archives, University of Minnesota, Florence Crittenton Collection, box 20, folder 5.

27. Solinger, *Wake Up Little Susie,* 95, citing interview with Frances Whitefield, September 1989; and Hannah Adams to Jules Saltman, March 1966, Box 1038, file 7-4-6-0 Record Group 102, National Archives.

Chapter 7: Birth and Surrender

1. E. Wayne Carp, *Family Matters: Secrecy and Disclosure in the History of Adoption* (Cambridge: Harvard University Press, 1998), 29. See also P. Maza, "Adoption Trends: 1944–1975," *Child Welfare Research Notes* no. 9, Administration for Children, Youth, and Families, Washington, D.C. (1984); Kathy S. Stolley, "Statistics

on Adoption in the United States," *The Future of Children* 3, no. 1, The Center for the Future of Children, The David and Lucile Packard Foundation (Spring 1993), 30, figure 2.

2. *Life*, February 19, 1951.

3. *Adoptive Families* magazine, calculations based on state laws compiled in 2004. Published as PDF file at http:://www.adoptivefamilies.com/adoptionlaws.

CHAPTER 8: THE AFTERMATH

1. Holli A. Askren and Kathaleen C. Bloom, "Postadoptive Reactions of the Relinquishing Mother: A Review," *Journal of Obstetric, Gynecologic, and Neonatal Nursing* (July–August 1999). This is a review of literature addressing responses to relinquishment. The authors cite the research of twelve studies in naming relinquishing mothers' grief reactions, including "separation loss" (Davis, 1995); "separation anxiety" (Lamperelli and Smith, 1979); "shadow grief" (Lauderdale and Boyle, 1994); and "a discordant dilemma" (Rynearson, 1982).

2. Carol Davis, "Separation Loss in Relinquishing Birthmothers," *International Journal of Psychiatric Nursing Research*, 1, no. 2 (1995): 55–66.

3. Askren and Bloom, "Postadoptive Reactions," citing Carol Davis, "Separation Loss in Relinquishing Birth Mothers"; and Leverett Millen and Samuel Roll, "Solomon's Mothers: A Special Case of Pathological Bereavement," *American Journal of Orthopsychiatry* 55 (1985): 411–18.

4. Michael DeSimone, "Birth Mother Loss: Contribution Factors to Unresolved Grief," *Clinical Social Work Journal*, 24, no. 1 (Spring 1996): 66.

5. "Coping with Loss–Bereavement and Grief," National Mental Health Association Web site, http://www.nmha.org/infoctr/factsheets/42.cfm.

6. Robin Winkler et al., "Birth Parents," in *Clinical Practice in Adoption* (New York: Pergamon Press, 1998), 48–68; Askren and Bloom, "Postadoptive Reactions"; Davis, "Separation Loss"; DeSimone, "Birth Mother Loss"; Robin Winkler and Margaret van Keppel, *Relinquishing Mothers in Adoption: Their Long-Term Adjustment*, Institute for Families Studies Monograph No. 3, Melbourne, Australia, 1984; Eva Y. Deykin, Lee Campbell, and Patricia Patti, "The Postadoptive Experience of Surrendering Parents," *American Journal of Orthopsychiatry* 54, no. 2 (April 1984): 271–80; Leverett Millen and Samuel Roll, "Solomon's Mothers: A Special Case of Pathological Bereavement," *American Journal of Orthopsychiatry* 55, no. 3 (July 1985): 411–18.

7. DeSimone reports 34 percent in "Birth Mother Loss." The figure is 37 percent in M. J. Carr, "Birthmothers and Subsequent Children: The Role of Personality Traits and Attachment History," *Journal of Social Distress and the Homeless* 9, no. 4 (2000): 342.

8. The National Infertility Association, information regarding secondary infertility. http://www.resolve.org/.

9. Askren and Bloom, "Postadoptive Reactions," 395–400.

10. Winkler and van Keppel, "Relinquishing Mothers in Adoption"; see also the guidebook to clinical practice by Winkler, van Keppel, Dirck Brown, and Amy Blanchard, "Birth Parents," in *Clinical Practice in Adoption* (New York: Pergamon Press, 1998), 48–68.

11. Askren and Bloom, "Postadoptive Reactions," conclusion, 395.

12. I highly recommend Winkler's *Clinical Practice in Adoption*. Intended for clinicians and adoption workers, it offers guidelines for working with mothers who have surrendered, adoptive parents, and adoptees.

13. R. Pannor, A. Baran, and A. Sorosky, "Birth Parents Who Relinquished Babies for Adoption Revisited," *Family Process* 17 (1978): 329–37. See also Winkler's "Relinquishing Mothers in Adoption."

14. There is no accurate count of the number of surrendering mothers in the United States today, but the number of children placed in nonfamily adoptions is believed to be 5 million to 6 million. D. Brodinsky and M. Schechter, eds., "A Stress and Coping Model of Adoption Adjustment," in *The Psychology of Adoption* (New York: Oxford University Press, 1990). Thus the corresponding number of mothers who have placed these children, less foreign adoptions, may conservatively total 4 million to 5 million. Davis placed the number of relinquishing mothers in the United States at 10 million. Davis, "Separation Loss," citing A. B. Fonda, "Birthmothers Who Search: An Exploratory Study," doctoral dissertation, California School of Professional Psychology, 1984.

15. Daniel A. Sass and Douglas B. Henderson, "Adoption Issues: Preparation of Psychologists and an Evaluation of the Need for Continuing Education," *Journal of Social Distress and the Homeless, Special Issue: Adoption* 9, no. 4 (2000): 349–59. The figure of 8 percent is probably low, because only half of the psychologists surveyed had asked their patients if they were part of the adoption triad.

16. Diana E. Post, "Adoption in Clinical Psychology: A Review of the Absence, Ramifications, and Recommendations for Change," *Journal of Social Distress and the Homeless, Special Issue: Adoption* 9, no. 4 (2000): 361–72. Post also cites other

researchers who have noted the absence, including J. Terrell and J. Modell, "Anthropology and Adoption," *American Anthropologist* 96 (1994): 155–67; K. Wegar, "Adoption and Mental Health: A Theoretical Critique of the Psychopathological Model," *American Journal of Orthopsychiatry* 65 (1995): 540–48; A. Jones, "Issues Relevant to Therapy with Adoptees," *Journal of Psychotherapy* 34 (1994): 64–68; and I. Altman, "Higher Education and Psychology in the Millennium," *American Psychologist* 51 (1996): 371–78.

17. Allen Fisher, "Still Not Quite as Good as Having Your Own? Toward a Sociology of Adoption," *Annual Review of Sociology* 29 (2003): 335–61.

18. Adoptees' Liberty Movement Association, http://www.almasociety.org, The ALMA Society, P.O. Box 85, Denville, NJ 07834.

19. Concerned United Birthparents, http://www.cubirthparents.org, P.O. Box 503475, San Diego, CA 92150. For a history of CUB, see also E. Wayne Carp, *Family Matters: Secrecy and Disclosure in the History of Adoption*, 204.

20. SunflowerFirstMoms-Reunited, http://groups.yahoo.com/SunflowerFirstMoms-Reunited, and SunflowerFirstMoms-Searching, http://groups.yahoo.com/SunflowerFirstMoms-searching/.

21. OriginsUSA, http://www.originsusa.org/.

22. Empty Arms, http://www.emptyarms.org/.

CHAPTER 9: SEARCH AND REUNION

1. For a complete overview of the history of adoption records, see E. Wayne Carp, *Family Matters: Secrecy and Disclosure in the History of Adoption* (Cambridge: Harvard University Press, 1998).

2. American Adoption Congress, http://www.americanadoptioncongress.org/.

3. Bastard Nation, http://www.bastards.org/. See Web site for information about birth-certificate access in individual states and legislation currently under consideration, as well as for lists of books and other links related to adoptees' rights. Bastard Nation, P.O. Box 271672, Houston, TX 77277, 415-704-3166.

4. National Adoption Clearinghouse, U.S. Department of Health and Human Services, http://naic.acf.hhs.gov/. Search: State Statutes, then Post Adoption, "Access to Family Information by Adopted Persons: Summary of State Laws."

5. Volunteer Search Network, http://www.vsn.org.

6. Melisha Mitchell et al., "Mutual Consent Voluntary Registries: An Exercise in Pa-

tience and Failure," *Adoptive Families* (January/February 1999). Also online at http://www.americanadoptioncongress.org/.

7. Carp, *Family Matters,* 140–41.

8. The ALMA Society, Inc., http://www.almasociety.org/, or P.O. Box 85, Denville, NJ, 07834. The $50 lifetime membership fee entitles members to a list of support-group coordinators around the country and to enrollment in the registry's database. Florence Fisher's book *The Search for Anna Fisher* chronicles the story of Fisher's search for her daughter and the founding of ALMA.

9. Statistics as of October 2005, provided by Marri Rillea. The Soundex International Soundex Reunion Registry, http://www.isrr.net/, P.O. Box 2312, Carson City, NV, 89702, 775-882-7755.

10. Statistics as of July 1, 2005, provided by Janice Pitts. The Oregon Registry and a link to obtaining preadoption birth records can be found at http://oregon.gov/DHS/children/adoption/adopt_registry/registry.shtml.

11. New Hampshire, Department of State, Division of Vital Records Administration. Monthly tally of requests online: http://www.sos.nh.gov/vitalrecords/Preadoption%20birth%20records.html#progress; see Track the Numbers: Preadoption Stats.

12. United States Department of Health and Human Services, "U.S. Surgeon General's Family History Initiative." Surgeon General Richard Carmona declared Thanksgiving 2004 the first annual National Family History Day and encouraged families to talk about health problems that run in their family when they gather for the holiday. The Web site comes with a computerized downloadable tool to assist individuals in creating a portrait of their family's health. See http://www.hhs.gov/familyhistory/. See also Vice Admiral Richard Carmona and Major Daniel Wattendorf, "Personalizing Prevention: The U.S. Surgeon General's Family History Initiative," *American Family Physician* (January 2005).

CHAPTER 10: TALKING AND LISTENING

1. E-mail response to article "RISD Artist's Project on Adoptees, Birth Mothers Hits 'Close to Home,'" by Marion Davis, *Providence Journal,* October 28, 2002, A-1, A-4.

2. E-mail response to article "The Girls Who 'Went Away,'" by Bella English, *Boston Globe,* July 28, 2003, B-5, B-10.

3. E-mail response to radio program, *The Connection,* WBUR Boston and NPR,

"The Women Who Went Away," aired August 5, 2003, hosted by Lyse Doucet.

4. Anonymous message left in comment book at *Everlasting* exhibition, January–March 2003, Decker Gallery, Maryland Institute College of Art, Baltimore, MD.

5. E-mail response to Davis article "RISD Artist's Project on Adoptees, Birth Mothers Hits 'Close to Home.'"

6. E-mail response to English article "The Girls Who 'Went Away.'"

7. Parliament of Tasmania, Joint Select Committee, 1999. "Adoption and Related Services: 1950–1988," 10.

8. Ibid., 13.

9. Ibid., 11.

10. Parliament of Tasmania, Joint Select Committee, 1999. "Adoption and Related Services: 1950–1988," Statement About Adoption by the Australian Association of Social Workers, June 12, 1997, 10.

11. E-mail response to English article "The Girls Who 'Went Away.'"

Acknowledgments

When I first began collecting the oral histories contained herein, writing a book was far from my mind. I had been producing short films, and audio-video installations on the subject of adoption for fifteen years. As a complement to the visual work, I often invited others to write about their experience of adoption and then published or posted their stories in conjunction with the exhibitions. Although the stories written by adoptive parents and adoptees were very moving, those contributed by the mothers who had surrendered children were so powerful that they transformed my understanding of adoption.

I began to tape-record the stories of these mothers in 2002. I initiated the oral-history project because I felt it was imperative that the stories be chronicled before they were lost to history, and that they be preserved in an archive to be available to future generations of sociologists and historians. This preservation is now ensured. The tapes of the interviews will ultimately reside in the Arthur and Elizabeth Schlesinger Library on the History of Women in America at Harvard University alongside the papers of notable women, including Susan B. Anthony, Amelia Earhart, Betty Friedan, and Emma Goldman. I am grateful to the Schlesinger Library for their commitment to preserving this collection and to Kathryn Allamong Jacob, curator of manuscripts, in particular, for her interest.

I intended the stories not only for an oral-history archive but also for use in audio installations and an independent film that would allow me to bring the voices of the mothers to an audience. The first interviews were made possible as part of an artists' residency and exhibition at the Maryland Institute College of Art. Curator-in-residence George Ciscle led a team of thirty students and their seven professional mentors in a year-long project that provided the resources and expertise necessary to create the first *Everlasting* exhibition using the recorded voices. I am immensely grateful to George for this opportunity. I know of no finer curator or educator than George Ciscle. It was he who understood the logic and symmetry of creating the first audio work at the college where it all began—where I had met the woman who thought I might be the daughter she surrendered.

In 2003 I was awarded a Radcliffe Fellowship from the Radcliffe Institute for Advanced Study at Harvard University to expand the oral-history project, conduct research, and produce a new region-specific audio-video installation. I am indebted to the Radcliffe Institute for this fellowship, which provided a year of uninterrupted time and contributed significantly to the development of the book. I am grateful to Judy Vichniac, director of the Fellowship Program, and to Drew Gilpin Faust, dean of the Radcliffe Institute, for the incredibly rich, stimulating, and supportive interdisciplinary environment they have created for the Radcliffe fellows, and to Lindy Hess, publishing consultant, Radcliffe Institute, for her advice and encouragement. I also want to thank the Radcliffe Research Partnership Program and Christine DeLucia for her research assistance. And a special thanks to Karen Walker, who volunteered countless hours and was an invaluable help to me during my fellowship year.

Since the inception of this multifaceted endeavor, many individuals and institutions have provided much-needed assistance. Foremost, I want to thank my home institution, Rhode Island School of Design. Without the support I received through an academic research leave, I could not have participated in the Radcliffe Fellowship Program, or spent the following year traveling to conduct interviews around the country and writing the book. I would like to thank four individuals in particular: Jay Coogan, acting provost; John Terry, dean of Fine Arts; Michael Schrader, former assistant director of corporate and foundation relations; and Ann Hudner, director of external relations.

I am also indebted to the organizations that provided financial assistance with the transcription costs: the Rhode Island State Council for the Humanities and the Pembroke Center for Teaching and Research on Women.

It was early in my fellowship year at the Radcliffe Institute that the idea of presenting the oral histories in book form first surfaced. I would like to thank Fred Seidel for introducing me to my agent, Andrew Wylie, who was incredibly supportive from the start. At The Penguin Press I have had the pleasure of working with a great team, led by Ann Godoff, president and publisher, and including Tracy Locke, associate publisher; Abigail Cleaves, senior publicist; Darren Haggar, art director; Amanda Dewey, senior designer; and Evan Gaffney, who designed the jacket. My editor, Emily Loose, has been an absolute joy to work with. Emily's sensitivity to the material and her expertise and intelligence as an editor have focused my ramblings and expanded my thinking.

All artists and writers who delve deeply into a project, neglecting all else in the process, know that it is a nearly impossible task without the generosity and encouragement of one's partner. I am grateful every day to have such a partner in my husband, Peter Andersen, who has given up a tremendous amount of the little free time he has to help with this project. His feedback, support, and love keep me afloat.

Lastly, my deepest gratitude is reserved for the women who were willing to share their life stories and who trusted me with their most intimate thoughts and experiences. My chief regret is that I could not include passages from the story of every woman I interviewed. The most painful part of writing this book was the requisite editing out of equally compelling stories. Thank you Ann, Anne, Annie, Barbara, Becky, Bette, Bonnie, Carol, Carol, Carole, Carole, Carolyn, Carolyn, Cathy, Cathy, Charlene, Charlenea, Charlotte, Christine, Claudia, Connie, Connie, Connie, Deborah, Debra, Denise, Diane, Diane, Diane, Diane, Dorothy, Dorothy, Edith, Gale, Gloria, Glory, Helen, Hilary, Jane, Janet, Jeannette, Jennifer, Jill, Joan, Joanna, Jonette, Joyce, Joyce, Judith,

Judith, Judith, Judith, Karen, Karen, Kathi, Kathleen, Laurie, Laurinda, Leigh, Leslie, Linda, Linda, Linda, Lydia, Lynne, Madeline, Maggie, Margaret, Marge, Marjorie, Mary, Mary, Mary, Mary, MaryAnn, Maureen, Maureen, Nancy, Nancy, Nancy, Nellie, Pam, Pamela, Pamela, Pollie, Rachael, Renee, Ronnie, Rose, Ruth, Sandy, Sandy, Serena, Sheila, Shelley, Sheryl, Sue, Susan, Susan, Susan, Susan, Suzanne, Toni, Wendy, and Yvonne. Your generosity astounds me. I only hope that I have done justice to your stories.

of only child, 215, 217–18, 242–43, 263, 303–4

positive view of, 131–32

second thoughts about, 181, 186, 189, 200, 219

signing papers for, 22–23, 82, 92, 128, 160–61, 170–71, 179, 181, 186–87, 192–93, 195, 199–200, 230–31, 282, 300, 304, 305, 315

without legal counsel, 186

reunion:

with active or passive searchers, 249

adoption agencies facilitating, 249–50

consequences of, 124–25, 221, 235, 244–45, 252, 264, 308

death intervening with, 257

emotions of, 51–52, 64, 95, 125, 194–95, 222, 247, 260–61, 265, 266–72, 277, 284–85, 307–8

with father, 65–66, 200, 255–56, 307

and healing, 66, 163, 247, 252, 269, 278, 317

honeymoon phase of, 260

interest waning after, 261, 263–64

laws against, 53, 315–16

in prison, 257–58

and privacy issues, 251–52, 291, 320

and registry movement, 250–52

reluctance for, 252–53, 258, 283, 289, 320

and sadness of lost years, 125, 236

search and, 1, 4, 62–66, 94–99, 124–25, 130–31, 241–42, 247–72, 275–78, 292, 314

and telling their stories, 53, 247, 253–56, 262, 263, 267, 278, 301

Riesman, David, 106

Rillera, Marri, 251

Roe v. Wade, 7

Rose, 116–17, 139

Ruth, 127–32, 301

Salvation Army, 133, 134, 137

Sandy I, 298–99

Sanger, Margaret, 41

school:

classes in maternity homes, 139, 157, 273

educational aspirations, 102, 109

expulsion from, 34, 72, 103, 167

returning to, 78, 82, 171, 192, 202, 230

Search Angels, 316, 317

searchers, professional, 194, 249, 283

secondary infertility, 217, 218

secrecy:

burden of, 12, 19, 83–84, 126, 207–8, 212, 278, 290

and family relations, 288, 294, 295–96

hiding the pregnancy, 72, 134, 152, 155, 156, 164–67, 229, 238, 314, 325

as protecting the baby, 194

as protecting the mother, 139, 205

and social mores, 9–10, 23, 71–72, 82, 123–24, 294

and telling the story, 267, 278

self-esteem, low:

Church and, 59, 70

marriage and, 161, 214–15

rebuilding sense of self, 192, 236

remorse and, 218, 236, 244

and sense of abandonment, 7, 78, 157

social mores and, 84, 153, 163, 211, 227, 241, 303

social workers and, 86–87, 151, 158, 187, 194, 195

Serena, 260–61

sex education, 7–8, 37–40, 44–45, 296–97, 317

shame:

burden of, 83, 97, 119, 131, 153, 202, 211, 290, 298–99

Church and, 59, 70

of family and friends, 11, 70, 72, 78, 103–4, 109

and social stigma, 8, 9, 11, 15, 25, 36, 40, 82, 103–4, 109, 126, 149, 188, 278

Sheila, 137–38, 221–22

Sheryl, 70–71, 104, 135, 154, 177, 224–25

social workers:

adoption promoted by, 88, 96, 150–51, 153, 187

change in philosophies of, 143–50, 294

false papers filed by, 130

inadequate counseling by, 180–81, 222

and increasing demand for babies, 183

low self-esteem fostered by, 86–87, 151, 158, 187, 194, 195

About the Author

Ann Fessler is a professor of photography at Rhode Island School of Design, a specialist in audio-video installation art. In 2003–2004 she was awarded a prestigious and highly competitive Radcliffe Fellowship at the Radcliffe Institute for Advanced Study, Harvard University, where she conducted interviews and research for this book. Her installations, among them *Everlasting*, out of which this book grew, have been shown in galleries and museums around the country. She is the recipient of grants from the National Endowment for the Arts, the LEF Foundation, the Rhode Island Foundation, the Rhode Island Council for the Humanities, Art Matters, and the Maryland and Rhode Island State Arts Councils. Her award-winning short videos have been screened widely at festivals and in gallery installations.